Couples in Conflict

Couples in Conflict

Inside the Counseling Room

DOROTHY R. FREEMAN

OPEN UNIVERSITY PRESS · Milton Keynes
Published in association with RELATE

Open University Press
Celtic Court
22 Ballmoor
Buckingham MK18 1XW

First Published in this edition 1990

British Library Cataloguing in Publication Data

Freeman, Dorothy Ruth,
    Couples in conflict : inside the counseling room.
    1. Marriage counseling
    I. Title
    362.8286

    ISBN 0-335-09422-8

Printed in Great Britain by
St Edmundsbury Press Ltd, Bury St Edmunds

*To my friend and husband, Jack,
whose consistent encouragement
made my professional career and
this book possible*

To see a world in a grain of sand
   And heaven in a wild flower,
To hold Infinity in the palm of your hand
   Or Eternity in an hour.

William Blake

Contents

II: Further Considerations

Foreword

This is a book for all of us who are fascinated by how couples interact in their relationships. Here we meet couples undergoing therapy, hear their stories as they tell them, watch their marital crises unfold, and are given a running commentary on how a sensitive and experienced therapist intervenes. We meet a variety of couples from different walks of life and different ethnic backgrounds; and they are being helped by a counselor who develops an empathetic relationship with them but also thinks sharply and diagnostically about them.

Watching Dorothy Freeman in action reminds me of a figure-skater whose skilled performance looks so easy that one forgets the many years of practice that went into the production. She is a clear and wise guide whose counseling is both active and problem-solving *and* humorous and compassionate. She is a pragmatist, and her definition of a good marriage is that "what works, works". She draws out the significance of the "little gains" in relationships which can lead to changes of a lasting nature: a therapist does not always need to tackle basic causes.

Above all, she provides couples themselves, counselors, and other professionals working with couples with both a good read and a learning experience. She deserves the wider readership which this paperback of *Couples in Conflict* will bring.

Dr. Miriam Stoppard

Acknowledgments

In writing this book, I have been keenly aware of the many others who have contributed to it, knowingly or unknowingly.

First of all, I must express my obligation to the many outstanding teachers of social work from whose knowledge and skills I had the opportunity to learn, and whose caring quality and social conscience contributed to my professional development.

Appreciation is also due to the late Dr. Baruch Silverman, pioneer in the field of mental health in Canada, under whose leadership the Marriage Counselling Centre of Montreal was established. I enjoyed the many years of congenial work in this agency with my colleague and friend, Dorothy Barrier.

I gained much from Dr. Nathan B. Epstein, presently Professor and Chairman, Section of Psychiatry and Human Behavior, Brown University, who instituted the first family therapy training program in Canada at the Jewish General Hospital of Montreal. Attending the weekly sessions and observing his skill as a family interviewer was an inspiring experience. Over the years he and his distinguished colleagues, Dr. Vivian Rakoff, Dr. Isaac Rebner, and Dr. John Sigal, participated with me in the Family Diagnosis course at the McGill University School of Social Work. I, as well as my students, benefited from their contributions.

My thanks to Dr. David Woodsworth, Professor of Social Work at

McGill and a former Director of the School, for his encouragement to undertake this project, and to Shirley Braverman, Professor of Family Therapy at the School, for her interest and helpful comments on my introductory chapter.

Then too I thank those friends who read case material and cheered me on my way—Nat Gerstenzang, formerly of the *New York Times*, Leon Levinson of the *Montreal Gazette*, and David Stevenson, retired Probation Supervisor, also of Montreal.

Special thanks are due to Dr. John J.O. Moore for the freedom given me during his sixteen years as Director of the McGill School to develop a number of new programs, and as well for his thoughtful reading and constructive suggestions on the two concluding chapters of this book.

1

Introduction: The Why and How of Short-Term Marriage Counseling

Everyone knows that the bookstores and magazine stands are bulging with material on marriage—old style, new style—on group marriage, no marriage, on singles, divorce, sex in all possible variations. Why yet another book?

The purpose of this book is threefold. Primarily it is designed to bring the beginning social work practitioner and therapist-in-training* into the counseling room, from the initial interview through the subsequent step-by-step events to the closing contact, in a series of short-term marital-conflict cases. Further, it is offered as a teaching aid to instructors of practice in schools of social work where a course on short-term counseling is available or under consideration. The work is also addressed to those professionals who by virtue of their calling are usually the first to be approached for help with troubled marriages. These are mainly clergymen, lawyers, and doctors, to whom a knowledge of the potential of time-limited marriage counseling is relevant, although it may be peripheral to their practice.

It should be borne in mind that this work was designed essentially as a casebook rather than as a formal textbook. The intimate exposure of one

---

*The terms therapist, practitioner, worker, and counselor, as well as therapy, treatment, and counseling will be used interchangeably.

1

worker's practice with a variety of troubled marriages, however, may provide a fresh learning experience. In my many years of teaching practice I have often heard advanced students in the final phase of training complain: "We usually see beginnings or bits of cases, but rarely a complete case showing the treatment method used. We often wonder at the outcome."

Along with my classroom teaching of practice methods I was for over twenty years consultant and part-time counselor at the Marriage Counselling Centre of the Mental Hygiene Institute of Montreal. These duties from the outset gave me the opportunity to develop and share my interest in short-term therapy.

A trend toward brief therapy has been growing in recent years. Why the trend toward short-term? After all, what can possibly be achieved in ten or even fewer sessions? Despite the persistence of the notion that length and depth of treatment indicate the best in skill and cure, this has been challenged from many quarters. Hans Eysenck attacked the efficacy of conventional depth psychology in the early 1950s. In 1961, Michael Balint, the noted English psychoanalyst, referred to "the highly embarrassing observation, recorded from all over the psychiatric world, that a very high percentage of patients . . . drop out from their treatment in the early stages" (Balint, 1961, p. 42). A high dropout rate from open-ended treatment has also been noted in social agencies and treatment centers. Such observations provide in part the rationale for time-limited therapy.

It is well known that most changes take place during the early sessions of open-ended treatment. If no change occurs during the early phase, clients are likely to withdraw from treatment.

Research by Reid and Shyne (1969) supports this view, emphasizing the greater value of brief services. And Hepworth has noted:

> Numerous concurrent research studies were also conducted, disclosing with unanticipated consistency that brief therapies were as effective as long-term therapies and, in some instances, more effective. [Hepworth, 1979, p. 317]

It seems to me that the *planned* use of time limits makes more sense than just "letting it happen." Indeed, the planned use of time in short-term counseling is a powerful dynamic which enhances client motivation. Rather than induce undue dependence and regression, as is often the case in long-term treatment, it is ego building. Instead of feeling inadequate and helpless, the client continues to feel that he has some control over the situation when he understands that the treatment is within forseeable bounds; that is, as he gets in, he can see his way out. It is encouraging for him to know that some help is possible in a relatively short period of time.

A further advantage of short-term over long-term therapy is that the client can more easily assert his right to question the treatment offered, and to seek other help or even change therapists if he believes no progress is being made, without undue feelings of obligation, guilt, or inadequacy. Too many clients are in the dark about "therapy" and are intimidated by being labeled "resistant" or "defensive."

There are other advantages to the short-term approach. More and more marriages require help today, the resources are limited: obviously more couples can be helped in a given time by a competent short-term therapist. The long waiting list is less formidable and frustrating for the worker as well, if the agency policy provides brief therapy. Then, too, as payment of fees for service is usually involved, it helps give the clients a good idea in advance of the financial liability to which they are being committed.

In short-term therapy the couple as well as the counselor are challenged to roll up their sleeves. As the counselor makes clear at the outset, the couple are expected to work at improving their unhappy state with his help.

The short-term counselor cannot become sidetracked into the leisurely relationship building, the passive listening, or the detailed and lengthy history taking that are characteristic of long-term therapy and that often confuse clients, who may not see the relevance of what is going on.

Although the historical perspective is important in short-term marital counseling, history taking per se is not the focus of attention. The guideline for the use of past material must depend on its impact on the present malfunctioning of the couple in their marital and parental roles.

Learning about and dealing with *how* people behave may well be more productive than learning about and dealing with *why* they behave this way. By raising only the derivatives of the past which disturb the present, the underlying conflicts may be eased, even if they are not resolved. The basic character structure remains. "Vaulting ambition which o'erleaps itself" is not for the short-term counselor. The selective and limited use of history is illustrated in the cases that follow.

My own experience with both long-term and short-term marriage counseling has brought me to the conviction that the short-term approach has more to recommend it—indeed it is more often the treatment of choice—than most practitioners believe. I do not propose short-term marriage counseling, however, as a Procrustean bed into which all couples in conflict must be fitted. Some of the contraindications are considered in Chapter 8.

My concept of "short-term" is flexible. It involves one, two, or three conjoint sessions for a marital assessment. Then, if a short-term approach is agreed on, a time limit or "contract" is established, for anywhere from six to twelve sessions. If the assessment indicates that short-term treatment is not appropriate, an alternate resource is suggested to the couple. This is explained in the first session, and the couple is also told that the decision as to whether or not to continue after the assessment will be a threeway one. The first session may last up to one and a half hours; subsequent weekly sessions are of one-hour duration. (The several phases of this short-term model are discussed in detail on pp. 11–16.)

Why marriage counseling? Why not family counseling? Family therapy, as many clinicians will agree, frequently moves away from the presented problem—usually the child as scapegoat—to the disturbed interaction of the marriage. At an institute I attended, I heard the late Dr. Nathan Ackerman observe that he watched for the moment when he could "get the kids out of the way" and deal with the marital problem. In other words, when the projections are uncovered, the focus of family therapy moves to the marital unit and its dysfunctional relationship.

Which services the family receives may depend on whose door they knock. If a couple present themselves to a marriage counseling center rather than to a family agency or mental health clinic, they have already located the problem in their relationship. It is then inappropriate to say to them initially: "Bring in the children, too." As will be demonstrated later by the case material, when the marital relationship improves, children often benefit without having been seen. In terms of systems theory, a positive change in the marital system may have repercussions in the family subsystems, the parent-child system, and the sibling system. Adolescents are occasionally seen separately; this occurs, for example, when a youngster and one parent have developed a tight coalition against the other partner and the problem does not yield to treatment in the joint marital interviews. This will be seen in the Green case (Chapter 7) in which three single interviews with the teenager took place.

ASSUMPTIONS OF TIME-LIMITED MARITAL COUNSELING

In time-limited conjoint marriage counseling there are some basic assumptions.

The marital assessment involves more than the sum of the assessments of each partner. It is not only the man, nor only the woman, but their relationship that is to be assessed. This assumes that there is a kind of marital axis or complementary balance of needs which brought the couple together originally, and that external or internal stress or a combination of both has upset the equilibrium.

I find the analogy to a seesaw to be helpful. A balancing movement is in operation, but an additional burden can result in excessive and precarious motion, causing the seesaw to swing wildly. Nor is the couple regarded as an isolated unit on a sort of desert island—that is, the marriage and the social environment are seen as an interactional field. The core problem may be essentially within an individual, or in the marital interaction, or in the outside social system. Usually, a combination of these is involved.

The assessment process therefore assumes that the worker possesses a basic knowledge of individual and interpersonal dynamics, skill in observation of the interactional process, as well as an awareness of the tensions and the resources in the family and the surrounding social systems. The counselor will appreciate that socioeconomic and cultural factors differentiate one lifestyle from another. It is assumed that he or she has skills in relating easily and communicating clearly, and self-knowledge regarding his or her assets and limitations in helping.

The counselor must be able to respond empathetically to each of the partners and to line up quickly with the adult part of their personalities. This serves to discourage regression, particularly important in short-term work. The counselor must be adept in active intervention, alternating support and confrontation to avoid "keeping the old fight going." It requires sensitive timing on the part of the therapist to engage the clients in a problem-solving process according to their value system, their readiness, and their capacity.

It is also assumed that the student and beginning counselor will have ongoing supervision available. Even for the more experienced, consultation is occasionally essential. Sound knowledge of referral resources and skill in the referral process are needed.

The therapist will draw selectively from a range of theoretical approaches, varying from the psychodynamic to the behavior-modification model. This is to say that an eclectic approach allows for flexibility in arriving at a differential assessment or diagnosis and treatment method.

In short-term marriage counseling, limited goals are assumed. All "t's" will not be crossed, all "i's" will not be dotted. The assumption is that after a meaningful experience during which clients were able to modify malfunctioning transactions in one or more areas of the marriage, they will be able to continue on their own to work through some of the "unfinished business." The related tasks are usually specifically identified in the course of treatment.

A further assumption is that a call for marital help is a crisis situation which requires prompt response on the part of the therapist. It should be noted that this interpretation of "crisis" does not conform strictly to the definition developed by crisis theorists.* Important principles of crisis theory are, however, applicable to the threat of marital breakdown.

When couples come with marital problems, the emotional features of a state of crisis are present, including a sense of hopelessness, heightened anxiety, frustration, inadequacy, and inability to cope with the situation effectively. The emotional fit or tie which drew the couple together originally and formed the marital axis is off balance. Former methods of problem solving no longer work and new solutions must be found.

A basic crisis-theory principle of prompt intervention applied at the peak of crisis, when tensions are high and failure in this most central of human relationships threatens, can therefore be a strong factor to encourage and mobilize motivation to change. Short-term service at such a time may well be more effective than protracted help deferred until later. To quote Lydia Rapoport, "A little help, purposefully focussed at a strategic time, is more effective than more extensive help given at a period of less emotional accessibility" (1967, p. 38).

The usual intake practice in social agencies of offering an appointment on the telephone, rarely for the same day or even the same week, could thus be the loss of an opportunity which may not recur. As the old Latin proverb puts it, "He gives twice who gives quickly."

It is in the very nature of crisis that its duration in time is limited. The upset state and disequilibrium at the outset of crisis are not static. One of the following consequences will result: return to the former level of functioning, regression to a lower level of functioning, or adaptation to an improved level of functioning.

The challenge which the crisis presents to the counselor, then, is to enlist the couple's adaptive capacity to reach for new and improved coping patterns. In other words, the counselor appreciates the growth potential in the marital crisis.

A further operational principle which is central to the process of helping in a crisis situation is the setting of a specific task or tasks to be undertaken relevant to the crisis. Task setting provides for purposeful activity which tends to reduce anxiety and to increase the energy available for problem solving.

Thus, crisis theory provides a valuable framework for helping troubled marriages. It is also compatible with a range of theoretical positions. The

---

*"The concept of 'crisis,' as formulated by its chief theoreticians, Dr. Erich Lindemann and Dr. Gerald Caplan, refers to the state of the reacting individual who finds himself in a hazardous situation" (quoted by Lydia Rapoport in "The State of Crisis, Some Theoretical Considerations," in Howard J. Parad, 1965, p. 23).

application of the principles outlined above will be demonstrated in the cases which follow.

Finally, the door is never closed with this time-limited approach. The assumption is that couples will feel comfortable in returning for a "booster shot" without a sense of failure, should the need arise.

METHOD OF CASE SELECTION AND PRESENTATION

The heart of this work is the case material presented in detail. Introductory notes and concluding comments, however, are provided for each chapter to clarify the process.

The method used to present the cases was dictation from notes made shortly after the close of the interviews. It was my wish and hope to present in this way a spontaneous and real picture of the interviews.

I recognize, of course, that the use of process in this form is bound to be selective. The reader will inevitably speculate as to what has been omitted. It is believed, however, that the material presented is sufficiently representative of the whole process as to be useful as a learning tool.

I considered using taped interviews as an alternate method of presenting the material, in order to provide a more complete picture of some of the sessions. In written form, however, this would have been too cumbersome. In the Martin case (Chapter 3) a transcription of part of the final follow-up interview, taped with the clients' permission, is supplied. The reader will note its length, despite the fact that segments considered not relevant to the follow-up were deleted from the transcription.

The notes provided in the left-hand margins of the process interviews are some of the worker's thoughts, both during the interviews and later. These notes are by no means comprehensive; again the reader is left to accept, reject, or fill in, as seems indicated. At the same time the learning principle of repetition is applied, so that concepts reappear in various forms.

The manner in which the two-column format is used will depend, of course, on the preference of the reader or instructor. Some students have found it helpful to read the cases first without reference to the side notes, to allow their own spontaneous reactions to the cases to come through. A second reading, including the comments and interventions, is then found more meaningful, permitting more critical evaluation.

To demonstrate my short-term method of conjoint marriage counseling in sufficient detail, I decided on a limited number of cases, using two criteria: that they be typical of the agency's caseload, and that they contain features related to four successive and major phases of the family life cycle. As early as 1931, Sorokin et al. presented a four-stage, family life cycle. Over the years, Glick (1947, 1957), Rodgers (1964, 1973), Hill (1970), Duvall (1971, 1977) and others have delineated eight and more stages in the family life cycle, terminating in widowhood or death.

Chapters 2 to 5 consider the following four phases:

Phase 1   The young couple in the beginning stage of marriage, without children
Phase 2   The young couple at the child-rearing stage
Phase 3   The middle-aged couple with teen-agers
Phase 4   The older couple at the child-leaving stage

What I have called the child-rearing phase embraces the three family stages identified by Duvall and others as infancy, preschool, and school age. Child-centered problems are peripheral to, not characteristic of, the caseload of the Marriage Counselling Centre. As already noted, family rather than marital treatment is then indicated. At the same time, during this child-rearing phase, the worker takes into account and deals with the marital discord as it affects the children. It may emerge that a child needs a specialized service, for example, for a learning disability. The worker will then arrange for this while the parents continue in counseling, or family therapy may be indicated.

A family goes through developmental stages just as an individual does, from infancy to childhood, adolescence, and adulthood. Each phase of the family life cycle presents tasks that must be coped with before the family moves on to the next phase, with its additional tasks. At each phase there is a transitional crisis until a new equilibrium is attained. Families differ as to how the tasks associated with each phase are or are not mastered, as well as how the interacting individual tasks are being dealt with. Of course, the phases are not cut and dried and they often overlap. It is understood, therefore, that no one case can be taken as truly typical of a particular phase.

The introductory notes for each of the chapters dealing with the four phases of marriage discuss some of the tasks related to the particular phase of family life. No attempt has been made, however, either in this general introduction or in the introductory chapter notes, to identify, discuss, or deal with *all* the tasks involved through the life cycle of the family. That would require another book! It is left to the reader to fill in what is relevant in relation to a particular couple.

While some common elements are present, each couple is unique in their manner of coping with their various tasks. My purpose is to establish an operational principle: that the worker should consider for the assessment and its treatment implications those tasks which are common and those features which are unique to a particular couple.

Similarly, the closing comments for each case are not designed as full summaries. They are intended, rather, to bring to the fore some but not all of the principles or learning points that may be derived from the given case and adapted to other cases. Again the reader will select, reject, or add what is relevant to his or her theoretical framework and practice. Professional development requires moving beyond the case, using hindsight learning to extract and apply principles, to test out what may or may not be effectively incorporated by a particular worker and adapted to his or her future practice.

Part II deals with some general issues in short-term marriage counseling. Thus, Chapter 6 includes three telephone interviews involving acute marital conflict, to illustrate both the need for immediate professional crisis intervention and also the importance of being sufficiently flexible to deal at a particular point with one partner alone, even though the conjoint interview is basic to this short-term model. Thus, in the case of the Victors (Chapter 2), Mrs. Victor was seen alone for one session, because it would have been too painful for Mr. Victor to hear some of the details of her extramarital affair. Similarly, in the case of Mr. and Mrs. Green, who were seen conjointly (Chapter 7), Mrs. Green's teen-age son by a previous marriage was seen alone for three sessions, as noted above.

A telephone interview provides direction for one spouse who at that moment is faced with making an urgent and critical decision. An important aspect of such an interview is that it often serves to bring both partners into a marriage counseling situation which might not otherwise ensue.

Chapter 7 discusses issues in divorce and remarriage. I do not believe that divorce counseling per se can be dealt with effectively on a time-limited basis; too much is involved and too much is at stake. Therefore, if the referral is for divorce counseling, or if divorce is clearly indicated in the initial contact, referral is made to a family agency, a clinic, or to legal resources.

In situations where ambivalence about divorce is present in one or both of the partners, however, the short-term service is made available. It sometimes becomes apparent after several sessions that divorce is indeed inevitable, and the short-term counselor is then obligated to continue working with the couple, or one partner, on the issues involved in the marital breakdown.

For example, it became necessary for me to continue working with Mr. Gray (Chapter 7) for over a year and a half, during and after the divorce proceedings. Thus, the short-term marriage counselor must be flexible enough to discard time limits and carry a case on a nonrigid schedule should the need arise.

Remarried couples often seek marital help, and a short-term service can be very effective. The case of Mr. and Mrs. Green (Chapter 7) contains some of the features common to remarriage and also illustrates how the problems of a teenager may be complicated by a strict or overzealous stepparent.

The contraindications to short-term marriage counseling are considered in Chapter 8. This list is subject to revision in light of further experience and research. Meanwhile it provides a workable guideline for the beginning marriage counselor who is using the short-term method.

Two cases are presented. In the case of Mr. and Mrs. Wood, conjoint marital therapy was impracticable because of the intense self-preoccupation of each of the partners. In the second case, Mr. and Mrs. Charlson, chronic alcoholism and violence required referral to other resources.

Although, following the initial phase, cases unlikely to respond to time-limited service are referred elsewhere, the assessment process itself has positive aspects. The client may experience for the first time a helping person who is understanding and nonjudgmental. In addition, the short-term counselor becomes skilled in quickly identifying and clarifying problems and is able to transfer an individual, couple, or family to a suitable resource without undue delay. Two-way referrals and collaboration with other resources, community and private, are more frequent when an agency provides a time-limited service. Thus, the provision of an efficient screening and a sensitive referral are in themselves of real value to the client.

In Chapter 9 there is a discussion on preparation for marriage. This includes my experience with short-term programs of ten sessions each for engaged couples in small groups.

The casebook concludes (Chapter 10) with my experience in sharing the short-term approach with key community professionals who by virtue of their roles as ministers, doctors, and lawyers are drawn into marriage and premarriage counseling.

LIMITATIONS

Of course limitations are inherent to the short-term approach described here, developed as it is from the practice experience of one worker. Its goals are limited, the client is left with "unfinished business," and the routine follow-up contact is of an informal nature only. The lack of specific research to test its effectiveness is also recognized.

It should be noted, however, that most of the couples with whom I have worked stated quite explicitly in the follow-up contact that the service had succeeded in being helpful to their marriage and to their family life. Of course the question arises: What is "successful"?

There is to date no unifying theory of marital therapy (Paolino & McGrady, 1978); consequently, related research is still in its early stages (Greer & D'Zurilla, 1975). But, as Carl Rogers puts it:

> I will settle for the simplest definition—If, a month after the group is over . . . most or all of the members still feel that it was a rewarding experience, which somehow moved them forward in their own growth, then for me it deserved the label of "a successful group." [Rogers, 1970]

While my own results may appear overly positive, it should be remembered that cases which did not respond to the short-term approach in the three assessment sessions were usually referred to other resources. The fact that most of the cases presented in this book show an improved relationship is, I believe, characteristic of the method when a sound assessment has been made.

This is encouraging and important for the beginning counselor, as well as for the couple. Beginning workers, like their clients, need the element of hope in order to function effectively. In fact, hope is an essential factor in fostering positive change in a marriage. Research has identified this factor as being related to successful therapeutic outcome, regardless of the therapist's theoretical position (Frank, 1968); that is, experiencing favorable even though limited results not only encourages and strengthens clients but also adds to the counselor's own professional development.

FUNDAMENTALS OF THE SHORT-TERM MARITAL COUNSELING PROCESS

The Initial Phase

In the initial phase (sessions one to three), four main tasks are involved (not necessarily in this order):

1. Assessment and determination of the precipitating factors
2. Interpretation to clients of the short-term service and "the contract"
3. Problem identification
4. Client involvement and task setting

1. *Assessment and determination of the precipitating factors*

The first interview involves a tentative social-diagnostic assessment. The joint interview quickly highlights patterns of interaction and communication as the couple respond to such questions as "What brings you here at this time?" If precipitating factors in the recent past do not emerge, the counselor may need to interrupt a confused or one-sided story to refocus on current concerns.

These usually involve one or more stress points commonly experienced to some degree in family life today. Some families manage to weather the disturbance, while others have great difficulty in coping. Such common precipitating factors include, for example, a move up the economic ladder. A return of the wife to the labor force, or a career woman's upgrading, are increasingly noted as stress factors between a couple. A promotion to a superior post can also become a serious stress factor for an individual, arousing fears of inadequacy that are not always openly expressed and of which he may even be unaware. The spouse will be affected adversely and a tenuous marital relationship may be thrown off balance.

A failure in business or loss of a job creates a stress that obviously affects both partners and the whole family. Transfer to another city, even a move to a new neighborhood, will create stress in the family system. A move from a larger home to a small apartment, involving the loss of possessions to which one has become attached, can be a strong emotional stress. The move from a modest to a larger, more elegant home may stir up feelings of unworthiness and guilt, and these have even been known to result in serious depression.

A new member enters the family system—an in-law, a grandparent, a boarder, a new child—or someone leaves the family—a son takes a job in a distant city, a father goes to war. Serious illness may strike a family member, affecting all aspects of the family system.

In the assessment, it is important for the counselor to be alert to the part that such recent events may play in precipitating marital crisis. At times the family may be assaulted by a series of such events, which contribute to escalating friction and tension within the marriage.

To round out the marital assessment, the counselor will take into account major role functioning related to work, household management, sex, parental control, class, culture, religion, values, and marital expectations. A brief glimpse into the families of origin is necessary in order to understand how the couple's marital roles may have developed.

2.   *Interpretation to clients of the short-term service and "the Contract"*

The counselor interprets the short-term nature of the service. The couple is told that after one to three sessions a three-way discussion will decide whether this service is appropriate for them. It is necessary to clarify the contract, emphasizing that the client role calls for participation and engagement; that the counselor acts essentially as a catalyst and an enabler who may shed light on what is going on between them or push ajar a dark door for a glimpse of a better way in the path ahead. In other words, the counselor, with the best skill and will in the world, is not a magician who can cause their problems to disappear without their own sincere effort.

It is sometimes necessary to form a *temporary* alliance with the more resistant partner in order to induct him or her into the client role. This is important in the first interview, in which a basic task of the counselor is to help both partners feel encouraged enough to return. To do this effectively, the worker must demonstrate a nonjudgmental approach to the couple's interaction, conveying the point that usually if one spouse is in pain, the other is also suffering—that it takes two to tangle, and therefore two to untangle. It is important to create an atmosphere in which some hope becomes possible.

3. *Problem identification*

As multiple problems are so often presented, the counselor must soon intervene to help the couple focus on a current problem, or a meaningful aspect of a problem, to be worked on in the beginning sessions.

Since it is important in short-term counseling for clients to meet with some early success, it will be necessary to break the vicious cycle of negative interaction, if only for the one session. With increased understanding and more satisfying methods of dealing with each other and affecting each other less negatively, the couple will begin to be able to work on unfinished business by themselves once the contract has been completed.

A focus on a segment of the core problem, a segment likely to yield to change, is therefore more productive than a head-on approach to a long-standing or major conflict area. In any case, this has usually spilled over into other areas of day-to-day living. The expectation is that a benign change in one area often produces beneficial repercussions in other areas, thus preparing the way for dealing with more central issues.

4. *Client involvement and task setting*

Before the couple leave even the first session, unless referral elsewhere is indicated, a mutually agreed on *manageable* task, related to the problem area, is established. The couple understand they are to work on this task before the next session. In this way client motivation is enhanced and the couple's responsibility for change is established. Defining a task also contributes to a beginning sense of hope that something can be altered or improved. The counselor must, however, be realistic and avoid false reassurance and over-support. We know that no movement can take place without some tension and anxiety.

The Middle Phase

People change only slowly, and by small steps. (As Talleyrand once said to his coachman, "Go slow, go slow. Don't you know we are in a hurry?") During the middle phase (sessions three to six), putting a searchlight on a small interactional issue immediately as it arises in the interview can provide the couple with a helpful learning experience. Any change or modification of behavior is highlighted positively. It bears repeating that early success is an important component in the effectiveness of short-term counseling. The worker encourages the clients to comment positively on any small improve-ment the partner has managed to make.

The issue under discussion may or may not be related to the assigned task. It may well relate to why the task was *not* undertaken. Such a client ex-change, however, permits the counselor to observe and point out what is of-ten a characteristic malfunctioning pattern. If so, the pattern will be repeti-tive, permitting the counselor to comment on how the partners affect each other—who pushes, who balks, who passes the buck, who picks it up—that when one attacks, the other withdraws; and how passivity induces aggres-sion, escalating frustration and hurt.

The short-term method is essentially a here and now approach but, as in-dicated earlier, when the past of one or the other partner impinges on the present, it must be dealt with. This is in line with Ackerman's concept of "the living past" (1958). For example, a woman may continue to react to her husband's social drinking as if he were her alcoholic father.

Communication-theory concepts are invaluable during the entire proc-ess. To enhance clear and direct communication between the partners, the worker consistently points out when one speaks for the other or thinks for the other or assumes how the partner feels, until they themselves realize that this "crystal ball approach" in their communication adds to rather than re-solves their problems. Nonverbal, unclear, or mixed messages are continu-ously clarified by the therapist.

During this process the counselor must himself provide a model of clear communication and be able to reach comfortably for unexpressed current feelings—not only the angry, hurt ones, but the tender, protective feelings as well. Distorted affect is interrupted and interpreted by the counselor.

A wide range of techniques, from the psychodynamic to behavior modification approaches, may be used to help the couple become more aware of how each is contributing to their difficulties and how each can contribute to improving their mutually unhappy state. For example, as indicated above, they are actively encouraged to use immediate positive reinforcement for any small improvement achieved by the spouse rather than rely on the all too common, mind-reading cop-out: "Oh, he knows I was pleased." Role-playing techniques are often helpful in the session, to demonstrate and help the couple in the use of new approaches to problem solving.

During this process, the counselor restates conflicts, points out inconsistencies, moves from confrontation to support. In other words, the counselor engages the couple by whatever means he has at his disposal to help them shift to more satisfying methods of dealing with each other. Of course, he works with the style that fits his understanding of behavior and his own personality. It is important, however, to feel free to test out new methods and to avoid a static position, which is usually self-defeating. As we say to clients, "If something doesn't work, why not try something else?" In counseling, if one approach is ineffective, then try another.

During this middle phase, as the couple begin to take over more actively, testing out new ways of reacting to each other, the counselor becomes less active, intervening only when they revert to their previous pattern or seem to be going around in circles. The counselor comments positively on observed changes which take place during the session. When the couple report that these changes are occurring *between* sessions, and this process continues, with allowance made for the realistic ups and downs that are a normal part of daily life and indeed of any growth process, the scene is set for further consolidation and termination.

The Ending Phase

This phase usually consists of a three-way summary of the gains made and identification of some of the unfinished business the couple still need to work on. The last two sessions are usually spaced two weeks apart, and a follow-up contact in two or three months' time is arranged for. The follow-up is important to maintain the principle of continuity of interest and to emphasize that the counselor's door remains open. Couples find this encouraging but often do not seem to require further counseling.

It should be noted that short-term intervention does not present the intense separation problems characteristic of long-term counseling. Of course, these feelings often emerge in capsule form, but they are more fleeting and less persistent and can usually be handled in the last session or two. This is understandable in that the brevity of the contact and its conjoint nature do not create strong dependency ties.

The couple are also helped to feel they are not being abandoned, and that returning for help need not signify a serious setback. Any resentful feelings of being left to cope on their own are therefore minimized.

Feelings of ending and separation from a helpful experience, or from a helpful person who has shared in their intimate marital problems, however, should not be lightly put aside. Mixed feelings of satisfaction, a sense of loss, or even anger can be anticipated by the worker. It is sometimes helpful to verbalize the naturalness of these mixed feelings for the client. A revival of early difficulties in the final sessions may reflect the clients' reluctance to separate from the therapist. In short-term counseling, however, we find that the pull toward autonomy is stronger than the wish for dependency, and any such transient feelings can be dealt with without difficulty.

The two-week interval between the last two sessions is designed to dilute the relationship with the worker. This gives the couple confidence to carry on without help; knowing that a follow-up interview is scheduled also serves to reassure them.

CONCLUDING COMMENTS

To repeat, this casebook is designed to serve as a springboard for consideration and discussion of the potential in the short-term approach to marital conflict by counselors in training and by those practitioners who have not yet seriously tested this alternative to open-ended treatment. There are many roads to Rome, and theoretical offerings in the literature are rich and varied.

Each instructor and practitioner will evolve a theoretical framework and will draw on techniques that are personally meaningful. This is as it should be, and I suggest that it may not be incompatible with the eclectic basis of the short-term model here presented. The model is itself not sacrosanct, and some experimentation with it, or aspects of it, may prove helpful.

It will be noted that I have myself drawn selectively from psychoanalytic theory, ego psychology, crisis theory, communication theory, general systems, and role and learning theories, and that I have also gained much from many of the leading family therapists, despite their somewhat different paths. I am therefore at times willing to modify a given concept in order to meet the unique needs of a particular couple. As I have often said to students, "Keep one eye on the book, but the other fixed firmly on the client!"

In short-term treatment, as I have already emphasized, limited goals and "unfinished business" are inherent. The helper must have the conviction, when clients have demonstrated the motivation to improve their lot, that they also have the capacity to do some further improving on their own.

The writer, too, has set limited goals for this book, knowing that there is much "unfinished business" left for its readers, confident that they will be able to continue further professional development on their own.

PART ONE
The Phases of Marriage

2

The Beginning Phase

In these days of drastic change it's difficult for young people to know what to expect from marriage. In the traditional marriage the man was the leader and the woman the follower. He brought home the bacon; she ran the home and took care of the children. Both knew what was expected of their marital roles.

Today the partnership marriage is more prominent and carries more potential satisfaction. It is, however, more challenging, more difficult. The individual roles and tasks are ill defined; they have to be worked out and worked at, and no established guidelines are available. In any case, neither the traditional nor the partnership marriage carries a prescription for instant happiness.

Bernard Shaw once said that if you put the names of all the eligibles into a barrel and pulled them out two by two, you'd have as good a basis for mate selection as any that has yet been devised. I don't quite go along with this, but it does suggest a significant, if implicit, message that marriage is not a ready-made affair. It involves a developmental process, which requires ongoing input throughout the family's life span.

The young couple settling into their shiny new apartment will have a number of issues to decide as they assume their new roles of husband and wife. What does he think a good wife should be? What does she expect of him? How realistic are their expectations? Sometimes each expects the other to make up for all the hurts and disappointments suffered in growing up. And what is expected of them by others?

Have they loosened those early emotional ties that may interfere with the new union? For example, does she telephone her mother ten times a day? Does he drop in on his mother on the way home from work, sampling some of her goodies before dinner?

To what extent do the parents, consciously or unconsciously, dominate the new marriage? Sometimes parental influences are so strong it almost seems as if not only the couple but their two sets of parents were married. Are the in-laws to become outlaws, something to battle over? Some regressive pull is natural and to be expected initially, but marriage is for adults, not for children. Of course, it is desirable to have and enjoy an adult relationship with one's parents, and marriage in no way implies severing that relationship. Still, it is essential for the new family structure to have priority:

> *Daughter am I in my mother's house,*
> *But mistress in my own. . . .*

This quotation from Rudyard Kipling applies equally to the new husband.

A range of emotional and practical tasks, often intertwined, have to be coped with. How is money to be managed? How is it to be spent? Will it be used to exert control or power over the spouse? As a way of giving or withholding love? How about the family chores, if both are working? Who washes the dishes? Who dries? And there's the garbage!

What about sexual adjustment? Do they share in making this an enjoyable area of experience for both? Will the bedroom become an arena for fighting out all sorts of discontents and resentments? What about the vital decision as to whether and when to have a child? Are their views similar?

Then there are religion, friends, decisions to be made about recreation, education, values, and goals. There is also the persistent notion that togetherness and intimacy are the most important aspects of marriage. Of course, the freedom to share thoughts and feelings—from sorrow to joy, anger to pleasure—is essential to a good partnership. But it is also of great importance to accept differences, to retain separateness and autonomy. The couple, after all, are not two peas in a pod; each individual does stand and walk alone.

The counselor facing young marrieds with these thoughts in mind develops a "hunch" about the marital assessment, which becomes clearer as the couple's interactional patterns emerge in the first or subsequent sessions. To assess a marriage the counselor needs a working definition of "a happy marriage." Alas! There is no simple definition. To put it simply, what works, works! The criterion is what is effective and functional for a given couple.

Almost a half-century ago, Levy and Monroe (1938) defined the "happy" family as one that was not problem-free but could somehow cope with its problems.

Any two individuals can presumably make a happy marriage if there is an emotional fit or meshing of their needs which makes for an effective balance between them. Sometimes, however, the balance may be precarious, and when a normal life stress comes on the scene, the applecart may be upset.

The counselor's role calls for a nonjudgmental acceptance of the lifestyle of any couple, married or unmarried, if it fits their needs. If it works for them, it is a "healthy marriage." Folk wisdom understood this, as reflected by the Mother Goose rhyme—

> *Jack Sprat could eat no fat*
> *His wife could eat no lean,*
> *And so between the two of them*
> *They licked the platter clean.*

In the case of the Victors, which follows, sexual adjustment was the presenting problem. They were assessed as a basically healthy couple. In fact, it is a good therapeutic principle to assume that people are healthy until proven otherwise. Too often, social workers and other counselors search for pathology, neglecting to seek out any healthy areas which may be built upon.

With the avalanche of sexual material available today, it is difficult for the beginning counselor to see the forest for the trees. Where to start? Where to stop? Should I refer them to a sex clinic? Is my working to improve their relationship a way of avoiding the sexual problem? Are these problems interrelated? Is giving permission for erotic pleasures really effective in relieving sexual guilt or anxiety, or should I recommend specific pleasuring exercises? Might pornographic pictures or movies turn them on? What about oral sex if one partner objects?

Of course, sex is an important and vital aspect of marriage. It is often, however, a magnet to which other sources of discontent adhere. Sometimes it is used or withheld by one or both partners as a way of getting even for some built-up resentment, neglect, or hurt. Indeed, there are many other factors that may and do enter into the sexual area and must be taken into account.

Despite the flood of information on human sexuality, despite the "sexual revolution," young people still find they have to work out their own unique sexual adjustment with their marital partner. Time is required to build up a satisfactory balance; I think that is why young marrieds so frequently say that the second year was better than the first. And although we hear so much about sexual freedom today, there are many couples today who are still insecure in their sexual roles.

In any case, it seems sound for the beginning counselor to peel the onion from the outside and not rush in with sophisticated techniques before understanding what the couple's needs are at a particular stage. One has to move sensitively with them, at their own pace, according to their concerns and readiness. The counselor must take care not to impose his or her own sexual attitudes and values on them.

The Victor case is offered as a starting point from which beginning counselors may consider current approaches to sexual disharmony (Kaplan, 1974, 1979) as well as decide what may be helpful on a time-limited basis. The short-term marriage counselor, however, need not be a specialized sex therapist, and at some point he or she may consider the usefulness of referring a couple to such a resource (Wyden & Wyden, 1971).

Mr. and Mrs. Peters, who are also at the beginning phase of marriage, came to counseling with a number of disturbing problems. Unlike Mr. and Mrs. Victor, the Peters had experienced a good sexual adjustment prior to marriage. After several years of living together, however, Mrs. Peters' not unusual concerns are expressed by the couplet—

> *Oh, let us be married!*
> *Too long we have tarried.*

Their relationship was thrown off balance by the move from single to married status.

MR. AND MRS. VICTOR

Jim Victor, age 23   Children: None
Ellen Victor, age 21

Married 16 months

Referral, October 14
Mr. Victor telephoned the agency. In a quiet, subdued voice, he asked if he could have an appointment for a marital problem. I

asked if his wife knew of his call and that he wished to see a counselor. He said, "Yes, she is interested, but shy," adding, "The problem came to a head a week ago and it is very serious." He sounded tense and nervous. Without querying him further, I made an appointment for the following day.

A crisis situation: quick intervention is important.

First Interview, October 15
Mr. Victor is a tall, blond, well-built young man of 23. In contrast, his wife is dark, petite, with large black eyes and an almost doll-like appearance. As they entered the room, Mrs. Victor sat on the settee and her husband sat close to her. He put his hand tenderly on her shoulder. Mrs. Victor looked stiff and tense.

Worker notes "body talk" but withholds comment at this early point. Increasing self-consciousness could inhibit the flow of the interview.

I asked whether or not they had ever sought help from a stranger before with their marriage and Mrs. Victor answered, "Not together." I asked what had brought them now and together. They looked at each other and Mrs. Victor finally said, "It's really my fault." At this, somewhat protectively, Mr. Victor took over with embarrassment, and in a hesitant voice explained that about a week ago he had learned that his wife was involved with another man. This situation had gone on without his knowledge for close to three months.

The question about previous help is raised, as worker should be alert to note if negative feelings and misgivings were the result.

Mrs. Victor was now weeping softly. I asked how he had come to learn of this situation. Still weeping, his wife managed to say, "I told him so." I asked why, and she answered, "I wanted to get out of it, of the affair—I had enough."

Is this self-punishment and/or partner punishment?

During this exchange Mr. Victor kept his arm on his wife's shoulder protectively. I remarked that he seemed to feel concerned and sympathetic toward her and asked how this made her feel. She replied, still weeping, "It makes me feel worse. I wish he'd get mad at me." She went on, "I'm also crying because the whole thing had to happen." Did she feel he should have prevented it? Between sobs she said, "He didn't listen to me so I hit him with this." By now, she was sobbing quite heavily.

Nonverbal interaction. His sympathy produces tears and guilt.

She projects blame on him for her affair.

Technique of moving the affect from one to the other. Here the partner is asked to respond when the

I turned to Mr. Victor, saying he must have felt very hurt when his wife "hit" him with this news. With obvious discomfort, he explained that their sex life had been unsatisfactory, and therefore he could not blame his wife for what had happened. He said he knew of nothing that could be done about their problem. He paused and added slowly, "I am very large and she is very tiny." I asked, "Could you tell me how this affected your sex life? An accommodation usually occurs."

He explained that they had been dating for about a year and had attempted intercourse a month before their wedding. I said in my experience it is like this today with most engaged couples; they get to intercourse especially if they have been dating for nearly a year. Here Mrs. Victor said softly, "It was the first time for both of us." But it had turned out to be an extremely painful experience for her. He had not been able to penetrate. A few days later they tried again, and it was equally painful and unsuccessful. I commented sympathetically that these episodes must have made them both feel very upset and frightened.

I went on to ask what they had done about the situation. He said he had arranged for her to see a gynecologist. After the examination, the doctor said penetration was just about impossible as the membrane of her hymen was very thick. The doctor recommended that she be surgically opened, and they agreed that a hymenectomy be performed. I remarked that they had jointly agreed on a sensible plan and asked how they had felt about all this.

It seems both were so preoccupied during this period with the fear their parents would find out that they felt only relief when it was over and that no one knew. Mrs. Victor, who had now stopped crying, said, "My parents are strict Catholics and would have been shocked. My mother would have hit the roof." He added that his parents too were Catholics with strong views about premarital intercourse. I said it was hard that they had no one to talk to about this very disturbing experience. Mrs. Victor said, "I didn't even tell my girl friend."

Had this "secret" behavior in any way made them feel obligated to go ahead with the marriage? "No," Mrs. Victor replied easily. "We went ahead because we really loved each other.'' They told each other the problem was probably behind them, but they didn't discuss it beyond this.

In discussing their courtship, Mr. Victor said that they had much in common, friends and interests, and she added, "We had fun. I admire and rely on Jim. He is tender and understanding." Mr. Victor said he had had a couple of girl friends before Ellen, but no one who really held his interest or love as she did.

He went back to the matter of their sex problem and the fact that he is "large and she is very tiny." He said that soon after marriage, when intercourse continued to be painful, he suggested that she go to another gynecologist. She commented, "That doctor was no help at all. In fact over the sixteen months of our marriage, I have seen three doctors, and the only advice I ever got was to have a baby. They said this would 'stretch me.' " Mrs. Victor went on, "We can't afford babies now," and he added, "We plan to save first for a small home." How, then, I asked, had they dealt with their problem? Here Mrs. Victor said, quite resentfully, "Over the past year or more, I raised the question of marriage counseling with Jim, but he was always reluctant even to discuss it, and so," she added hopelessly, "I just dropped it." Yes, she agreed that she had felt hurt and angry at this lack of response from him. Had she told him she was hurt and angry? No, she did not want to upset him. He interjected his regret that he had not responded before now, but he had really thought there was nothing that could be done about it. He added, "I suppose I was afraid I might lose her." No, he had not shared this feeling with her. I said it seemed that they shared good feelings but appeared to have difficulty sharing angry or frightening ones.

Since marriage, their sex life has been very sporadic, every three or four months. He said, "I would like us to sit in the living room and have some preliminaries, but Ellen would just get into bed, slip under the sheets, and urge me to get on with it." "Yes" she admitted, "because it is always painful, I wanted to get it over with quickly." I said it seemed that their first encounter with intercourse had unfortunately shattered their confidence, and left them both very frightened and uptight. She said "yes" and he nodded agreement. I added that they had

---

Useful information for the marital assessment.

Mr. V's problem solving is to identify the problem as "hers."

Note the interaction: he resists her attempt to involve him in mutual problem solving, and she gives way too easily.

When he attempts a solution, she resists.

Worker gives permission to enjoy "forbidden" behavior.

A glimpse at the "proper" home atmosphere—its implications for sexual attitudes and marital expectations.

Assessment information—growing up, Mrs. V. had few boundaries or limits placed on her behavior, Mr. V. probably too many. Both are only children. Parents will tend to indulge or be overstrict. The couple were likely drawn together as each could provide the unmet needs of the other.

The marital assessment—exploring what's right as well as what's wrong is important.

Strengths in the marriage: both are responsible in areas of financial and household management and they function well together. Also, family, religion, and social life seem essentially satisfactory.

missed out on the fun of learning and exploring intercourse as a pleasurable part of their relationship.

In both their homes the subject of sex was carefully avoided. He thought his parents were companionable; they were affectionate, and the atmosphere at home was tranquil. His parents had married rather late in life. His father was very much the leader at home and rather strict. They went to a lot of effort to avoid spoiling him as an only child; he had friends, was good at schoolwork, and enjoyed sports. No, he was not really close to either parent, perhaps a little more toward his mother, who was more outgoing and affectionate.

Mrs. Victor said her family got along well. She was her father's darling and an only child; he pretty much let her have her own way. Her mother was more of a disciplinarian, but Ellen knew it would be "no big deal" if she didn't keep the curfew, and she usually didn't. (Here she gave a little grin.) Her mother always encouraged friends and cousins to visit so that she would not feel too much alone. Her parents still know nothing of their marital difficulties. She thinks they are "old-fashioned" about sex.

In briefly exploring other areas in their marriage for a tentative assessment of its potential or lack of it, it was learned that Mr. Victor is working in a responsible position for a large drug company. He is taking two courses at night to obtain a further degree. Mrs. Victor has also been working, as a part-time secretary. They have been saving for a down payment on a home. They share household tasks, and he willingly gives her a hand. They bowl once a week with two other couples. Her family lives in the United States, his parents in Canada, and they visit occasionally. Mr. Victor's parents are fond of Mrs. Victor and Mrs. Victor's parents think a great deal of Mr. Victor. Mrs. Victor's undergraduate education was interrupted when she married and she did not complete her degree. They are agreed that she should be able to do this in another year or two. Religion is not an issue between them; both are somewhat liberal in their views. Mr. Victor had suggested during the engagement that she talk with her doctor about taking the pill, and she has been on this without any complication.

I commended them for the practical step they had taken with regard to birth control. I asked if they had ever talked to-

Weakness in the marriage: Lack of intimacy and of clear communicating about "emergency feelings" such as fear and anger. Lack of sexual information.
Failure to perceive the sex problem as "theirs."
Attitude change and educational procedures are indicated.

The use of generalization as a supportive technique —i.e., "you are not strange or unique."

An active "hope-giving" comment is offered.

Worker explains how their "solution" reinforces the problem.
Worker thus demonstrates no *one* partner is to blame.

Important to raise the option of dissolving the marriage.

gether during whatever lovemaking occurred between them. "No, not really." Verbally, they never communicated in this way. No, Mrs. Victor said she had not known about a lubricating jelly until the last gynecologist had advised it. She said it helped a little, but not much. She still felt tight and small, although intercourse was not as painful as before marriage. I said I thought the early painful experience had persisted in a scary way into the marriage.

I said I thought they were handicapped by attitudes they had brought to their sexual relationship—the restrictions, inhibitions, and myths about sex, which had got in the way of their being able even to talk about sex with comfort and ease. I said this would be one of the goals in working together with them.

I also said I thought it was important to understand that a sex problem is not the responsibility of one or the other partner but is a mutual problem, and that both would need to accept the responsibility for working out a satisfactory adjustment. I added that it is not at all exceptional for the woman to feel she is the inadequate one, and for the husband to feel it is "unmanly" to seek help or understanding about sexual functioning. I said they had taken a constructive and courageous step in seeking help now and together. Mr. Victor added, "Hopefully, better late than never." "A good attitude," I commented, "and it's not at all late." I pointed out that both had perceived the problem as being hers alone, and that this was reflected in her going to the gynecologist after marriage, in his hoping the problem would go away, in her urging him "to get it over with quickly," thus preventing him from trying to give her some preliminary sensuous pleasure. "Yes," she repeated, "I refused because I kept on thinking it's going to hurt anyhow." I told them their "solution" had only made the problem worse, and that they had both gone along with it. They had both experienced hurt and anger in a highly sensitive area, and this had not been dealt with, so that their painful beginnings had continued to haunt them.

I raised the option of separation, which should be considered as both were young and without children. Did either of them feel the marriage should be dissolved? Mrs. Victor said, "No, I really want to keep my marriage; I'd feel lost without Jim." And he said he only wants the marriage to improve and knows he wants to keep her.

I wondered how they had coped with their natural sex urges in the period when they were keeping away from each other. After a little silence, Mrs. Victor said, "I had some desire, but was too frightened to approach Jim." He was looking pretty self-conscious, so I commented that most young people in their situation would resort to masturbation, the usual solution when intercourse is not available. Yes, they acknowledged that they had done so and had masturbated before marriage. I said it was excellent that they had released some sexual tension in this way. I added that I was pleased to know that Mrs. Victor was able to have an orgasm through masturbation, as this was an indication of her capacity to achieve sexual pleasure.

Worker verbalizes for them to remove fear of criticism.

For attitude change: worker turns a "negative" into a "positive," and demonstrates nonjudgmental attitude.

More details of her affair or his fidelity would complicate the joint first session and slow up the process of therapy.

Summarizing—a helpful technique.

By way of summary and clarification of goals toward the end of the session, I commented that despite all that had gone wrong between them, it seemed that each had a strong regard and affection for the other, and that each of them wanted to keep and improve the marriage and their sex relationship. Today, they had been able to share some intimate feelings and concerns with a stranger in a forthright manner, which I thought would help them in mutually working on their problems.

The element of realistic hope is reiterated.

Mr. Victor had had a painful shock but, I explained, he had unwittingly contributed to his wife's infidelity by not feeling secure enough to face up to their sexual problem as a mutual one. This was, however, understandable and part of the traditional myth, which Mrs. Victor had also accepted, that if something goes wrong and the man is potent, it follows that the woman needs to be "fixed up." It seemed that they had been groping in the dark, hampered by cultural and religious misconceptions as well as by some misinformation. I explained that the vagina is capable of accommodating the penis regardless of size, with rare exceptions. This must surely be possible, I added, since a baby finds its way through the vaginal passage. I said that this present crisis, painful though it was, could be a factor in bringing them to a closer level of intimacy.

Crisis anxiety induces problem solving. Concept of growth through conflict.

The "contract" and a short-term goal are established in the first session. This is based on a rapid and tentative marital assessment. These individuals seem basically healthy; the marriage has not really got off the ground. Their motivation seems good.

I suggested that we work together for another four or five weekly sessions. The purpose of these sessions would be to have them deal with their fears and inhibitions around sex and to loosen some of the hurt and angry feelings both of them must have at the present impasse. I went on to explain my belief that as they became freer to share intimate feelings, this should help them respond with growing pleasure to their sexual needs. I did not think they would need longer therapy; if, however, further help seemed to be indicated, we three could discuss this after our sessions were over. Mr. Victor remarked that he hadn't thought they would be able to talk to me as they had, and Mrs. Victor said she was glad they had come.

I explained that a physical and emotional relationship evolves slowly and that it often takes months, even a year or more, to build a really satisfactory balance. Did they want to invest such time in working together toward this further goal? They agreed they did, and I added that our plan would be for ongoing development to take place after they left the sessions, asserting my conviction that they would be able to carry on by themselves to improve their situation.

Worker shares her confidence in them. This is ego building.

The task of nonperformance is set. Simple and manageable aspects of the task are spelled out as "homework."

They were specifically asked to avoid any sexual contact during the coming week. I suggested that they could share and show any affection they wished to show each other spontaneously, and that they might talk together briefly about our meeting. I asked also that they try to avoid "stewing" over their problem. I thought it would be good, however, if they could talk a little together about the parental attitudes toward sex they had mentioned, and about any concerns or experiences they had had in their teens.

They both left looking more relaxed and, I thought, somewhat encouraged.

Worker's Tentative Assessment and Treatment Plan

This reaction at the close of the first session often indicates a positive outcome of treatment. The sex problem with this couple appears to be due to misinformation, guilt, and a traumatic experience with coital experimentation. In addition, family taboos have contributed to sexual anxiety and poor communication.

Active permission to enjoy sexual pleasure is indicated from the counselor, who represents an authority or parental figure. Some directive guidance should relieve anxiety. Encouraging freer communication in this area should improve the marital relationship as well.

Second Interview, October 25

Mr. and Mrs. Victor arrived punctually. Both greeted me with pleasant smiles. He hung up her coat, and they sat together on the curved settee, facing each other. Again they sat quite close. I pulled my chair away from my desk and sat facing them both. I asked, "Who wants to begin?" They looked at each other, and Mrs. Victor said somewhat coyly, "Last week was much better." Mr. Victor went on, "The session was a big relief for me. Talking about things here was like getting a weight off my chest." One evening during the week they had gone out to dinner, and a few days ago they had a couple whom they had not seen for a long time over for the evening.

Mr. V. again takes the initiative.

Then Mr. Victor said, rather abruptly, "Things are more relaxed, but still it has become complicated between us now." It seems that her lover had called her on the telephone the night before last. He added with great anger, "He had the nerve to call at my home!" Mrs. Victor had answered the telephone. Mr. Victor said, "I guess he would have hung up if I had answered." Now Mrs. Victor interrupted, "What could I do if he called to speak to me? He was very upset." Mr. Victor said to her, with a sense of urgency, "Look, this telephone calling has got to stop." He clenched his fists and said angrily, "I'll do something terrible if it happens again."

It crossed my mind that the affair had not ended but I withhold questioning about this. It is more important for Mr. V. to demonstrate that he is capable of expressing appropriate anger.

I commented on how much rage he was feeling, and he said, "Yes, I have a terrible rage toward him. He let us down. I know him personally. He is a professional, and he acted in a foul way by taking advantage of my wife behind my back." I said his anger was indeed understandable. Did he also feel that his wife had acted behind his back? "Well," he answered tentatively, "I know she has been taken advantage of." Here I turned to Mrs. Victor questioningly. She then said, "Oh, I know it was me that caused it all, I know I was the aggressor." I looked at Mr. Victor. He still denied anger toward her. He said, "I understand her problem." Could she tell her husband how she feels about his kindness and understanding? She said to him, "You know that you're upsetting me. It upsets me that you just forgive me." Mr. Victor looked thoughtful, but did not respond.

Worker feels Mr. V. needs help to release his anger toward his wife. This intervention, however, is not effective.

Worker therefore promotes interaction between them on this.

I said, "Mr. Victor, your reaction may be logical, but you must have some feelings too. In any case, you see you do manage to upset your wife." More silence. I asked Mr. Victor whether he was afraid he would lose his wife if he got angry with her. "Well," he said, "I know I am afraid to lose her." He went on that he is very hurt but insisted he had been inadequate. I told him he couldn't take full responsibility for what had happened. His wife had made a decision and had acted on it independently. This led to some discussion of Mrs. Victor's feelings of guilt and inadequacy as well. I said I thought each one was still feeling individually blameworthy, and also that each one somehow thought that the partner was to blame. What was missing was the "we" part of the problem.

When I mentioned Mrs. Victor's sense of inadequacy, she said, "That's why I looked for satisfaction outside the marriage." She had wondered whether she could function better with someone else. She wanted at least to see whether it was possible. She turned to him and said, "I did try to tell you before I went outside, but when I talked about it you always would say, it will go away; we should give it time."

Mr. Victor responded that he hadn't wanted to talk about it before now. I said, "It isn't easy now either," and he agreed. I pointed out that Mrs. Victor had not been very persistent in raising it with him. She agreed that she would touch on it and then let the matter drop. She added, "But without encouragement, it was hard for me to stay with it."

I said their reaction was understandable, but this holding back of their real feelings had handicapped them in finding an appropriate solution, he by hoping that it would just go away and she by not being more persistent about her concerns. This had increased their sexual anxieties and fears, resulting in this unhappy situation.

I again raised Mr. Victor's feelings about his wife's lover. He said, "Thinking of him makes my blood boil." With tight fists, he went on, "If this continues, I'll ruin him professionally." Mrs. Victor said, "That's why he phoned, when he heard from my girl friend, who is his secretary, that I had told you about us. He told me I was acting very stupidly. He said it was dangerous, as it could ruin him professionally, but I reassured him that you would do no such thing." Here I interjected, "But

---

Mr. V. is expressing fear of anger and fear of losing his wife, and these are interrelated.

Technique of restating the presenting problem as being a mutual one.

Her telling him of the affair could be a way of forcing him to take counseling.

Pointing out the mutually maladaptive response has reinforced their problem.

He can express negative feelings, but is more inhibited in a love relationship, fearing rejection. This will have to be picked up again at a later point.

Worker brings out reality of

the risk involved in V.'s rage. Also, this is supportive of his right to anger.

Mr. V. is trying to be more assertive.

Mrs. V's ambivalence comes out clearly.

Here I translate Mr. V's anger into hurt, to which he can relate.

Confirmation that he *is* afraid to get angry at her and/or to lose her.

Support for Mr. V. to take a stand.

Mrs. V. goes along, but "the confession" could also have been a way to punish Mr. V. However, I thought

your husband has just indicated that he might well do that very thing."

I asked, "Shouldn't this man know what risks are involved for him in this affair?" Now Mr. Victor came on firmly, "He damn well should—even another phone call—"

Mrs. Victor then went into a vague discussion of how this man was really trying to be considerate. He had phoned her simply to find out; he was concerned, concerned about himself, it was true, about what her husband was going to do, but she also thought he was concerned about her.

I said, "Perhaps you feel some regret at having broken off this affair?" "No," she said, somewhat uncertainly, "I've had enough. It was really just a physical relationship, he never even got to know me as a person." She went on, "However, I'm not really sure he was all that unkind."

This got Mr. Victor very excited, and he turned to her, "Can't you see what that bastard is doing? He's trying to get back to you, the way he was at the beginning, just pretending to be interested, pretending to be concerned." To this, Mrs. Victor responded, "Well, I'm not sure whether I really do like him." Then, a little more daringly, she added, "I've even wondered, maybe I even love him."

Mr. Victor looked defeated. I said, "Mr. Victor, you look very hurt." He remained quiet. I added, "You know, it seems to me you are so frightened of losing your wife that you won't even show the hurt you must feel at this disclosure from her." Then he responded, "That's true, I am hurt, and I do fear losing her, but I'm full of anger at him." I asked Mrs. Victor how she felt about the anger her husband was expressing toward this man. She said to him, "I didn't know you had such very strong feelings about him." Here he said, "I was afraid to tell you too much. I didn't want to spoil things between us this week; I wanted to discuss this in a three-way session before I took my position." I said, "You have a right to your position, and your wife has a right to know it too." I asked, "Is it possible, Mrs. Victor, that you wanted some limits put around this situation. Is this why you confessed to Mr. Victor?" Here she nodded agreement and I pointed this out to him.

raising this would be too much for Mr. V. at this point.

Techniques of generalizing and verbalizing for the client.

Without spelling it out, worker is separating his past from his present. His wife is not his mother.

The problem-solving processes are identified for the couple with the assumption that they will work on it further together.

Worker links past unfinished business to present patterns which are now dysfunctional. Some working through can go on outside the session.

Worker reinforces the reality problem that must be faced.

I asked Mrs. Victor to tell her husband how she would feel if he did show her his anger. She said, "You know, Jim, I'd feel better." I asked whether his anger would chase Mrs. Victor away from him. She said, "Why should you feel that way?" Here he replied thoughtfully, "I suppose I never let off much steam in my own home." I said he had learned, as many youngsters do, to hold back his anger. I wondered, did he feel then that he would lose love if he didn't hold his anger back? He was silent.

"Would you tell your wife what happened when you did blow your top, the way all teenagers do?" He said to her, "I only know my dad would say, 'Don't raise your voice to your mother,' and then I would feel sorry." I said, "You're an adult now, and your wife is saying she would rather you didn't store up hurt or angry feelings." She repeated, "I'd be relieved. I wish you wouldn't do that." I said this is something he would have to test out and work on with her help; it would take time until he could risk showing her some negative feelings and still feel safe.

I added that in growing up, she was used to being protected and had somehow passed this message on to her husband—i.e., "Go easy and let me do what I want." She said, "I suppose that's so." I said this could make it more difficult for Mr. Victor to express anger since he had already had the problem before his marriage. Here he said, "I never thought of it like that." I suggested this was something they could talk over further on their own.

Meanwhile I returned to his anger toward the third party. What was he going to do about this? Mr. Victor said to Mrs. Victor, "He's got to be told that unless he leaves you alone he's going to regret it. Either you tell him or I will." Mrs. Victor looked scared. "I don't want you to talk to him—that would be awful. But I don't know how to do it—it's so awkward." I put in here, "It's a tough problem; what's to be done?"

Mrs. Victor continued defensively, "Well, it's complicated," and he explained to me, "Yes, it's complicated, because she works in the same building as this man. He's a doctor, and she works in the lab in the same building. Her best friend is his secretary." He continued, "I'd like to stop that friendship, and I would like her to change her job. But," he added, "I realize that's asking a lot."

I asked Mrs. Victor whether she sees this man during the day, and she said, "Yes." What does she do when they meet? "Well," she said, "I greet him." She added, "I think it's very childish not to even talk to him, as Jim would like."

Worker engages them in problem solving.

Here Mr. Victor came on strong: "I'll get him for sure if this goes on." I turned to Mrs. Victor. How was she going to deal with this? She thought maybe it would be easier to tell him something on the telephone. Mr. Victor agreed this would be okay if he could hear just how clear she would make it.

Use of role playing to enable Mrs. V. to deal with an awkward situation.

I asked Mrs. Victor how she could put it. She felt and sounded quite awkward with the conversation, stumbling a good deal. I asked Mr. Victor if he could help with this. After several efforts on his part, she finally agreed to say that she and her husband were working on improving their marriage, that he had told her to make this call and to make it clear there would be unpleasant consequences should any further intimacy occur between them, including even a phone call.

Mr. Victor then said that if things were cleared up in this way and the man was told directly where he stood, "I wouldn't mind so much to my wife continuing her job. She could even be formally polite, if a contact should arise in relation to her work." He added, "I know it's difficult for her to find another job so near to our apartment, especially a half-time one."

It is necessary that Mrs. V's ambivalent feelings be openly discussed.

Mrs. Victor said soberly that she was relieved she didn't have to leave her job. She liked her work, and they are saving for the down payment on a home. I said that although Mrs. Victor went along with the telephone plan, it had been on her husband's insistence. Did she still feel somewhat reluctant about this? Did she feel she was being pressured to close the door on this outside relationship?

Mrs. Victor said, somewhat sadly, "No, it has to be closed." I commented on how sad she looked. Perhaps she really wants out of the marriage, even apart from this man? She responded firmly, "No. I'm proud of Jim. I know I'd miss him and can count on him." Perhaps, then, she was hanging on to the hope that the other man had not just used her. This, I said, would be quite a blow to her already low self-confidence as a woman. She softly replied, "I don't really know, but I'd hate to think I was of so little consequence to him."

At this point I suggested that it would be useful to have a separate interview with her about her conflicting feelings around the other man. I turned to Mr. Victor. "Actually," I said, "it's important for you to know where you really stand in this." I went on to say that I thought Mrs. Victor would feel freer to talk to me in a separate interview about something so painful to him and to explore what potential there was, if any, in the future of their marriage. Their decision to stay together should be freely made, and not too readily taken for granted. Mrs. Victor said she *would* like to see me alone. An appointment was set up for the next day. I explained to Mr. Victor that I would not be free to tell him about this interview, but that his wife could tell him whatever she wanted to about it. I also made it clear that I was ready to see him alone as well, but he said he would prefer to leave it for the present.

Individual Interview with Mrs. Victor, October 26

Mrs. Victor was prompt. She looked tense. I told her that our meeting together was to give her a chance to speak freely about some of the unsettled feelings she had about the other man and about her husband, touched on in the last interview.

Mrs. Victor said, "Yes, I'm glad to talk to you alone." She felt very badly that the affair had ended so abruptly. Actually, she still felt she would like to see the man again; she would like to leave it "nice." She felt terrible that the man had got so angry at her at the end. In talking about how the affair had ended, she brought out, "Actually, *he* was the one who stopped first."

Her eyes filled with tears as she explained how much this had hurt her. He had, however, explained this to her nicely, saying, "I'm afraid my wife might find out, and it's going to hurt my family." I said this must have left her feeling very rejected. Yes, and it hurt her even more when her girl friend told her he had another woman, and had lied to her about hurting his wife. At first she didn't believe it and had quarrelled with her girl friend. "Now, I've lost her too." Mrs. Victor had seen him, however, in the coffee shop with another woman and began to feel that her girl friend was right and that she had just

Once raised, it was important to see Mrs. V. quickly. Allowing a whole week to go by might unnecessarily complicate their situation. I thought it would be too hard on Mr. V. for him to be present and that it wouldn't help for him to hear details of the intimacy that had gone on between his wife and the other man.

Worker makes explicit the purpose of the interview.

Mrs. V. is enabled to express her feelings of hurt and disappointment.

Worker is empathetic.

been used by him. All this was a big letdown. She wept profusely. I gave her some tissues and sat quietly for a few moments, then said I was sorry she had been so hurt.

I asked her how she had felt when they were alone and the affair was actively progressing. She said, "It was exciting—it was pleasant." No, she never did have an orgasm with him, but it had not been painful. He had stimulated her breasts, and she had become lubricated so that entry was not hurtful. Had she and this man ever discussed her reactions? She said "No, not really." At first he had asked her, but she had said it was okay, that she liked it in spite of not having an orgasm. So he did not raise this any further.

A repetitive pattern is pointed out.

I commented this was somewhat like the way she had reacted with her husband, and she agreed that she tends not to pursue situations that are uncomfortable. I told her this was something she would have to work out with any sexual partner —this tendency to give way too easily and not to explain her needs. Unless she changed this pattern, she could not get what she wants and is entitled to from sex and from life.

The past pattern is not functional.

After some discussion, she agreed that she expects the other person to do more for her. She also could see it had been like this in her own home. Both parents had always extended themselves and paved the way to make things easy for her, so that she didn't have to struggle too much. I said this childhood pattern hadn't really served her well, that, like her husband, she still had some growing up to do.

Mrs. Victor then confided she still felt warmly toward the other man, and that this worried her. I said, "That's only natural. You can't just switch off your feelings suddenly." I added that she had for the first time experienced a sexual encounter without pain, and this was important and meaningful for her as a woman.

Divorce as an alternative is raised.

When I asked why she had told her husband, she said she had wanted to "get a rise" out of Jim, so "I hit him with it." She went on, "I always wanted to improve our sex, but I never could get him to listen." I suggested that "hitting" him was one way of showing her anger and blaming him. I asked, in view of her feelings of warmth toward this other man and her ongoing affection for him, whether she had ever thought of divorce.

We discussed this further, quite apart from the other man, as realistically she could never marry him. Mrs. Victor said, "I've thought about this. I've been very cross and angry with my husband for not taking my complaints more seriously." "Did you feel the need to prove you could be a real woman?" I asked and added, "I wonder if you hoped that going outside would give you some reassurance." She nodded here and said that was exactly how she had felt.

There was some further discussion of divorce, and she said, "It wouldn't be practical. I don't earn enough to live alone." I asked her what other alternatives were possible for her, and she said, "Well, I suppose I could go back to my family, but I just couldn't take that." I asked if carrying on with her marriage as the lesser of two evils was enough for her to look forward to. After a silence, I said, "There could be a rough road ahead for you, and this marriage has had a poor start."

I pointed out that there were no children, that she was still young. She said, "Actually, I'm qualified enough to earn more money." She went on, thoughtfully, "I know my husband would help me with support if we were to break up, until I become more self-sufficient." The more this alternative was discussed, however, the more Mrs. Victor began to withdraw from it.

She went on: "After all, my husband is consistently concerned about my welfare." They did get along, in a very companionable way. They had a lot of things they liked together; he was kind and gentle. She liked having someone to look up to and she thought he was very clever. Getting back into the dating game seemed hateful to her. Besides, she thought she really did love her husband and that she couldn't be without him for long. She turned it over. "You know—I really do want to keep my marriage."

I asked, "Even if he gets a bit more assertive?" She answered, "I'd like that." "Then," I added, "you could be somewhat less protected." She asked me what I meant. I said, "It's not easy to grow up and give up some of the advantages of being a child." She said, "I know I was too much the little kid at home, and that's why I don't want to go back there."

I emphasized that whether her marriage lasts or is dissolved

Other alternatives to the marriage considered.

Worker reiterates Mrs. V.'s right to dissolve the marriage, particularly as no children are involved.

Anticipating a better emotional balance in the marriage.

She is faced with the task

of modifying her behavior in the future, and of relinquishing childish advantages to achieve more adult ones.

is an important adult decision, and she had a right to do what is best for her. Staying together because it is the easiest way or the "right thing to do" may be contrary to her future well-being and not even fair to her husband.

Mrs. Victor went on, "I do believe things will improve between us, and, on the whole, nearly three years of knowing each other has done a good deal for me." We talked about their dating period, and she said it had been fun. They had fun, too, when they were necking and petting, before they had got into the actual act of intercourse. We spent some time discussing her feelings of guilt and shame around her early sex behavior with Mr. Victor, and she related this to a dreadful fear of being found out. I wondered whether what had happened in the premarital sex had seemed something like a punishment.

Mrs. Victor said she wasn't sure; she only knew she felt terrible about the whole thing, that had it happened after marriage she might have felt better about it. Then, she might have shared it with her mother, and the whole situation would have been different. Again I commented on how alone she must have felt during this upsetting experience before marriage.

Worker give support for her feelings.

I went back to the subject of the other man and asked how often he came into her thoughts. She said she thinks of him a good deal, especially when she falls asleep at night. I said having these feelings about the man who gave her her first pleasure and excitement with nonpainful intercourse was very understandable. In fact, he had actually helped her feel less inadequate as a woman. She sobbed a lot here as I pointed out that she couldn't help her feelings or her thoughts, that she was going through a form of mourning for the loss of a relationship which had meaning and importance for her. I said fantasies about this man or any exciting thought could help her in future sex activities, would be a normal reaction, and would hurt no one.

Worker continues to give Mrs. V. acceptance for her feelings and relieves guilt.

The positive aspects of the crisis are explained. It is not uncommon in counseling for disclosure of infidelity to help move the marriage forward, if greater understanding results.

She continued to weep, and I told her it was good to let her feelings of sadness out, and she should not criticize herself for the way she felt. I added that this crisis had actually, in a way, been the means of their getting together on their marital problems, and that it could prove to be a helpful turning point for the years ahead.

On leaving, she said to me, "This has been a great help, particularly that I don't have to feel so awful when I think of him" (the lover). I pointed out, and she said she could see, that thinking and feeling were not the same as doing.

I raised the possibility of a further single interview, but she thought she would like to carry on with the joint interviews right now, since they had never before talked so openly together and she thought it was helpful. I said I'd like her to keep the option open should she feel the need for another single interview. As to this session, we agreed that she would simply tell her husband of her freely made decision to stay with him and work with him to improve their marriage. I had her permission to bring out, if I thought it was necessary or useful to do so, that her behavior had been a desperate attempt to prove herself a woman rather than have a serious love affair.

Third Joint Interview, November 2

Mr. and Mrs. Victor arrived promptly. She opened the interview by saying she had told her husband after our separate session that she now was clear about wanting to keep her marriage, and of her wish to work with him on improving it. Mr. Victor took her hand as she was speaking. "Yes," he said, "and it sure made me feel a lot more encouraged." She said, "I realize, Jim, I could have been more persistent about getting some help with our problem."

Mr. Victor looked pleased and told me that when she came home from the interview with me, she went to the telephone and spoke to the man, as had been agreed. Mrs. Victor said the interview had given her courage and her husband had helped her; in fact, he had held her hand while she was talking. "When it was over, he kissed me," and Mr. Victor added, "It was a relief for me too." I complimented them on the successful mutual problem solving they had accomplished. I said they both deserved credit for how they had worked this out.

Mrs. Victor was feeling pretty good at this point, and she went on to tell me that the next day she had invited her former girl friend to lunch. They had had a good talk, and this cleared the air between them. She was glad they could be friends again. I pointed out how well she had taken the initiative here, which

Margin notes:

She responds well to worker as a permissive, noncritical authority figure.

They are working together on problem solving. The counselor freely credits this behavioral change. It is important to model for the couple that rewards (i.e., praise) should follow accomplishment.

Mrs. V. demonstrates she

can take initiative and be "more persistent"—that is, more adult.

Worker wishes to build on former pleasurable experiences.
Worker encourages experimentation and confidence to extinguish fear.

demonstrated that she was capable of more persistence in dealing with uncomfortable situations than she had thought.

Since both agreed the air was being cleared, I asked if they felt like talking now about that part of sex which had given them pleasure during their courting. There was a shy exchange, which I pointed out was only natural. How had they showed the affection they felt for each other? Mrs. Victor said, "Of course, we did a lot of just kissing." They had enjoyed this, and soon experimented with petting. This too had been exciting and enjoyable, but they had stopped short of intercourse. I said this was a usual pattern. "You know," I added, "I think it would be useful if you two, until your next session, would keep to this type of sexual behavior, without completing the sexual act."

I then asked where outside their bedroom they could get this going. He said, "I get the idea—we haven't had much fun in the bedroom." They looked at each other as I waited. Then Mr. Victor went on, "We have a neat couch and lounge in our living room." Now Mrs. Victor was smiling. I asked her if she had any suggestions and she said, a bit daringly, "There's the hall, and even the kitchen!" We all laughed. I remarked that they had the right idea—to begin slowly, to enjoy each other, and to build on previously satisfying intimacies. I said I would like them to go slowly in building feelings of security and freedom in their sexual behavior, adding that intercourse before both were ready might slow up the process. I pointed out that they had unlearning *and* learning to do—to shake off the fear and to put in the fun.

During this discussion, one difference in their sexual exchange was agreed upon. Instead of her usual passivity, Ellen agreed to be more explicit in helping him understand and gently guiding him in the type and tempo of stimulation she enjoyed. He said that would be great. I added lightly, "A man doesn't exactly want a traffic cop in bed when he's making love, but some verbal and nonverbal cues are always welcome."

I then raised the matter of masturbation again. They said that one evening they had talked together about this, about some of the fears and inhibitions they had experienced in growing up. Mrs. Victor said, "We laughed when I told Jim about my mother warning me when I had my first period—'Now, Ellen, you have to be careful of men.' " I commented that it wasn't funny at the time, and she agreed. Mr. Victor said he had picked up a lot of negative feelings about masturbation and how shameful this was. He recalled being spanked by his mother for "touching himself" when he was 5 or 6 years old. As they had never done this kind of talking together before, I said it was a fine beginning in developing more intimacy and freedom in communicating. We talked about fantasies which I indicated were associated with masturbation and which often persist, and I pointed out that this could be a useful and helpful way of becoming more relaxed during intercourse.

Generalization about fantasies, again to reduce guilt.

I said that since each of them had experienced and was familiar with masturbation as a form of pleasure, it might be an important phase for them before they got to actual intercourse. If they felt like getting release in this way, why not?

Again, encouraging earlier satisfying behavior as a helpful technique.

I asked Mr. Victor if he knew where her clitoris was. Had he discovered this delicate and potent sensory area? He seemed less shy now as he said, "Not really." She said, in response to my questioning that yes, she knew how much, when and where a little pressure excites her to orgasm, and she would share this with him. I said it would be nice if she could do so, although again it might take a little time before she got to it. He said he could understand that and would be patient.

Worker uses informative and educational procedures.

I asked him whether or not he could share with her what gave him pleasure during masturbation, and he said he would like to be able to do this but felt a bit shy. Again I pointed out that there was no hurry; what we were doing today was talking together frankly. The idea was for them to continue this openness on their own in the period ahead.

Repetition of the principle of nondemand for performance.

At this point, Mrs. Victor volunteered that she had never actually looked at her husband in the nude. She turned to Mr. Victor and said, "You know, my mother used to boast that she had never undressed in front of my father." She went on, "I know that's antiquated, but I too feel shy about your nudity and touching you sexually."

Here too, I suggested that they slow up the process. I said a little would be a lot for them in view of their backgrounds, but I wondered if it would perhaps be fun for them at some point just to try a brief exposure, a sort of "peek and run"? They both laughed here. Even this suggestion, I said, could well be deferred, but meanwhile they had just now taken a good step for-

Worker gives a gentle nudge; at the same time a small success is pointed out as being important.

ward in sharing their mutual shyness. I left it to them to continue this type of talking together. They would need leisure and time to experiment in developing their sexual interests and pleasures. With time too, I said, the past hurtful experience would be absorbed.

Information is given, generalization used as a reassuring technique, repetition used as a learning principle.

As the session was drawing to a close, I repeated that it was not unusual for young couples to take months to understand each other's sexual needs, and that young marrieds often told me the second year was much better than the first. I indicated there are ups and downs in sex as in other areas of the marital relationship, and that making haste slowly is the important principle here.

Worker prepares for possible "downs," anticipating that hurt and angry feelings will recur.

I said it was good that Mrs. Victor no longer felt desperate to prove her adequacy, and that Mr. Victor understood his fear of losing her was no longer a reality. I thought this should help them tolerate some expression of the leftover painful feelings resulting from the affair which had brought them to marriage counseling. These feelings, though greatly lessened, could not be expected to dissolve quickly. At this Mr. Victor said that the relief for him from just knowing that they were not "mismated" was best of all. This fear is something he had lived with since their marriage. They left in a cheerful mood.

Fourth Joint Interview, November 9
Mr. and Mrs. Victor arrived punctually and greeted me with pleasant smiles, looking relaxed. They sat together on the settee. I asked how the week had gone. He looked at her and asked after a pause, "How do you feel it went?" Mrs. Victor said, "It was very nice."

The opening question permits them to raise what is uppermost. Worker then gets them to define what was nice about it.

Are they "testing" worker for disapproval?

I asked what they thought was nice about it. He blurted out, somewhat proudly, "We went the whole way." She added, with a touch of coyness, "Well, I felt like it." Yes, he had stimulated her successfully, on their living room couch, and though she didn't have an orgasm, she found it very pleasant and not painful. She had used a lubricant, but didn't think she really needed to.

Worker demonstrates flexibility and gives positive reinforcement for behavioral

I said I was pleased they had both enjoyed themselves. Also, I said it was fine with me they had gone beyond the limit I suggested. They both knew that what I really wanted was for them

change and reduced sexual anxiety.

to take the pressure off expecting a quick success, which might only serve to slow them up. However, I went on, this was indeed a special event and a mutual achievement. He nodded enthusiastically. He said, "Ellen is beginning to tell me what she likes," and Mrs. Victor added warmly, "Yes, and you have been very responsive." She then announced somewhat daringly, "We took a shower together, and it was fun." I said, "You're really going places and that's great," and they both laughed.

I said experimentation was fine, but at the same time, I thought they should know it was important to carry on in a casual manner, even anticipating finding themselves at a plateau in terms of their growing sexual gratification. All this should be accepted as part of a normal process. Sometimes one would feel like sex and the other not a bit turned on, and I encouraged them to talk together about how they would feel and how they would deal with this. The myth of simultaneous orgasm as the only way to have satisfactory sex was also discussed. I found them both considerably freer today in talking with me about sexual questions and interests.

They are drawing on resources away from me. A good sign.

They asked about books and reading matter. I said I did not consider it important for them to get too intellectual about their growing sexual pleasures. There were, however, many good books on the market. I knew they must have heard of the works of Masters and Johnson, and some of their techniques might be of interest and helpful. Actually, I said, they could read anything they liked, but the principle and guideline here was that sexual material should be read and talked about together, more as fun work than as homework.

Toward the end of the session, Mrs. Victor raised the question of her visiting her parents for a week alone as Mr. Victor could not get away. I asked her to discuss this with him now. He said he would go if he could, but he would like her to go in any case, although of course he would miss her. She still wanted to know what I thought. I said, "Your partner has given you a green light. I think you can separate without risk of losing each other."

The couple are encouraged to do their own decision making.

We discussed the fifth session and the prospect that this might complete our contract, with perhaps one more session to follow. Both said they felt more ready now to go ahead on their own. I said they had used this brief experience very well and indicated that the door was open for both or either to return should they feel the need to do so, or if they felt little progress was being made on their own. An appointment was made for the fifth interview two weeks hence.

Fifth Joint Interview, November 23

Mr. and Mrs. Victor arrived together. They sat side by side, but his overprotectiveness is no longer apparent. Mrs. Victor began by saying, "We got along better, but he's had a very hard week at work." Mr. Victor said he had had to fill in for a colleague who was ill.

Note the couple's concerns are broadening from sex to other areas in the marriage.

Mrs. Victor said, "I wish you'd work less hard; you take on too much responsibility." He agreed this was so. She said, "I resent it when you come home late and bring work home with you." He said he intends to do less of this in the future. She replied he should complain at work about this. "It's not as though they'd fire you."

I said, "It seems you feel you can't complain too easily, either at work or in your marriage." He responded, "It's true, but I'm getting better at it." Here, he turned to her, and said, "Remember the other night, I got mad at you when you wouldn't come to bed? You just said, 'In a minute.' I was waiting later to turn the light off, and then you said, 'Just another article.' So I stomped after you into the front room, kicked open the door, and said, 'When the hell are you coming?' "

He's going great guns!

Here she replied, almost approvingly, "Yes, that was quite a change for you." I commented that she didn't seem to mind. "No," she said, "I like him to be more assertive."

It appeared, however, that later on when she did get into bed, she suddenly jumped up, "to put the bread dough into the oven," telling him, "It takes fifteen minutes to preheat." At this point, he said, he became more upset than angry.

Mr. V.'s confidence in expressing anger is still somewhat shaky.

With these leading questions, worker may have missed the boat about Mrs. V.'s delay in getting to bed and jumping up to see to the dough. One should not overlook the obvious—

I asked her whether she knew he was upset. She shrugged, "What could I do? I told him I was coming back." I asked him how he felt about this disappearing act. He shrugged and merely said, "It's annoying."

maybe she just didn't feel sexy! Perhaps he just wanted to turn off the light and get to sleep!

Worker retrieves and good work follows.

I wondered if he fears he is not pleasing her enough, and that her taking off is a way she has of showing her dissatisfaction. He thoughtfully said this could be so. Mrs. Victor interrupted, "You know, maybe I am still angry, that you just assumed there was nothing we could do about our sex problem." Here she turned to me and added, "I think I get what you mean about the leftover feelings."

I then pointed out that at the same time she was now saying "we" and "our" sex problem, which was a big step forward. She replied, "I know now it is us." To him she said, "You can get mad at me too, Jim. I really don't want you to feel you mustn't get angry because you're so afraid of me. I'm not going to take off."

Mr. Victor responded, "Don't worry—I'll let you know when I'm mad."

I pointed out they were now sharing their feelings more freely and were realizing that past hurts take time to dissolve. I added that continuing this kind of exchange would serve them well in the future.

Worker reiterates the non-functional interaction that had led to the unworkable solution.

I asked whether they could now see how both had felt helpless and inadequate, that neither had felt able to cope with the problem. His way was to push it aside and to keep his hurt in. Hers was to resent and deal with it by going "outside" and blaming him for her behavior.

I pointed out that Mr. Victor, feeling more secure, is now becoming a little more assertive with her, and that this adds to her security. This might well be reflected in his work situation. Here too, he could experiment in being more assertive; of course I was confident he would do this at his own pace, using his own judgment.

Note how he responds to my recognition of his potential.

Suddenly, at this point Mr. Victor burst out proudly, "She's had several orgasms lately!" I said I was delighted to hear this. Mrs. Victor smilingly added that this was the first time in her life she had experienced orgasm in intercourse. He had manipulated her manually, and they then had coitus. He could tell she had an orgasm, and it was a thrill for him. She

Mrs. V. has learned the principle of immediate reinforcement.

added warmly, "It was very nice indeed." I asked her what she had done at the time to encourage him. "Well, I did kiss you, and told you I was pleased."

Mr. Victor then said, "Maybe we don't need to come back any more." I said that would be fine, if they felt ready to experience those ups and downs we talked about last time as part of any good sexual adjustment. Here she volunteered that she even woke him up an hour or so after he had said he was tired and didn't feel like sex. She had aroused him, and they had had fun. He said it was a great idea, and I said they were using initiative and imagination, and that there were a variety of ways they could get to know each other's needs. I thought they were demonstrating that, given time, they could work these out on their own.

I pointed out that they had again done an effective piece of problem solving on their own. This way of working together would help them cope with the unfinished business of consolidating and building an improved relationship. Encouraging small changes in each other was just what was needed. I commended them for making excellent progress in so few sessions.

Referring to Mr. Victor's point about not coming back any more, I said I felt his leadership in this was sound, but I did want to be sure it wasn't part of his old pattern of not expecting help from an outsider. "On the contrary," he said, "it would be very easy for us to come back here if we need more help."

I said that was fine, but I would like a follow-up session with them in about three months' time, which could be either at the office or on the telephone. We parted cheerfully.

December 15
I received a holiday greeting card from Mr. and Mrs. Victor with "Many thanks for your good help."

Follow-up Telephone Interview, March 20
Mrs. Victor was pleased to receive my call. They had talked about a possible office interview but didn't think it was necessary. She said she felt that their marriage had really begun when

A more adult relationship with her mother is developing.

her affair ended. When she visited her parents, she had told her mother that she had had a sex problem. Her mother had been understanding, and even told Ellen that she herself had taken a long time to adjust to sex. Mrs. Victor had not mentioned her outside affair but had told her mother of the counseling help they had received.

Mr. Victor had asked for a raise in salary, and got it! She still thinks he works too hard, but he gets more done on the job, bringing work home only rarely. Mrs. Victor found herself a new part-time job about a month ago. She will register for one or two courses at the university and plans to complete her degree. Mr. Victor was eager that she do this.

She had wondered whether she would miss seeing her former lover, now that she had changed jobs, but was surprised at how rarely he entered her thoughts these days. "We both feel we were helped over a very hard time," she said.

I sent my regards to her husband and reminded her that the door was open for their return should the need arise, without any sense of failure or even the need to wait for a critical situation.

With lowered anxiety, more energy is released for work on the job.

She is building up more competence and he is encouraging her independence. He will have less need to overprotect her. The maturing process is going on.

June 20
There has been no further contact with this couple, and the case was therefore closed.

CLOSING COMMENTS

The assessment of this couple as basically healthy, with potential for a satisfactory marriage, was borne out. Further maturation and life experience will probably lessen the sexual insecurity each brought into the marriage. Both recognize that they had been groping in the dark, hampered by cultural and religious misconceptions as well as by sexual misinformation. Closer intimacy has been achieved, along with an awareness that marital problems belong to both, not to one or the other, and that joint problem solving can be very fruitful. The sexual problem seems to have been resolved adequately in relatively few sessions. This confirms the assessment that their problem was neither profound nor tenacious.

If the sex problem had returned after some initial success, or if it had persisted, the counselor would then have indicated that this was understandable, that possibly they were trying too hard. Reassuringly, the counselor would have said, "It's okay. This often happens. Let's go back and slow up." This "going back," again reinforcing the need to remove the pressure of performance, may be necessary to remove the fear of failure. Several more sessions would then be arranged.

The counselor must keep in mind that each couple is a unique combination and has to develop its own particular partnership. A mutual search for solutions, physical and emotional, requires time, and one cannot build up a really satisfying balance in short order. The wife needs time to learn to use the words, gestures, and movements gently to let her husband know her needs, and yet not weaken or undermine his self-confidence and self-image. He too has the right and obligation to share what he enjoys and how she can be helpful in their mutual search for pleasure.

Beginning counselors will find that simple, uncomplicated procedures, such as giving permission to enjoy erotic pleasure and reviving sensual satisfactions of the courtship days, are often effective, as is reassuring couples that fantasies, whatever their nature, are normal and indeed useful in obtaining sexual pleasure. The counselor encourages free discussion to clear away old taboos and myths. Setting tasks of nonperformance is essential in the process of helping couples become more relaxed and more satisfied with their sexual responses.

If the counselor is comfortable and ready, other techniques may be used, such as pleasuring exercises, with the partners taking turns in enjoying erotic responses without feeling selfish or responsible to the other. A good deal of literature is available to increase the counselor's repertoire of techniques that may be appropriate to a couple.

It should be recognized that beginning counselors or practitioners should use only those techniques with which they are comfortable, and about which they have conviction. It is quite in order for the counselor to limit himself or herself in this way. There is nothing wrong in a counselor's building up confidence slowly through discussion with colleagues, or occasionally referring to a consultant if this seems indicated. If the couple are going to overwork, and the counselor is going to overwork, the outcome can hardly be a happy one!

In the Victor case, the focus of treatment was primarily on the sexual adjustment. This was the area for which they sought help. Had the identified problems been in the area of the in-laws, or had they been bickering over household chores or money management, the process would have similarly involved the relationship issue, which is central to marriage counseling. It would also have involved helping them develop more skill in communicating their feelings and improving their joint problem-solving ability. As systems theory tells us, a change in one part or in one conflict area will have repercussions in other areas.

In the case of the Victors, transactional analysis, with its concept of the three components of personality—parent, adult, and child—could also have been used effectively. For instance, overpermissiveness and lack of boundaries in her growing up had left Mrs. Victor's "child" too dominant in relation to the adult aspect of her personality. Mr. Victor's "parent" (his incorporated strict upbringing) was too strong and inhibiting, preventing him from expressing appropriate anger against the loved one.

A movement toward a more adult-to-adult relationship would be the goal of the transactional analysis approach, and the direction for the ongoing work (that is, the unfinished business) could be identified for the Victors if short-term service were offered. Workers who are more at home with the transactional approach could well have achieved a somewhat similar result as this worker did with a more eclectic method.

MR. AND MRS. PETERS

Walter Peters, age 33
June Peters, age 28

Married 5 months

Children: None

Referral, November 12

To seek help so early in the marriage, the situation must be critical, and early intervention is called for.

Mrs. Peters telephoned, saying that after only five months of marriage, so much had gone wrong she can't think how they can get out of the mess they're in. She hesitates to move toward divorce or separation. An appointment was made for the following afternoon.

First Interview, November 13

The receptionist called me when they arrived and whispered, "Wow! Are they ever a stunning pair!" As I shook hands with them, I could see what she meant. Mrs. Peters, tall and slender, was an attractive woman, dressed with quiet elegance. She had an air of poise and sophistication. Mr. Peters, tall, broad-shouldered, and blond, was strikingly handsome with an easy and casual bearing.

Worker notes nonverbal behavior, as this could be an indication of their interaction.

When they entered the office, she sat on the sofa. Mr. Peters hesitated, then joined her on the sofa, but somewhat apart. She leaned forward and now looked quite tense. He lit a cigarette. I decided to ease the atmosphere for them by asking for some brief background information before finding out what the problems were.

In summary, Mr. Peters is American-born, Mrs. Peters is a Canadian. He comes from a well-to-do family, has an M.B.A. from an Ivy League college following an engineering degree, and was transferred to Montreal about four years ago. He carries a responsible position, heading up the Canadian branch of a large U.S. consulting firm. He likes his work and is doing well.

His mother died when he was in his early teens. His father, still a widower, and his older brother, recently divorced, live in the States. A younger sister ("she's my wife's age") is also divorced, with two young children. Although he feels friendly toward his family, they are not close since he has been separated from them for so many years.

Mrs. Peters completed her B.A. at age 20 and worked for over seven years as secretary to the senior member of an important law firm. She gave this job up shortly before they were married, so as to find and furnish their new apartment. Her father, whom she adored, passed away suddenly four years ago. Her mother and an unmarried sister of 23 live together.

These preliminaries took only a few minutes, and I then asked what the problem was, after only five months of marriage. Here Mrs. Peters quickly took over. She said they had lived together for over three and a half years in an apartment near both their offices. It was a happy and beautiful time for both of them. She turned to him, and he nodded in agreement. She thought they had made a wonderful adjustment, rarely argued, had many common interests, and liked the same friends.

After three years had passed she couldn't see why they shouldn't formalize the relationship and get married. He took nearly six months to make up his mind, and his reluctance was very upsetting to her. Here Mr. Peters interjected that he would have been content to defer the marriage for another year or two. She said she was afraid his marriage might end as his brother's and sister's had, and this made no sense to her at all. He merely shrugged, but made no protest.

I asked him what had made him change his mind about marriage. He replied that he had had an ultimatum from his wife, who was pushed by her mother and sister. He finally

---

Margin notes:

Such information is essential in a first interview but often emerges later. It is nonthreatening, and may ease the situation.

Worker takes note of the two divorces in his immediate family. Also that he brings in his wife when he mentions his divorced sister.

Strengths in couple—they have maintained a relationship which worked for over 3 years.

I take note that she is speaking for him, and that his silence is probably assent. Getting into this with them so early in the session would be time-consuming as well as likely to detract from the priority of gaining a broad assessment picture, with pressing problems identified, in a first interview.

agreed to the marriage rather than face the possibility of losing her. Here she interrupted to say it wasn't her mother and sister pushing, but that she herself had had enough of being "tried out" and wanted to get settled. She realized she wasn't getting any younger. All along they had agreed they would eventually have a family. "Look," she said, "I've already turned twenty-eight, and a woman should have her first child before she's thirty." At this point he turned to me and said, "That's her mother talking."

Sarcastically he went on, "Her mother has always resented me for 'taking advantage' of her daughter." I asked Mrs. Peters whether she felt that way too. "No," she answered, "that would be unfair. After my father died my mother went to pieces and she depended on me for comfort, as I was the older. I had the responsibility of settling the estate and arranging her affairs. I was glad to do what I could, but she became more and more demanding of my time. I had only my job to keep me going."

Around this time she had met Mr. Peters, and her mother had resented her dating him. After a few months, Mrs. Peters said, it was *she* who had suggested they take an apartment together. Several of her friends were living in this way, and she as well as Mr. Peters wanted time to get to know each other better. Marriage at that time wasn't an issue. I asked him for his reaction here. He said, "That's it exactly—June has a strong sense of fairness."

Here I commented that her own grief and sadness on the loss of a beloved father had been submerged by having to take care of her mother and sister. Meeting Mr. Peters must have been a great solace to her. Yes, she said, he had been wonderful. In fact, "He was just what the doctor ordered. I was really down."

A serious rift developed between her and her mother and sister on account of her "unseemly behavior." I remarked she had shown strength in asserting her right to live a life of her own. She said that at first she had felt badly about "Mom," but after many upsetting arguments, she had withdrawn gradually, and then almost entirely, from her family. Eventually she maintained only a superficial relationship with them, calling once or twice a month to find out how they were getting along,

---

Margin notes:

Note reversal of the child and mother roles.

Her mother has difficulty in releasing her.

As she readily accepts responsibility for their live-in plan, I now ask him to acknowledge this. Technique of teaching client use of positive reinforcement begins.

Now worker gives support to Mr. P., which Mrs. P. freely acknowledges.

I demonstrate acceptance of her right to live *her* way, thus separating myself from her mother—an important therapeutic principle.

but her mother could never accept her unconventional way of living. It had been a relief to learn from her sister that after she left, her mother had taken hold of herself. Here I said she had done her mother, as well as herself, a good turn by leaving.

"Now," interjected Mr. Peters, "Mom's back in full force and making up for lost time. I'm now expected to turn up like a dutiful son every Sunday for dinner." Mrs. Peters commented, "You don't go anyhow—I go alone." I asked her whether she now also felt obligated, to make up for lost time. She was silent for a while, and then said she knew her mother was too bossy, and perhaps she was letting her interfere too much in their marriage. She said that now Mr. Peters was becoming so argumentative and critical, and after all it was *her* mother who was trying to be friendly. I said it looks as if mother has now become a means of their getting at each other. I asked what else bothered them. She replied, "Now we have arguments about money." He said that he is good and fed up with her mother's expensive ideas.

Now she blew up. "No," she said, "it's you—you've become tight about money. Everything was fine when I was sharing the rent and footing half the bills!"

Now he became angry, saying he had done more than his share, and happily too, taking her on expensive holidays, giving her nice gifts. They ate out two or three times a week. He went on, bitterly, "I resent being called 'tight.' " A free-for-all now developed between them. She said that he doles out money, begrudges the fact that they're in a larger apartment for which he has to pay, resents having to dip into his substantial savings to furnish the new apartment, and rarely takes her out. He accused her of being lazy and self-indulgent, and of not pulling her weight.

"You used to darn my socks," he got in, "and used to arrange a candlelight dinner, to surprise me. You're not working now—why shouldn't you prepare dinner?"

I continued: "So much has gone wrong since you got married—problems with mother, and problems about money—how about sex?" She responded that this wasn't a problem as he knew how to stimulate her to orgasm, but it was less frequent since they were married, and the "afterglow" was missing. He put in, resentfully, "You stay up for the late T.V. show, and when I leave in the morning you're asleep. It would help if we

---

This comment serves to relieve her guilt at leaving "Mom," physically and emotionally.

When a new role is taken on, some regression occurs until its expectations are learned. Mrs. Peters has regressed to her former daughter role.

Here he is again fighting her indirectly, through mother.

Her leaving the job is a transitional crisis for both, with drastic changes in their lifestyle.

I move on to raise sex as a possible issue to broaden the marital assessment and for identification of problem areas.

got our hours together." I commented, "Marriage has certainly changed your whole lifestyle, which upsets both of you."

Here I pointed out to them how one thing led to another, and that we could go on like this for the rest of the hour. I said it was clear enough that they were in deep trouble, that both were very unhappy. Many problems were mushrooming, but it looked to me as though they stemmed largely from the fact of their formal marriage.

Worker shares her assessment thinking, up to this point.

For over three years they had enjoyed an intimate and carefree relationship, but it appeared that the legal commitment of marriage had thrown their relationship off balance. I said that many couples are unprepared to take on the new roles of husband and wife, that they weren't clear as to what to expect from each other as they moved from single to married status. More is involved than "love." In their case, they were even less prepared and therefore more vulnerable to difficulties, in that they probably *thought* they had already made the necessary adjustment to marriage.

Technique of clarification by pointing out the negative interaction between his fear of marriage and her urgency to marry.

Actually, I explained, their problems had preceded their marriage. When he withheld his consent, she felt hurt and rejected and had brought these feelings into the marriage with her. Her pressuring him to get married had intensified his fear of marriage and the possible risk of divorce. These feelings *he* had brought into the marriage, so that he also felt hurt and short-changed. He added he now felt that he was giving more and getting less.

I said his previous reluctance to marry and his present discontent made her feel insecure in their relationship and caused her to develop grave doubts about the future. She brought out how humiliated she felt asking him for money. I noticed that she had by now become a little tearful.

For women today, the loss of financial independence is a serious blow to self-esteem.

Now I am testing a hypothesis for their response.

I wondered whether part of her wish for a baby was to save her relationship with him. She said this was certainly part of it. I turned to Mr. Peters and asked him whether he realized this. He said "no," he thought it was simply a matter of her hanging on to an old wives' tale.* I asked him how he felt about what she had just said about saving the relationship. Now he looked

Technique of persistence. I am trying to draw a posi-

*Viz., a woman should have her first child before age 30

tive response from him to her. It works!

Worker credits him for this.

There is much work ahead, but realistic hope is provided—a necessary element in short-term marriage counseling.

As she is the more motivated and initiated the counseling, I direct the problem solving to her, hoping to draw him in.

Technique of partializing; worker identifies a concrete aspect of the parent-in-law problem.

at her warmly and took her hand. "We're both afraid of the same thing; it looks like—we really don't want to lose each other."

I said it seemed to me that Mr. Peters realized their relationship still had a lot going for it. It was not surprising that as a consequence of the rapid changes which had taken place in their lives, one problem had compounded another, and now there were many difficulties to sort out.

Were they prepared to work together with me to see whether they could get this marriage off the ground? Each agreed, rather solemnly. At this I suggested a short-term service of, say, four further weekly sessions. Both were pleased with the possible brevity of the counseling.

I then said that before they left the interview it would help for them to agree on something by which they could get a beginning wedge into the vicious circle of escalating problems that they were currently facing. I said I would like them to agree on some contentious issue, something simple and concrete, that they could work on during the coming week. The idea would be to make haste slowly.

To Mrs. Peters I added, "You are probably turning more to your mother these days because you feel neglected by Walter; maybe you also want to make up to her for leaving home the way you did." She nodded. I turned to Mr. Peters and said, "This new closeness between June and her mother must leave you feeling out in the cold." "Yes, it does." Here I asked Mrs. Peters, "What about those Sunday dinners which upset you both? Can anything be done about that?"

After a short silence, she came up with a suggestion. Perhaps if he would come with her to her mother's every second week for dinner instead of every week, she would stop going there on her own every week. She wasn't that keen on going anyhow. Here Mr. Peters put in that her mother was sometimes a real pain in the neck, and did persist in trying to control them.

I said they couldn't expect to work out all their feelings about her mother in a week or two, but this could be a beginning for them to get their priorities in order. Even when our sessions were over, their feelings about her mother would still need to be worked out.

He then offered to go with her to her mother's, not the coming Sunday but the next, provided that they could get away early, before mother began telling them what to buy and where to get it. Here Mrs. Peters, obviously pleased, said she was even prepared to tell her mother she was interfering far too much, that she, Mrs. Peters, wanted to save her marriage, and that they were now involved in marriage counseling. I asked Mr. Peters what he thought of this, and he said she now sounded more like her old self.

Using reinforcement.

I said they had made an excellent beginning and pointed out that Mrs. Peters had taken the first step toward compromise, for which she deserved credit. He had responded encouragingly, for which he in turn deserved credit. These first steps were the hardest. That is why I suggested that they go slowly but be quick to acknowledge any positive change by the other, no matter how small.

Teaching reinforcement.

Assigning manageable tasks.

I asked Mrs. Peters to see her gynecologist before our next session if possible, to find out specifically his opinion on the importance of her having a baby before she reaches age 30. I suggested to Mr. Peters that he take his wife out "on a date" during the coming week.

Second Interview, November 20
The Peters were punctual and greeted me warmly. Mrs. Peters told me quickly that they had had a more relaxed week. He agreed, saying they both had the feeling now that they could work things out. She had talked to her mother soon after our last session here and had told her she couldn't see her this Sunday, but that they would both come the following Sunday.

Mrs. P. has regained some of the distance from her mother she had established before marriage.

Mrs. Peters said that her mother had at first objected—why couldn't they both come this Sunday too? Mrs. Peters had held her ground and had told her mother that their marriage was in trouble, that they were getting counseling, and that she, for one, was very pleased that Walter had agreed to come with her to visit her family every other week. "In fact," said Mrs. Peters, "I went even further. I told my mother that if she didn't see this as an improvement, then perhaps we shouldn't come at all, for the time being."

He, too, is a quick learner.

Mr. Peters, smiling broadly, said, "I told her then, 'Bravo,' and I say it again." I added, "Let me echo that too." I said I was pleased that what he was doing was exactly what was needed—to reinforce and encourage any change in behavior immediately as it took place. In our work together, I said, each partner has the task of giving credit to the other, quickly and unreservedly, for any improved change, no matter how small.

Mrs. Peters told me her husband had taken her out for dinner one evening. He had even put on the act of telephoning her from his office to ask if she was free that night! It was a special treat.

Also, she had managed to see her gynecologist on Wednesday. In essence, he told her that she had a wide pelvis and that child bearing shouldn't present any difficulty. As for age, a year or two over thirty would make no difference in terms of risk for her or for the baby, but he suggested that waiting five or six years, apart from any risk factors, wasn't advisable, as by then parents may have less patience to undertake the necessary care of an infant.

She and Mr. Peters had talked this over. She still favored the idea of starting a baby as soon as possible, adding that one doesn't always become pregnant when one wants to; it can take months, or even years. He, however, wanted to wait.

It is important to make explicit the dangers of bringing a baby into an unsettled marriage.

Here I said very directly that until they had resolved their many problems and had consolidated the marriage, a baby would only add to and complicate their difficulties. I stressed it was a mistaken notion that a child would repair a troubled marriage. This put an unfair burden on the child and on each of the partners. Parents often compete for the child's affection or try to gain an ally against the partner. It was essential to get their marriage off to a good start before taking on the additional commitment of mothering and fathering.

The marital relationship is of central importance and is their priority.

I said that Mrs. Peters had a need to feel secure and to be wanted for herself as a wife, and that unless Mr. Peters readily agreed to bring a child into their lives, his fears of not being wanted as a husband but as a provider and a father similarly would continue. His fears of divorce could be heightened and might then threaten the marriage.

Anticipatory guidance, by encouraging them to find out for themselves.

I told them that even the happiest couple are often thrown for a while by the advent of a baby. It's hard to anticipate this before the reality. I suggested that they ask some of their married friends how the coming of the first baby had changed their way of life.

At this point Mrs. Peters said thoughtfully, and rather sadly, that she wanted them to have their baby under good circumstances and would agree to defer pregnancy while they were

I empathize with Mrs. P.'s difficult decision.

sorting out their differences. I said this wasn't an easy decision for her. She had set her heart on having a child and had even given up her job with this in mind.

He is pleased, but I continue to empathize with her, in order to enlist some consistent support from him.

Mr. Peters commented that it was a big relief for him, and he certainly appreciated her attitude. I pointed out that Mrs. Peters was being reasonable and sensible, but feelings don't go away so easily. I asked Mr. Peters whether he could understand this. He said he thought he could. I wondered how he would respond if at times his wife expressed some natural feelings of sadness in not having a child. Could he show her his support, with some affection? Here, he turned to me reassuringly and said with a smile "Don't worry, Mrs. Freeman, I get the message." We all laughed.

The realistic budgeting task is set, to help them deal with the money issue, an emotionally charged area since the marriage began.

I then asked: "What's on the agenda for next week?" Mrs. Peters said, "We do have to talk about money." I responded that their assignment for next week would be planning a budget. I asked them, however, to hold off on such a discussion until they had made the Sunday visit to her family.

Third Interview, November 27

The session opened quietly. Mrs. Peters said the Sunday visit to her mother had gone well. Mr. Peters said her mother had behaved like a lamb, but that he and his wife just couldn't see eye to eye about money. They had gotten nowhere, only upset.

Soon the interview turned into a free-for-all. Each accused the other of being irresponsible, he by being unwilling to furnish a nice home, and she by overspending and being pushed by her mother's snobby friends. "Why blame them for your tightness?" she retorted.

Worker tries to focus the interview more realistically.

I commented that these cross-accusations seemed to be an expression of their mutual fears and the anger that accompanies it. There was no response. I went on to suggest: "Let's try to sort out the reality from the hurt. Can we start with the new apartment?" He agreed more quietly that he liked their apartment, which she had chosen. Yes, he felt he could easily handle the rent. She reminded him, "You told me you would leave the furnishing to me." "Yes, but I had no idea you would go haywire."

He feels manipulated and threatened. He clings to

He said he was particularly annoyed that a decorator friend of her mother had taken a hand in giving "free" advice. The

money to retain some control over his position.

cost of the drapes alone, he thought, could furnish an apartment. She reacted angrily, saying, "I paid for those drapes out of my own savings, and I've spent every cent I had." She continued, "The living room is only half-furnished because you're not willing to spend any more." He responded that he should have put his foot down earlier instead of just complaining while she ran up the bills.

They are still at the "free-for-all" stage. Worker tries again, this time by asking how had they managed previously.

She said there are still some bills to pay, "and this still worries me, but you just let it ride." Here I interrupted and asked how they had managed about money during the three years before marriage. It seems that they had taken a furnished apartment and shared the rent, the food, and the cleaning bills. Each had bought his or her own clothing. He had paid for all the extras.

I asked, had they discussed what giving up her job would mean? Yes, he had told her it was okay, he didn't need her money. She said, "Apart from your investments, you manage to save at least a third of your salary." He retorted, "What are you trying to prove? How mean I am?" He went on, "All my adult life I've managed to make a good living and have always spent freely." She too had previously spent freely, had worked hard, and had been well paid. Now she again brought out how humiliated she felt having to ask for money.

However, they need to continue to bring out hurt and angry feelings.

Now, worker responds more supportively. I point out the new stressful roles for each of them.

I said a lot of pain was involved for both in the money issue and pointed out that she had suddenly been thrown into a new dependency role, having given up her job, and he had suddenly assumed the role of the sole breadwinner. I thought the mutual insecurity in their married relationship created a great deal of emotional stress. This seemed to be reflected in their difficulty in handling money. I asked, did he consider her basically reckless and irresponsible about money? Not really, he answered, "She always liked nice things, but I used to think she was practical."

Worker's approach here is productive—technique of confronting each of them, as they seem ready for this now.

I asked her, "Mrs. Peters, do you really believe he's mean and irresponsible?" "No," she responded, "but it looks as if I have more confidence in his future than he has himself." I asked, "In his career future, or his family future?" This stumped her. I then wondered aloud whether somewhere Mr. Peters equated marriage with divorce. He replied thoughtfully, it did concern him, especially since his sister's recent divorce—

they had seemed to be such a fine couple—yes, he was especially fond of her.

I commented, "After your brother's divorce, this second divorce must have been even more upsetting." Yes, and he worried, as his father took it particularly hard. When they talked on the phone, his father would always end up urging him to "be careful" and not to be the third in the family to have a broken home. After a long pause, he brought out, slowly and with some difficulty, how sorry he felt for his father, who was a gentle man and had done his best for all of them, without a wife to help him. He had deprived himself to give them a good start. I commented, "I can see you want to protect your father from further hurt, as well as yourself." Here he could only nod, obviously touched. He seemed unable to continue.

Mrs. Peters had been watching closely and said sympathetically, "I'm so sorry, Walter. You never told me about your father, how badly he felt about the divorces."

Now I encouraged Mr. Peters to talk about his sister, who had always been the family pet and very spoiled. As a little girl, she had followed him around. His older brother had ignored him and bullied him, but she was always his little pal. It appeared that he and his brother had little in common. The brother had dropped out of college, and although he was bright, he was always in and out of jobs. Now they rarely got together.

His sister has a year-old baby girl and a three-year-old boy. She has become involved with another man, about whom their father has serious doubts. I said his father must feel inadequate as a parent after all his efforts, and his fears for Mr. Peters and his daughter were understandable.

However, I continued, Mr. Peters had been able as an adult to separate from his family and had demonstrated his maturity in doing so as effectively as he had. He had developed a successful career on his own and had maintained a meaningful love relationship for several years. Neither his sister nor his brother had managed to do this.

Here Mrs. Peters, who had been listening intently, said she had met them all one Christmas, and that she liked his family, particularly his father, but had found her husband head and

---

Margin notes:

Important to face him with his feelings about divorce.

The disclosure from Mr. P.'s past brings out an empathy response from Mrs. P.

My intention is to help him to separate his marriage from those of his siblings, and particularly to separate his wife from his divorced sister.

Note how this discussion brings out a further supportive response from her.

shoulders over his brother. I said that Mr. Peter's anxiety about divorce wasn't surprising, but his situation was very different.

I then reminded him, "When we first met, you told me that your divorced sister and June were the same age. Are they similar in other ways, too?" "Well," he considered, "they are both warm and affectionate, have a sense of humor, and are outgoing, but June has had to carry her weight at home and make her own living."

I said their differences were more important than their similarities, and that he and Mrs. Peters could work out their own kind of marriage, without the burden of his siblings' failures and problems, over which he had no control and in which he had played no part.

This was an emotional session, particularly for Mr. Peters. I said that Mrs. Peters had been tender and responsive, that this sharing of his worries had helped her realize what he was going through. She nodded. He said he felt she understood, and that the discussion had helped him.

I said this had been a constructive session. I suggested that they could now take on a more rational budgeting task and try to put the money issue to rest. It seemed to have been a kind of testing ground, to see how much each really cared for the other. We could discuss money management and any other concerns they had next week.

Fourth Interview, December 4

The Peters arrived looking cheerful. They had had a very good week. She said that the last session had been an eye-opener for both of them. She said, "I realized I was trying to prove how much I meant to Walter. I also wanted to prove this to my family and my friends." He added, "This has been the most relaxed week we've had since we've been married." I said I was delighted.

She went on to tell me that her former boss had phoned her several times in the past two months asking her to go back on any basis, part or full-time. "It looks as if he can't quite replace me"—this with some pride and satisfaction. "Actually," she continued, "I think I've been pretty bored the last few months. Walter and I have been talking this over, and I think I'm going to take it on four days a week. I really love the work, and I miss the stimulation during the day."

Marginal notes:

Worker brings out that Mrs. P. and Mr. P.'s *divorced* sister are different—that is, that Mrs. P. is not necessarily a candidate for divorce.

Money often becomes a focal point for a last-ditch stand, as with this couple.

Note that clients can learn with hindsight.

A satisfying work role is reinstated—of special importance for women today.

I said this made a lot of sense to me. He said they had worked out a cost-of-living budget. She said, "We have arranged for me to have a good monthly allowance, and I am very pleased. It is more than adequate." Mr. Peters said he will cover any additional expenses and wants her to keep her own money and use it in any way she likes.

I commented that they were both good learners and had worked this out intelligently. They had talked about a further session but thought they would now like to cope on their own. I said they had a solid relationship behind them. They had shown skills in problem solving and decision making, and I thought they had found ways in which their communication could become more open. They agreed each had the responsibility to continue the ongoing work of building up their marriage. I said the experience here should stand them in good stead when problems occur. Again I indicated that there would be ups and downs. These are part of the pepper and salt of life, and they shouldn't be easily discouraged.

Before they left, I said they would be wise not to hurry into the role of parents. I hoped they would allow themselves time to enjoy being married before taking on the additional responsibility. One of their ongoing tasks would be a decision as to their readiness to have a child. They went along with this and thanked me warmly. I said I would call them in three months' time to see how they were doing, as is our usual practice.

Important to prepare clients for some setbacks.

It is good practice to indicate that a follow-up contact is routine. In this way clients won't feel I have doubts about how they'll manage on their own.

Follow-up Contact, March 15

Mrs. Peters called me today to say they were getting on just fine. She wanted me to know about her work and enthusiastically said she had just gotten a raise and would be on full salary for her four-day week. "No money fights," she said, "it's amazing—and I have my own little nest egg." Walter is also doing well in his work, and his company thinks that the Canadian branch is sufficiently under way for him to return to the New York head office in a year or so. They are both looking forward to this. I asked about her mother. She laughed and said, "She's still full of advice, but we don't take her so seriously any more. We exchange visits occasionally." I sent my regards to Mr. Peters. Case closed this day.

CLOSING COMMENTS

This competent and intelligent couple were able with some help to disentangle the recent crises of marriage, for which they were unprepared despite the years of living together. One could argue that with their capacity for insight, a great deal more could have been achieved. This is probable, but they have done pretty well on their own, and there is no reason why they should not have the opportunity of accomplishing further growth on their own, both as individuals and as a married pair.

It will be noted that no effort was made to discuss the dynamics of Mrs. Peters' relationship to her sister, her mother, and perhaps most importantly, to her late father. To what extent was she motivated by guilt, to have served her mother to such an extreme degree for nearly six months? Did she marry Mr. Peters to replace her lost love object? Exploration of this material, I believe, would have protracted the counseling without benefit to the marriage at this point.

On the other hand, allowing Mr. Peters to ventilate his current fears of marriage and divorce in relation to his early growing-up years was necessary. Opening up this material helped his wife to empathize with him and to understand his apparent change in behavior. It was also a form of catharsis, a release of feelings that served to separate him from his siblings, enabling him to perceive himself as someone who need not necessarily equate marriage with divorce, as he had been doing.

In terms of role theory, this case demonstrates how ill-defined role expectations, particularly those of husband and wife, can result in a negative chain reaction. In terms of systems theory, it shows how outside systems—the economic system, the extended family, the recreational and social systems—all interact with and affect the interpersonal system of the married couple themselves.

Of special interest was the Peters' emphasis on spending and withholding money as a way of testing their relationship. In a money economy such as ours, money is used in many ways, apart from the acquisition of goods and services. Many people perceive it as a measure of their worth. Spending money or refusing to spend money may be a means of retaliation; it may be used to assert independence, control, or power. Money may be used as a bribe or withheld as a punishment. It may be a way of giving or withholding love and affection.

The case also illustrates how problems that have recently escalated may be halted and dealt with by early and brief intervention, with the ongoing unfinished business to be worked on, understood, and accepted by the couple.

3

The Child-Rearing Phase

Now a little stranger arrives on the scene. What a happy event! Congratulations pour in from all sides. The young couple, back from the hospital with their precious bundle safe in the shiny new crib, beam at each other with pride and pleasure.

But take a look a week later. Despite prenatal lessons and Dr. Spock, the apartment is topsy-turvy. Mother looks a little bleary-eyed. Father, home from work, may have to change, feed, and even burp the baby to give mother a chance to throw a hasty meal together.

The first child propels the often ill-prepared young parents into the roles of mothering and fathering, into a whole set of new tasks to be coped with in the care and nurturing of an infant (White, 1975). Reared in a small nuclear family, few young couples in Western society have experienced caring for an infant brother or sister, as was usual when families were larger and the age gap between oldest and youngest offspring was wider. The extended family of former years, which provided young couples with supports and built-in babysitters, is now scattered to distant parts. Grandparents, uncles, aunts, nieces, and nephews are no longer in close proximity. Particularly in large urban areas, young couples usually have to rely on their own resources and those which the community may have developed in response to their needs. It is well known that such community resources do not begin to fill the gap created by the mobility and fragmentation of the family in modern life.

The mother's first priority is, of course, the loving care and nurture of the infant. This necessary and close biological tie is gratifying, but it permits the mother less time and freedom to attend to household and other tasks. The father, often with the best will in the world, feels somewhat put aside and is of course ashamed to admit it, even to himself. Anyhow, who cares about not having a decent meal after coming home from a hard day's work? And if his wife is not ready or is too tired for sex, so what? He can still feast his eyes on little junior!

A whole new set of tasks is now added to those of the beginning phase of marriage. What has taken place is a temporary disequilibrium in the marital balance which the couple had previously established. The entry of a baby into the family system is a "normal" life crisis. Those who have coped adequately with the tasks of the beginning phase of marriage and who have learned to communicate freely will adapt to the new tasks in a mutually helpful way, and before too long a new equilibrium will be established.

The new responsibilities undertaken by the young couple may result in reduced financial resources if the mother has given up her previous employment. The father may need to take on additional work. The tasks of budgeting time and money therefore take on a new light. Babysitters are expensive and hard to find, so carefree outings and even relaxed evenings with friends seem things of the past.

As time goes on, the father will probably earn more money, and when the child grows to school age the mother may go back to work. The child-rearing tasks move on, requiring change and growth on the part of the parents as the child grows and develops. The advent and timing of each additional child will have an impact on the marital pair and their parental tasks.

In my experience, parents have often wished that they had had their second child first. The second child is usually more easily integrated into the family, although normal sibling rivalry has to be coped with. "The first and only" now becomes the elder child and has to make way for the new interloper. The picture changes again when number three arrives on the scene; role changes again occur. The elder is now "the oldest," the former baby is now "the middle one," and the role of baby is now passed on to the new member.

The expectations of these new roles are affected by the siblings' ages, sexes, health, and other individual differences, by the size of the family, the gap between the parents' ages and those of the children. All this has an important bearing on the developmental process of the children and on the family system (Maier, 1978). Meanwhile the outer system continues to interact; class, education, values, culture, economic, ethnic, and religious factors will all affect the couple at the child-rearing phase. It seems that the one constant is change itself. This provides for challenge and satisfaction as well as possible hazards for the family during this phase, as indeed for all phases of the family life cycle.

Parenting is learned behavior, and the tendency for young parents to repeat with their children what was done to them by their own parents, or to do the opposite, may not be appropriate to the needs of their children. For example, we may hear a young mother say, "Spanking didn't do me any harm—I grew up all right." But did she? Or a father may say, "I want my child to have all I missed when I grew up," including a university education. Such a child may then be pressured to overachieve.

The parental tasks in raising children call for ongoing collaboration and joint decision making, in order to provide an atmosphere where emotional as well as physical and intellectual growth takes place. It has been wisely said that "more is caught than taught." Do the parents freely show and express affection and pleasure? Are emotions of anger, fear, and sorrow, as part of the human condition, also expressed appropriately and experienced by the child? Family styles and rules about emotional expression emerge: "In our family no one shouts," or "We always argue," or "We kid and laugh a lot," or "We're a kissing family," or "We keep in our sadness," and so on.

The counselor forming the assessment in the child-rearing phase will be alert to how parents are coping with these and other child-rearing tasks. Do children have time for study and play (Bruner, 1975)? Do they share appropriately in household chores? Do parents jointly set controls and limits to pave the way for self-discipline in their children, or is one parent too permissive and the other too demanding? Or are the children in the driver's seat? Do parents establish time and privacy for themselves, or is the bedroom door never closed? If the mother of young children is working outside the home, have adequate child-care plans been made?*

Broadly speaking, does the child's behavior seem appropriate to his or her age group? Such questions are usually clarified as the couple discuss their complaints and conflicts. If not, some questions will need to be asked, although a questionnaire approach should be avoided.

---

*Half the children of school age in the United States have mothers who are working. The Canadian scene is not dissimilar. In a society beset by inflation and the rising cost of living, the proportion of working mothers is increasing. This adds pressure to the family system, as it entails parental role changes and the need for outside child day-care services. Such child day-care services are a vital social policy issue, to which marriage and family counselors can and should provide valuable input.

Sometimes beginning counselors tend to identify, even over-identify, with a child against the parents. This situation is better coped with if one stops to consider that the parent was once a child too. When we find ourselves too critical of a parent, it helps if we speculate on that parent's own childhood years.

Child-rearing problems may be the arena in which other marital conflicts are being inappropriately worked out. Engaging the couple in problem solving in this area may be a fruitful treatment focus related to the marital conflict. Marital crisis may provide an opportunity to improve the child-rearing process, and not necessarily be a disaster for the children.

A word of caution—during the counseling process when parents describe persistent and unusual behavior in a child, this should be taken seriously. Consultation is indicated to consider whether family therapy, individual and/or conjoint marital therapy, or some other treatment modality is required. A collaborative plan with other disciplines may be called for. In this case, the short-term counselor should be flexible in the use of time limits.

Thus, parents today face many and complex challenges during the child-rearing process. But the full burden does not rest on the parents alone. Much of the child's waking life is spent outside the home, in school and in the neighborhood. To what extent children's needs in these areas are being met is again a broad social concern.

It follows that there can be no one ideal way to be a parent. Parents do the best they can with the inner and outer resources available to them. Fortunately, children are resilient. I recall attending a series of lectures on child rearing given many years ago by Melanie Klein. When the series was over, she commented that it was indeed difficult to meet and perform parenting tasks effectively. One final sustaining sentence remains with me to this day: "It's better to do the wrong thing in the right spirit than to do the right thing in the wrong spirit." In other words, love and understanding may not be enough, but they certainly help to get us through the rough and tumble of family life during the child-rearing years.

The majority of parents today still hold to traditional child-rearing attitudes. It is interesting to note that many of the couples who had adopted values born on college campuses in the 1960s are, as contemporary parents, reverting to the traditional values they had previously rejected (Yankelovitch, 1974).

Now, turning to the case of the Martins, we will see that the family structure has already absorbed three children. While child-rearing problems were not a main concern when the couple were first seen, they soon emerged as an important issue interacting with and affecting the marital conflict. We will also see how mothering and fathering have been influenced by the couple's own parenting. We will see how the impact of a series of precipitating factors and the consequent role changes disturb the family system. With role conflict and parental role ambiguity, with mounting pressures, the Martin marriage is in jeopardy.

MR. AND MRS. MARTIN

Mr. Martin, age 36
Mrs. Martin, age 34

Married 11 years

Children: Michael, age 9
Richard, age 7
Phyllis, age 2

Referral, February 18

The telephone call has crisis implications.

Mrs. Martin, very upset, called in the morning for an appointment. She said her husband had been to see a lawyer the day before about a separation. She didn't want him to leave, and she had gone to their minister for help. The minister had called her husband in, and he then agreed to see a marriage counselor. I arranged to see the couple that very evening.

Quick intervention. Clients are more malleable during the crisis period.

First Interview, February 18

Worker notes early nonverbal clues: he leads, she follows.

Mr. Martin walked into the office with a firm stride; Mrs. Martin followed meekly. He sat in a chair, facing me directly. She huddled in a far corner on the sofa. I asked whether she'd like to remove her coat. She thanked me, but said she felt a bit cold.

Mr. Martin is a dark, thick-set, good-looking man, carefully dressed. He had an air of purpose and independence about him. He immediately took the initiative.

Mr. M. is an angry man, not a client. My task will be to induct him into the client role. Defending a colleague is a "no-no" before a working relationship is established. This entails listening with respect and an effort to be understanding. One need not agree but must relate to the client's feelings

Bluntly, in fact belligerently, he said, "I have no use for social workers. I had an experience with one of your colleagues on a committee, and I have absolutely no respect for them. However, I gave my word of honor to the minister to come, and I'm here. You should know that my decision to leave my wife is not a hasty one. It's a principle of mine never to go to anyone for help, and this counseling is quite pointless."

rather than to what has been said. The interviewing principle is the same, and applies whether a doctor, a teacher, or other professional, or oneself is involved.

I accept his feelings, without discussing the content of his message.

Some interpretation of the service, part of the "contract." One has to do this at various points in the interview as clients often do not retain the initial explanation.

I said he had a right to his feelings, and he might very well be correct. At this point I could not know, but here he was anyhow. When this session was over, he could decide for himself whether it was pointless or not. At this, he relaxed somewhat.

In any case, I added, all I could do was to help them understand more clearly what had gone wrong between them. The outcome for the marriage itself would have to be their own decision, and not mine in any way.

Meanwhile Mrs. Martin sat tense and frozen, like a scared rabbit. She looked older than her thirty-four years. Her long hair was parted in the middle, and plainly combed. She was without make-up and dowdily dressed.

I asked what had brought their marital situation to this point of crisis. Mr. Martin took over, "I've done my best. We've been married eleven years. We have two nice boys, nine and seven, and a lovely daughter of two. The problem is, I can't respect my wife. I can't talk to her—her interests are petty. She leans on me constantly for the smallest decisions. When I come home tired, I never get a greeting, nor is there a meal ready for me. All I get are problems and complaints."

A glimpse of the emotional axis. She is passively hostile; he is aggressive.

Note this fear of the son's failure as a precipitating factor. It reflects on the father's adequacy.

He went on bitterly: he works hard to provide well for his family, but the whining and complaining have increased. On the odd occasion when they do have a social engagement, he's always embarrassed because she's late. Now the strained atmosphere is affecting the children. The older son is going to fail in school. Mr. Martin continued, "All my efforts and energy are for nothing. I've had enough, and I want *out*!"

I turned to Mrs. Martin and asked her how she felt about all these criticisms. In a thin voice all she could say was, "I only know I don't want him to leave me." I asked her why she was not able to say anything on her own behalf. She brought out that he always argues her down, tells her she has no brains; she feels she can never win.

He broke in sharply, "We've been through this routine before. The point is, I'm trying to provide for you and the children, and you deny me the right to do this."

I commented that this sounded hard to understand. Could he explain?

He brings out a further stress factor—the new role of shopowner.

Still angry and excited, he continued, "I work hard at a full-time job, which is demanding and boring." About two years ago he began planning to supplement his income, and finally a year and a half ago, in order to better himself, he and his friend opened a small toy shop "on a shoestring." His partner is a very good man and carries the bulk of the work during the daytime, but to make the business go, Mr. Martin has to work there after his own job, from 5:30 P.M. till late at night during the week, and on weekends too. The prospects for this shop are promising, and on the strength of this he was encouraged to go to his bank and managed to arrange for a loan and mortgage about a year ago, to buy a small house convenient to the new store, located in a good suburban area.

Worker takes note that Mrs. M. was pregnant at this time with the third child.

Further stress factors—the move and buying a house.

Here I credited him for unusual initiative. I went on to ask how this affected his family life. Still angry, he insisted that he was doing this *for* his family, to support them, to give them what they needed, and to keep them from the disgrace he had seen in his own family when he was growing up.

Confrontation with an arm around the shoulder.

In response to my question, he explained, "My father drank heavily. He was a weak person and rarely worked. He never provided decently for his family. He borrowed, and brought shame to us all. I despised him, and I vowed that I'd *never* be like him." With strong feelings, he added, "In fact, my guiding principle has always been to be *different* from my father."

He raises "the living past," i.e., the past that is active in the present.* Worker decides the impact of that past has to be interpreted now.

At this point I knew I should move in quickly and sharply if Mr. Martin were to be enlisted. I pulled my chair forward, looked him straight in the eye, and said, "It seems to me that your father *still* has you by the throat."

Technique of nonverbal communication, to strengthen the message.

This seemed to stun him. He looked at me for a long moment. "What do you mean by that?" he demanded. I replied, "You seem to be devoting your life to proving how different you are from your father. Isn't it time you had the right to be yourself?" He was silent, and I let him turn it over.

*A phrase I heard used by Dr. Nathan Ackerman at a workshop.

His value system: "Be a material success." She demeans his worth by looking unkempt.

In a little while he went on, less belligerently, "Look here —I work hard. I put in all this energy for my wife and family. I come home; nothing is ready. My wife is sloppy, wearing slacks or an old robe, without lipstick. I feel my efforts are all for nothing. There's no companionship. She is dull, interested only in petty details."

Mrs. Martin ventured tentatively to take a stand, and I plan to support her by challenging his aggressive counterattack.

I again asked her how she felt hearing herself downgraded like this. She still sat stiff and wide-eyed, watching me, watching him, hardly able to speak. Then, in a soft little voice she turned to him. "Why should I get dressed and do things for you? When I try to make myself look nice, it makes no difference. You never notice it or compliment me. And what is there to talk about when you're not there? I feel that you leave everything to me. You don't even phone to say when you'll be home."

He interrupted abruptly to say that she pesters him constantly on the phone with all her silly indecisions and petty interests.

I use a technique of exaggeration to limit the flow of downgrading criticism.

I stopped him to ask whether or not he really thought his wife was stupid. "No—not really stupid." He laughed a little. "In fact, there are times when she has given me a good argument."

It helps!

I asked whether there was anything worthwhile about her. He conceded, more quietly, "She's a good mother. She's warm-hearted with the children." I said, "I'm glad to learn she has something going for her."

The children are brought in.

I can now involve Mrs. Martin.

Turning to Mrs. Martin, I asked about the children. By now less fearful, she said they were all bright and healthy. Little Phyllis, two years old, is a joy to her, and now much easier to manage. Richard, now seven, is well liked and likes school. The nine-year-old, Michael, is good and bright too, but not so happy at the school. He seems a little shy. Mr. Martin agreed that they were all good children and healthy, but he is concerned about Michael. He isn't getting on in the new school, and is doing poorly. I said that must be a worry to them, but they certainly had the love for their children in common.

I do not explore the problem of Michael at this point, as I wish to pursue the general picture, for the assessment. Enough problems have already been raised. So many problems are often offered in a first interview, the worker may find the time has gone without having settled something to be worked on. Clients must not leave confused, without knowing why they should return for another interview.

Sex and age differences make her a welcome sibling.

Note the impact of this third unplanned baby, in crowded quarters.

Support for Mr. Martin, as well.

Added financial responsibility.

Now the in-law problems.

Has Mrs. Martin's excessive dependency been brought into the marriage with her?

I relate only to the reality issue of his leaving town.

Mrs. Martin added, "The children are lovely; they all love him and he says he loves them too. But now they hardly ever see him." Here he became angry, "This annoys me. I do my best. I get the boys off to school. We have breakfast together when you're busy with Phyllis. Besides," he went on, "you're home all day. You complained enough about the old apartment being crowded, and how the baby cried on the balcony. Now you have a garden, and you say yourself it's easier."

I inquired whether Phyllis had been planned. No—it seems this baby was an "accident." Both said, however, they were happy to have her, and particularly because they had both wanted a little girl, and the two boys were delighted with their little sister.

How had they managed when Phyllis was born? He came in, "It was a shambles. You'd think she'd never seen a baby in her life." Here I stopped him with, "I think Mrs. Martin can speak for herself."

Quietly she said, "My mother lived a few blocks away from our apartment and did her best for me with the two boys and with Phyllis too, but our place was so small, it was hard to manage."

I said, "This must have been a hard time for you, and for you too, Mr. Martin. I think you began to plan for the new store around this time?" "Yes," he said, "I had to find ways to increase my income and make a decent home for my family. Even four years ago, I was eager to leave town to get a better job, but she wouldn't go." He went on heatedly, "She's afraid to leave her family and phones her mother constantly. She claims she loves me, but she loves her mother more."

She tried to deny this, saying she turned to her mother because there was no one else to talk to. He snapped, "If you really loved me, you'd have picked up and left town in three weeks, but you refused." She fell into silence again, and here I asked him how practical it was to move away with the family on three weeks' notice. Did he have a job to go to elsewhere?

Repetitive material is always significant. Note his use of "principle."

"Well," he said, "it's the *principle*. If your wife loves you, she will take her chances and go with you. I would be satisfied to know that she would go in three or five months, for me to get a job lined up and then go, but whenever I discussed this matter with her, she kept saying, 'No! No! No! What will happen if we do go, and how can I leave?' " Here she said, "Richard was still a baby, and you remember he had one cold after another."

Worker could get "lost" in exploring this past problem, and returns focus to the present and to the assessment.

Important for worker to credit him with a successful work effort. This is an area which the spouse often ignores.

I asked him about his present daytime job, as a computer programmer, which he has held for the past five years. He finds it a strain to be in a large corporation. I commented that he had stuck to it nevertheless. This pleased him. He feels he doesn't get enough scope in his situation for initiative and has little chance to advance. The toy shop he has opened is his only satisfaction. He thinks it is working out amazingly well, though he cannot draw too much from it as yet. He feels sure he can build up this new business and in a few years will have financial security and time to spend with his wife and with the children, as he formerly did.

Finally, he stressed that his wife should understand this. He is doing it all for her, and she should be prepared to wait the few years out. I suggested that he ask his wife how she felt about this. He turned to her, "What's unreasonable about that? And you know there's no other woman."

Useful to get one to talk directly to the other.

Rather than respond to her fear, I confront her by pointing out that her non-response frustrates her husband.

She sat looking frightened but didn't answer. I asked if she knew that her not responding must be very frustrating for him. At this point he was gearing up for a further attack.

To hold a balance, it was necessary to confront him quickly.

So I asked him, "Do you *really* believe you can keep a wife and children in cold storage for three years while this process goes on?" This, too, seemed to shake him quite a bit. I went on to say that I thought he would have to take a look at some of those "principles" of his, to see whether they were working for him or against him, whether he was riding them or they were riding him. Again there was a long pause.

Necessary to raise here what's right as well as what's wrong, for the assessment.

I turned to Mrs. Martin and asked, "Have there been good times between you in the past?" Yes, they'd had a happy courtship, and she often thinks of the early years of their marriage. They had fun then. They talked and planned together. He had helped a lot with the first baby. They didn't have much money, but it didn't matter. She admired and looked up to him, but now she feels neglected and belittled.

Note that sex is a plus for this marriage.

I asked about their sex life. He said, "There's never been a problem with this. We've always been very natural." She readily agreed that this had always been a satisfactory part of their marriage.

An important area to clear, particularly as her depressed mood causes me some concern.

I raised the question of their health. They both had had medical check-ups a little over a month ago. Yes, she said, she sleeps well, and eats okay. I asked whether she had lost weight? Only two or three pounds, she said, since they had moved. She said there was so much to do in the house, and with the three children.

Worker's tentative assessment and treatment plan at this point

My feeling now was that the couple didn't really want to separate. The man, under his angry tone, felt helpless and frustrated. He was intelligent, hard-working, and had shown a capacity to take the challenges I had put to him.

Despite his rather rigid rules for living, I thought he could be enlisted, that he did not want to fail at marriage. I also knew he would resent a dependency relationship with me, that it was essential in this crisis situation to work quickly and limit my goals in order not to threaten his "independence," equated by him with manhood. The goal could be to reestablish their former level of functioning.

Over the past few years Mrs. Martin had put up a passive resistance campaign out of fear, insecurity, and low self-esteem, fed by a need to be submissive. Although she seemed mildly depressed at this point, her motivation to hold on to the marriage was strong, in contrast to his. Mrs. Martin, despite her passivity, had taken the initiative of going to her minister rather than to a lawyer. The crisis of a legal threat brought some change in her pattern of coping, which I wished to reinforce quickly, with brief and firm time limits. I decided on a limit of three sessions, the present one and two more.

Summary and sharing of plan at close of interview. This is a useful practice.

By way of summary, I told them that their mutual disappointment and their great frustration over the past few years had come to a head with the pressures that arise from another child, setting up a new business venture, buying and moving to a new home. I added that Mrs. Martin was also hurt and angry, but seemed too frightened to show it openly, as her husband

The negative effect each has on the other is explained—i.e., the pattern of interaction is interpreted.

Contract is clarified to define client and worker roles.

Technique of expressing confidence. When this is genuine it is ego building and adds the important element of hope.

A small but acceptable task is set—coffee outside the home, away from the area of tension, may serve to interrupt a negative pattern of communication.

did. He drives himself hard; she feels pressured and tends to withdraw and neglect herself, which upsets her husband. He pushes harder, and she feels still more helpless. This creates a sort of vicious circle of mounting hurt and resentment.

It needs two to improve a marriage, I continued. If we are to work together, they will each have to contribute to bettering their situation. I had no magic powder to sprinkle over them, much as I might like to. In my opinion, there were assets as well as problems in this marriage, and in each of them as individuals.

I mentioned that they had a joint investment of eleven years and three children involved in the pending decision. I said that with their help, I would like to sort out some of their present difficulties, to consider with them more effective ways of coping. I suggested two more sessions, a week apart. In my judgment, should they decide to stay together, I thought they were capable of continuing to work on "unfinished business" in the marriage on their own. Mr. Martin responded enthusiastically, "I'll buy that!" At this, Mrs. Martin brightened visibly.

I asked her how she felt, hearing this plan. "I'm so glad he came," she said, "and I too want to come back." We set up an appointment a week hence. Before they left I asked them to take off just one hour during the week, outside the home over coffee, to talk over some of the things we discussed today.

On leaving, Mr. Martin shook hands with me. Mrs. Martin smiled at this and went off looking quite pleased.

Worker's reflections at the close of the first interview

It is important for the worker not to get caught up in the couple's "system." Mrs. Martin's weakness induces help and protection. In reviewing this session I wondered whether to some extent I had fallen into this trap. It was important, however, to her as well as to him for me to demonstrate a woman unafraid of his aggression. Gaining his respect was crucial to motivating him, and of course encouraging her to shift from her defeatist attitude.

Having achieved a basic goal of a first interview, to enable the couple to return prepared to work on improving their relationship, a more balanced confrontation is indicated for the next interview. Mr. Martin now seems firmly enlisted. His central need to be independent was respected, and I therefore thought it best to set a modest, nonthreatening task at this point, suggesting only that they discuss the session together.

As this case was planned to be exceptionally brief, limited to three sessions, it was important in this first session to cover the generic elements of the beginning phase of short-term marital counseling as outlined in Chapter 1 (namely, the assessment and the precipitating factors, interpretation of the service and "the contract," problem identification, and client involvement and task setting).

Second Interview, February 25

Mr. and Mrs. Martin arrived promptly. He took her coat and hung it up, and today they sat on the sofa together. I noticed that Mrs. Martin had lipstick on and looked more at ease.

I asked whether they had spoken of last week's session and the plan of work. Mr. Martin responded quite pleasantly and said they had talked together a good bit and had agreed that they would really try to straighten things out.

I turned to Mrs. Martin for her reaction. She said she really wanted to do what she could. Here he interjected, "But you've made promises over the past four years, whenever I said I was leaving." It came out that she would cry, beg him to stay, and resentfully he would give way. In fact, a few months ago he had actually made her sign an agreement that if the friction continued she would go to a lawyer without hanging on to him and whining. He made a point of saying that he would always provide for her and the children. By way of explanation, he added, "That's why I was so angry with her for going to the minister."

I commented that it also showed that Mrs. Martin was capable of initiative and of behaving differently, by taking action rather than resorting to helplessness. I thought he was about to argue on this point, so I went on to suggest that we use this session, now, to get started on some practical problem solving, the kind they will have to do on their own in the days ahead.

I asked them what they felt was an immediate issue that troubled them. I could see that Mr. Martin was now lining up his bill of complaints, getting ready to count off his grievances on his fingers. "Sir," I said, "let's stick to one for a starter, and I would like Mrs. Martin to lead off." He shrugged, and said "Okay."

After a pause, Mrs. Martin said, "We're always fighting about the accounts. It's a job I hate and dread every month."

Mr. Martin responded, "That's true enough—she never takes proper care of the accounts." I directed him to talk to his wife. He went on, "You misplace the bills. I have to pay extra

A positive response to the "task."

In crisis situations, new coping methods emerge. Worker reinforces this.

The purpose of the interview—it must be task-oriented—focus is essential with such brief time limits.

It is important to get Mrs. M. actively involved.

To promote and stimulate interaction, worker directs one to talk to the other, rather than to her.

on the electric bill. It's a mess, and the waste annoys me; you know that.''

Mrs. Martin replied that she never knew what money was available to pay the bills and that was why she got discouraged and put it off. Mr. Martin, getting irritated, said, ''If you kept the details in order, kept everything in one place, added up the totals, and told me exactly what's needed, I'd see that the money was there.'' Mrs. Martin then said, ''If I knew what money was there, then I could take care of it. Anyway, it's a job I've always hated.''

Worker plans on negotiating changes in the marital relationship.

I pointed out that they were going around in circles. He said, ''It always ends up in a fight and in the end *I* do it.'' ''Well,'' I asked, ''why not just do it, then, and avoid the fight?'' Here he laughed good-naturedly, and said: ''Okay. I'm ready—I'll take it on.'' She looked pleased. I suggested that she comment on his offer. She said, ''I'm happy about that.'' I said, ''Good. It's important to express openly appreciation of any helpful change the partner makes.''

He accepts this task and shows he can be flexible and giving.

Teaching the couple the use of immediate reinforcement.

An effort to improve the equilibrium. Tasks are set for each partner.

I then asked Mrs. Martin what she thought she could do to ease an irritant bothering her husband. ''Ask him to specify one he would like you to work on.'' He interjected, ''She knows very well.'' He wants her to fix the house up, get herself looking like someone to be proud of, to be punctual when they have somewhere to go, and particularly to get Michael to stick to his school work, especially in math—in other words, to organize herself.

Technique of using one's own reaction to check whether the spouse is being affected in the same way.

''Hold it,'' I said, ''I'm getting breathless, just listening. You're like a racehorse. Does he do that to you, Mrs. Martin?'' ''Yes. I feel I don't know which way to turn or what to do first to please him.''

Pointing out their negative interaction. He pushes; she balks.

I commented, ''You feel pushed around, into an impossible corner, when too much is expected of you at once.'' She agreed. ''So,'' I went on, ''it seems that you then go into a sit-down strike.'' They both stared at me. I said, ''When you, Mr. Martin, criticize and drive too hard, Mrs. Martin feels helpless and stalls. This gets you even more worked up—you see, it's a vicious circle. Perhaps you, Mrs. Martin, could suggest one thing that you know would please your husband?''

Technique of encouraging negotiation.

He said, "That would be something," but added somewhat protectively, "She's good to the children; she takes care of them, gives them affection, and is very patient. You know, I think a lot of her trouble is due to her lack of confidence."

In relation to this lack of confidence and her difficulty in standing up for herself, I asked whether this was a pattern she had grown up with. Had she been greatly dominated in her own home? She replied she didn't really know, but didn't think so.

At this point there was a general silence. I said, "It just now occurs to me that you have helped Mrs. Martin off the hook." Mrs. Martin looked surprised, and Mr. Martin questioned what I meant. I went on, "Instead of staying with a specific change in your wife's behavior that *you* want, which I had raised a few minutes ago on your behalf, you have instead diverted the issue to your wife's lack of confidence. As a matter of fact, I too was becoming diverted by this. It's as if you don't want her to face her need to contribute, so you excuse her, and as if you, Mrs. Martin, are quite willing to be sheltered in this way."

Mr. Martin replied, "I'm not sure I see it like that, although I agree we got off the subject. What I'm really upset about is that Michael is doing so poorly at school." Turning to his wife, he said, "You're home all day; you should help him with his homework. His failure in math upsets me. I worry that the boy may fail the year."

She brought out there was plenty to do in the house, with no help, and added, "Besides, you know I'm not that good in arithmetic, and that's why I'm not good at the accounts."

I pointed out that when parents assume the role of tutor, it rarely works. Could she think of an alternative?

After some hesitation, Mrs. Martin spoke, "Michael likes a boy who lives a few houses down the street." This youngster is twelve years old, goes to the same school, and is very bright. Mrs. Martin said she had sometimes thought that for a little extra pocket money, this boy would help Michael regularly with his weak subjects.

Mr. Martin: "That's okay with me. I'm ready to go along with that. Go ahead—arrange it."

I remarked, "It's encouraging that you've been able to agree on this," and to Mr. Martin, "What do you think of your wife's coming up with this plan?" He laughed, "She surprised me." I said, "That's fine, and I'm sure that a little credit from

---

Margin notes:

Technique of linking present to past. However, it doesn't work here.

He keeps the system going by protecting her helplessness with a topic switch— i.e., "It's her lack of confidence."

My interpretation doesn't take, but it does serve to refocus on a specific problem.

Does he see the boy's failure as *his* failure?

Actively engaging the couple in problem-solving work.

Worker reinforces their joint effectiveness here, then leads Mr. M. to reinforce Mrs. M.

you means a great deal to Mrs. Martin, and can only help in building up her confidence.''

Mr. Martin went back to the subject of the children in general. ''You tend to fuss too much with them. They're good kids, but they should learn to tackle things on time and take more responsibility for themselves.'' He began to sound off on the need for them to develop ''important principles'' early in life, so I reminded him that he himself has a sorting-out job to do. He needed to decide which of his principles worked for him and which did not. I suggested that perhaps Mrs. Martin does too much for the children because he does so little. Mrs. Martin nodded, saying it was all left to her.

He is driven to provide materially, and perceives child rearing as her *task.*

I pointed out that the children, the boys in particular, needed a father to look up to. ''You know this so well, Mr. Martin.'' I wondered whether he would give this some thought, in spite of his heavy schedule. Mrs. Martin nodded supportively, that the children do love him and miss him at bedtime. He indicated that he doesn't exactly ignore them. He loves the kids. ''You know how they get my interest and affection in the mornings.'' She agreed that he usually gets them off to school in good spirits.

It is important to help him face his almost unfilled father role.

I said, ''There's more than breakfast involved in raising children. You've thrown so much of your energy and time into being a responsible provider—'' He interrupted, somewhat resentfully, ''What's wrong with that?''

I said, ''It's a very important part of fathering, but it's only a part. I recall you said last week in three years you'll have time for your family, but in the meantime it seems that Mrs. Martin is expected to make the decisions about the children's upbringing and training, but you find this unsatisfactory.''

''Just a minute, now,'' he said, ''it's not that bad.'' I agreed it wasn't that bad, and the children appear to have fared pretty well. Again he interrupted, ''Naturally, I worry about them— that's why I raised it just now.'' Mrs. Martin got in here, ''That's what I'm always complaining about—there's no time for us. I can do with less—I know you'll make money anyhow.''

I added, ''Bringing up three children can be hectic in the best of circumstances, but with all the changes of the past few years, it's even tougher for both of you. It's hard for the boys too, getting used to a new school, finding new friends. Even a little more time from father would go a long way, while they're still young and impressionable.''

I leave the initiative to him.

He agreed to think of a way to budget his time, so as to make more room for his family.

In closing the session I pointed out that a good beginning in problem solving had taken place, Mr. Martin agreeing to take over the accounts and Mrs. Martin to plan for Michael.

To Mrs. Martin I indicated that a constant diet of home duties and the company of the young children week in and week out wasn't very stimulating, nor was this in the best interests of the children. She said she'd like an afternoon off, but had been too discouraged even to think about it. At this Mr. Martin said he'd be glad if she got a sitter and went out, and at the same time perked herself up a bit.

Setting manageable tasks so that the couple can meet with early success is essential in short-term counseling.

Mrs. Martin added she would go ahead with the tutoring plan as soon as possible, and would try to arrange for an afternoon outing. Mr. Martin then volunteered to phone home when he expected to be late, and he also agreed to look at his time budget.

An appointment was confirmed for the same time next week.

Third Interview, March 4

Mr. and Mrs. Martin arrived together, on time. Their greeting was friendly. Mrs. Martin was more animated and Mr. Martin more relaxed. She volunteered that one afternoon she had arranged for a sitter, and had gone out with a friend. She added that most evenings her husband had phoned, and she had dinner ready for him. In fact, twice this week he had spent some time with the boys before bedtime. I said they had both taken a good step forward.

Mr. Martin then said to her, "I know you're trying to please me. But remember when I asked you to call the T.V. man, and you forgot again? You have a way of forgetting things. You know how this annoys me—why do you do it?"

A basic rule of communication: one cannot not communicate (Watzlawick, 1967).

Mrs. Martin tightened up, and didn't answer. I waited a bit, then said, "You do know, Mrs. Martin, that you not answering is doing something?" Mr. Martin put in, "It sure makes me mad." She said, "I just want to keep the peace."

Pointing out that her behavior is not functional, and explaining her passive hostility in words she can understand.

I said, "But don't you see it's more likely to bring on a fight?" I added that by withdrawing, she put herself into a vulnerable position where Mr. Martin comes on so critically. To this Mrs. Martin responded, "I never thought of it like that." I said, "Not answering and forgetting things can in fact be a form of fighting. It doesn't keep the peace. Instead it brings on an angry response."

At this point Mr. Martin said that ignoring her appearance also provoked him, but he added supportively that with a little effort she could look quite attractive. She responded that she had lost heart to try.

Teaching positive reinforcement.

I asked him if she did try, what response would this bring from him? He said he would be really encouraged. I wondered whether she could do something about this, and she said, "If it means that much to you, I'll gladly do so." I commented that this sounded just great.

I asked what help the boys gave her with household chores. It appears the boys both like to help with the baby; in fact, they used to fight about this. She got over this by having them take turns. Richard comes home first and then gives over to Michael when he gets back from school. It seems that Michael willingly clears the table and helps with the supper dishes, but that Richard just runs off to play. Mr. Martin said here that he didn't know Richard was getting away with so much. I suggested they discuss this now and try to work something out. He came through with suggestions for Richard to take on some specific jobs, asking her what she thought would be most useful. They agreed that Michael should be given some privileges as he was the older boy; he could be allowed to go to bed a half-hour later than Richard.

A child-rearing issue is used in assigning an exercise in joint problem solving now.

I commented that this was a good way of working, and suggested they discuss their decision together with the boys.

Technique of reinstating former satisfying roles.

I then raised the possibility of outside interests and asked her what she had done before her marriage. She had worked as a secretary for six or seven years and had several girl friends, whom she rarely sees nowadays. She used to enjoy a pottery class with one of them.

Mr. Martin said he'd be glad for her to get out once or even twice a week on a regular basis, to take on some outside interest. He went on, "In this way, we might become a little more companionable, and have something to talk about."

I pointed out that she too had resources for increasing her own satisfaction and improving the marriage and need not depend so much on her husband.

Here Mr. Martin said with warmth, "Somewhere I do love her—she's a good kid." "That's fine," I said, "but your wife is an adult too, and if you'd treat her like one, you might find her more competent and have less to complain about."

In closing off the sessions, we spent some time summarizing how each had been affecting the other adversely. Putting excessive demands on Mrs. Martin was nonproductive, such as expecting her to rear the children on her own, or to move out of town on short notice to prove her love. Her method of withdrawing and losing interest in her appearance and in her home, even in herself, resulted in hurting not only her husband but herself as well.

I indicated that in these few sessions, each had effectively demonstrated ways of contributing to solving some of their problems. It was up to them now to continue this type of give and take on their own, and I thought that they were quite capable of doing so, and in particular, they were able to work together on raising their children.

She asked him, rather coyly, whether he would continue to phone her when he was going to be late, and he agreed to this. I questioned whether his reluctance to "report" to her was a way of showing that he was the man his father wasn't. He said, "Maybe, but I get the idea—I should be myself."

I left him with the ongoing task of budgeting some time for his wife as well as for the children, in ways possible for him, again indicating that even a little could go a long way. Here, she said she would be very content if she could have even a little more of him.

I repeated that they had modified their expectations of each other and so had broken into the "vicious circle." I said this should help in getting at the "unfinished business" in their marriage. Of course, it was only natural to expect ups and downs in any marriage.

As they were leaving, Mr. Martin thanked me warmly and asked whether there was anything he could do for me, as I had been so helpful. Mrs. Martin asked if she should send the minister some flowers! I said I thought he would be content to know that they had agreed to stay together.

Worker lines up with the adult part of Mrs. M.

Unfinished business—some ongoing tasks identified.

Important to prepare for inevitable down period.

As far as I was concerned, I would be pleased to have a follow-up session, possibly in a few months, to see how they had worked out some of their differences on their own. I added that I would also like to tape that session for teaching purposes, because of the brevity of our work together. Mrs. Martin expressed some concern about confidentiality, but Mr. Martin said he knew all about tape recording and would arrange everything. He would also erase names if they were used. He made one condition: that I come to their home for the interview. He added that he would place the recorder in such a way that neither his wife nor I would be nervous!

For a variety of reasons—summer holidays intervening, their children having a round of chicken pox, followed by a repainting job at their home—we did not get to this follow-up interview until ten months later.

Excerpts from tape-recorded follow-up interview in the home of Mr. and Mrs. Martin, 10 months later

I arrived at 9:30 P.M., as arranged. The Martins live in a pleasant residential suburb. The house is one in a row, all with neat small gardens and newly planted trees. They greeted me warmly at the door and showed me proudly around the ground floor, as the children were sleeping upstairs.

I was struck by the change in Mrs. Martin's appearance. She had lost that drawn look and had gained a few pounds. Her hair was cut short. She was tastefully dressed and wearing a little make-up. She smiled freely and was very much at ease.

After a period of preliminary chit chat:

A question to either partner. Note that Mrs. M responds first.

WORKER: Let's hear how you two have been managing since we last met.

SHE: Things are a lot better and even the children are happier, Michael especially. He's doing better at school this year, although he still has his tutor.

HE: I agree. I find we're getting on better, and even when we have an argument it doesn't drag on and on, the way it did.

SHE: Yes, there was a time when you wouldn't speak to me for a week.

HE: And I used to sleep on the couch, and this I haven't done since the interviews.

WORKER: Well, that's good. It seems you've done a lot on your own, with just three sessions. What do you think happened?

HE: I don't really know what happened. All I know is that if it had taken many sessions we wouldn't be sitting here tonight—I promise you that. If I can remind you—

WORKER: I don't think I quite follow you—

HE: The marriage would have been over.

WORKER: If it had been—

HE: If it had been drawn out, there would be no marriage today. I was at the end of the line.

WORKER: In other words, the fact that it was brief, and—

HE (emphatically): That's it. It was left up to us to act like *adults*. Every time we walked out of your office . . . well, I looked forward to getting out. I always walked out holding my wife's hand. I remember the first years after we were married, we used to walk like that. But to be quite frank with you today, if someone had asked me, who did it? I would have to say that my wife and I did it.

WORKER: Well, this certainly is true. I don't believe I could have been of help unless you two decided to work together.

SHE: I know that I was fighting, by not cooperating.

HE: And I felt, not only felt, I knew that my father had no ambition. I didn't speak to him for ten years after I left home. He had no principles, and as a result I refused to permit my children to be part of that kind of life. Whatever I've done, I've done on my own. I can go to people, I can get help, have been offered help, but I've refused. I might have a little less, but I don't want anyone to throw anything up to me. I think I've told you this before, that a man without a basic set of principles is not a man. But you pointed out to me, and it was important, that principles are okay as long as they work for

Note application to systems theory. That is, there are often "fringe benefits" and changes occur outside the home as well as inside the home.

you. As a matter of fact, I've used this idea in my job, and people tell me they notice I'm easier to get on with. I'm earning more now, not that much more, but you can see where it's going, to make a nice little house that is our own.

As this is a follow-up session, worker is more passive.

WORKER: Yes, it's a very attractive one.

HE (to her): Yet you would deny me the right to provide.

SHE: No, I didn't mind when you worked late to earn extra money. I was resentful when I was left all alone by myself with the children.

HE: But it was for you.

Mrs. M. is more assertive.

SHE: I know it was for me and the children, but how much can one person stay alone? I feel that anything we'd have in the house—it's not worth it. You weren't home—why didn't you call?

HE: So now I call and tell you I'll be home at 7:30 or 8—mostly it's 11 o'clock, or I'll be home at 12 o'clock. This makes it worthwhile? this phone call?

SHE: Yes, and you manage to be home for dinner once and sometimes twice a week, and that's great. Last week when it was your birthday, you were home. We had a cake for you; the kids were waiting up for you. You were home, you thought of it.

In effect he says: I don't need a birthday fuss—I never had it. Maybe I don't deserve it.

HE: Wait a minute—I came home for the sake of my family—

SHE: But it used to mean nothing to you. You felt it meant nothing to your family—if you weren't there, so what? And last month you made it a point to be home on Halloween with special candies for the kids. I feel that's part of family life.

HE: And I did it to please you.

SHE: I felt so good, and the kids were so excited. (To worker) Sundays, he doesn't run out to be with his business partner. If he does, he's with us till lunch, and then he goes.

Note his discomfort about praise, linked to his not being used to this in his growing up.

HE (uncomfortably and a bit facetiously): So I've become a reformed character!

WORKER: Apparently, though you're still carrying two jobs, you've managed to give more time to your wife and children, and this was one of the important issues we talked about.

HE: This is correct. I have more leeway to develop my ideas on the job, and we get out more.

SHE: Now I feel like getting dressed, going out, talking to people. Before, I was just in a rut. I just wanted to stay in the house with the kids.

For him, admitting change is admitting he needed and took help—that is, he is not as "independent" as he needs to feel.

HE: But you give the impression this was all due to me, to *me* changing—

SHE: No, it's the way I felt—

HE: And you changed because I treated you differently. I happen to feel that I treated you differently because of the ways you changed.

(They go back and forth on this, he insisting that she has done most of the changing.)

WORKER: If I can intervene here, does it matter who changed, if the effect you have on each other has changed for the better?''

HE: Maybe so, but these are things I expected from my wife. Actually, I love my wife, I love my children, whether my wife looks after the accounts or not. I don't mind now. We used to argue at the end of every month, so now instead of arguing with her, she doesn't do them any more. I took it off her. To me, this was the easiest way, to do it myself.

SHE: I used to dread that job. I always worried if the money was there.

Mr. M. defines the traditional type of husband/ wife roles, which she accepts, but she goes on to reject his inconsistency.

HE: I had a belief, an impression, or whatever you call it, that I would look after providing essentials. This would be my job, and my wife would look after the home and the children, and paying the bills was part of it. Included in looking after the home was buying wallpaper, picking a pretty color, which to me were small details, and you know how much it used to annoy me to be involved with such matters. Anyhow, we don't fight about the accounts at the end of the month any more.

She seems to be more confident, saying: "It's Okay now, but you used to confuse me."

SHE: Yes, but you would say to me: "Go out and buy it," and if I did buy it, or look and say I saw something, you'd say, "How could you possibly like that?" I was stuck in between. I didn't know if it was nice or wasn't. That's why I always looked to you to come shopping with me.

Restating the conflict.

WORKER: You didn't know whether to be independent or to lean on him totally.

SHE: I just didn't know where I stood.

He uses projection here, saying *she* won't admit change. Although it is he as well, worker decides to

HE: This makes me think that really not so much has changed. Maybe the importance I put on certain items has changed. In the past I wanted my wife to do certain things at once, immediately. Now, if she changes a little bit more to what I want, every week or every month or so, I'm quite satisfied. I feel she has, although she won't admit it. I feel she has changed a lot. She's ten years younger in her attitude.

leave it, rather than to push this.

WORKER: You look ten years younger—your hair—

SHE: I cut my hair. I fought with him all the time that my hair was long, for two and a half, three years. I really don't care for it too much, but because my husband wanted it, I keep it short and he likes it.

Note she likes the traditional role. It is functional for them, with some modification.

WORKER: One of the things you were both unhappy about was the lack of openness and companionship between you.

SHE: That's right. And now if he has something to tell me, he says it. He doesn't keep it stored in, and then burst all of a sudden, out of a clear blue sky.

HE: Because you never had anything in common with my interests. You can sit till one-thirty, two o'clock in the morning now, and listen to music with me, but before you used to go upstairs and go to sleep.

Mrs. M. is again showing more assertiveness.

SHE: Why? Do you know why? You'd put on a record, and as soon as I said, "Gee, I like that, it's nice," you'd switch it off and put on something else. Now, I really enjoy sitting and listening to music.

HE: I'll give you another example. I don't think that I ever once took my wife to a movie that she didn't fall asleep. Or if we stayed up at night to watch a show together, I know exactly what she'd do—sit at my feet to keep them warm, and fall asleep. I didn't need a hot-water bottle; I wanted company, and a sleeping woman to me is not company.

WORKER: Does she fall asleep now?

HE: No. Since we have met with you, she will sit up, even if we're in bed, with the T.V. in the bedroom. She's sleeping occasionally, but she's mostly up.

Note she now has a sense of hope.

SHE: I feel better—I like to please my husband. I want to do things—my outlook is so different; perhaps I was running away, and that was my way of showing it.

WORKER: When there is a fencing match between two people, you find ways of doing things to irritate each other, whether you know it or not.

SHE: We were just fighting each other continuously.

HE: These things are so hard to explain. As I said before, the stress has definitely changed.

WORKER: But how do you settle a difference nowadays? Do you just let it go? Don't you talk it out?

HE: Not much—maybe we don't talk about it enough—

SHE: Sometimes we do—

More changes—but it was important that he retain control, by making choices himself.

HE (to worker): Yes, but I know the most important way you affected me was by showing me my blind spots. What did I value most? My principles, my wife or my children? So I don't drag out the fights the way I used to.

(Here the Martins went on to discuss in some detail what happened to friends who are getting a legal separation. They discuss how upset this couple's children seem when they come to visit the Martin children. They go on to talk about the pleasure they get nowadays from their three children.)

HE: I still say we have a lot of improving to do—

WORKER: Who hasn't? (laughter) The main thing is, I thought you two could do a lot on your own. It was a matter of opening a few doors, to help you see the way you were affecting each other, and you did pick this up very quickly. (To him) You were the first to pick this up.

Crediting him with leadership.

SHE: I was too scared. All I knew was that I didn't want him to leave me. That's all I had on my mind.

He is more supportive of how her past made spending difficult. Before, it was a painful aspersion on his adequacy as a provider. Her spending money has helped to further differentiate him from his father's inadequacy.

HE: And you were pushing me further away. Mrs. Freeman, even today my wife is still a bit fearful to spend money, and I think it's because of her upbringing, because she came from a relatively poor family. Now, I don't want to die a rich man. I'm not interested in that. I'm interested in living a good and full life with my wife and family. Isn't it true we used to argue every time we had to buy something? Lately, when I said, "Let's go out and buy a couple of armchairs," she said, "Okay, let's go." I was the most stunned person in the world. This wasn't my wife speaking.

WORKER (to her): Maybe you've gained in confidence from feeling more respected and valued.

SHE: Yes, I do feel better about myself.

HE: If I may bring something up—I've always been very frank with you, Mrs. Freeman, right from the beginning, even when I told you I didn't think much of social workers.

WORKER: Indeed, you were very frank.

Note that I hold back when Mr. M. now raises sex as a

HE (after a pause): I've always been frank, but in our sex relationship I find that when we were at odds with each other, I

new concern. I had wanted to confine myself to a follow-up interview. It crossed my mind that a further contact should perhaps be involved. I bided my time by picking up on the quarrelling but soon realized I would have to get back to the sex issue.

Further evidence that he's changed.

don't know if this is the reason, but I find that before, when we were apart, the desire was much greater, and now that we're closer, the desire is much weaker. I don't know if this is anything to do with the fact that we don't argue much any more.

WORKER: You hardly argue?

HE: Very little, very little—we soon drop it.

WORKER: Let's go back to some unfinished business here. There's no reason why you shouldn't get annoyed or angry with each other, if you feel that way, and talk it out afterwards.

HE: I like it when she gets annoyed. I wish she'd get annoyed more often. I don't mind this. I shouldn't say that we always change the subject—

SHE: We had a dilly of an argument this summer, and we didn't change the subject—

HE: Which argument was that? It was so unimportant that I can't remember it now. Before, this was something I could do. I had a filing cabinet up here (points to his head). Until the time we went to see you, I could draw out any argument that we had in the ten years we were married, up till the time we came to see you. But now, when we refer to arguments in the last ten months, I can't remember them.

SHE: I think it was about my mother—I'm not sure.

WORKER: I'd like to come back to this later. You were connecting this with your sex life. How was sex before?

HE: It was terrific.

WORKER: Well, was it frequent?

HE: Yes, very. (To her) Correct?

SHE: Yes.

WORKER: And now?

HE: Now, I'm satisfied to lie in bed and cuddle up to my wife and go to sleep.

WORKER: You have no sex at all now?

HE: Oh yes, we have sex—

WORKER: And it's no good?

HE: Oh, very good, but it's just that maybe I've reached that age now where—

WORKER: Do you really think in ten months you can deteriorate that much?

HE: No (laughs), I think there is something underlying here, I don't know.

WORKER: Well, before, so much seemed wrong with the marriage, and this was one area, one place, where you were satisfied, and your wife said she was. Now that you are both more relaxed, I wonder whether this is affecting you adversely. Did the fighting make sex more exciting?

HE: I wouldn't say that, but I've noticed it's definitely not as it was.

Clarification.

WORKER: Is it less exciting?

HE: Oh, it's exciting, when we have it.

WORKER: But it is less frequent?

HE: Yes.

WORKER: How, less frequent?

HE: Well (pauses), now that you've asked the question, and I'm thinking about it, I think it may only seem less frequent, because of the fact that we slept apart so much before. When we did sleep together we had sex, whereas now that we're sleeping together every night, I guess there's nothing wrong with it—it's just normal—(pauses) so I've asked you a question, and I've answered it myself.

WORKER (to her): How do you feel about this? Do you enjoy your sex life now? Is there less satisfaction for you?

SHE: No, I'm quite content. I'm very content to cuddle up to him.

WORKER: Do you approach him sometimes?

HE: Oh yes, in this we've always had an understanding; we never had trouble.

SHE: That's true.

HE: No inhibitions whatever.

WORKER: Well, it sounds pretty good to me.

HE: I feel also that this is something else—since we met with you, I feel that any relationship that we have together, or even going out for a drive, or discussing something, it's real, it's not false, whereas before, we'd go for a drive, I'd take her to the car, we'd keep driving around the block. She'd say, "Well, where are we going?" I'd say, "Where do you want to go?" "Out for a drive"—"Well, we're driving," and I'd drive around the block again. I realize now this was childish, and that I did it to annoy her. It wasn't real, taking her out.

SHE: You didn't *want* to take me out.

HE: I didn't care—I just didn't care. (A bit defensively) you didn't see that what I was doing was right. I work; I'm not working for nothing. I'm working for a little better life, to spend a few dollars, to have my home look nice. Why work twenty-four hours a day? I could go out and get a job as an elevator man in a building. The point is that *you* didn't need any new furniture—the old couch was good enough for you—that was selfish.

SHE: Because you weren't here to share it with me, to sit with me.

HE: This was selfish. Why didn't you want that new couch for me? Maybe if we had bought the new couch, I would have come home earlier. Mrs. Freeman, I honestly believe she was wrong here. She was perfectly satisfied with the old couch, and that was that.

WORKER: Also, she was satisfied to walk around in old slacks. I mean, this was all part of the same thing, because—

HE: Because she thought only of herself.

SHE: No, because I thought you didn't care enough for me.

HE: Anyhow, this is not that important to me now, because I realize I wanted to get back at you, and you wanted to get back at me—

WORKER: There was quite a struggle going on, you with two jobs, and you with three children, only you each used different tactics. Mr. Martin was more actively attacking and downgrading, but Mrs. Martin was doing it passively—by falling asleep, by not buying furniture, by not getting dressed, by not having dinner ready. (To him) You went off to make good in the world, and you, Mrs. Martin, felt left by the wayside.

SHE: Yes, I felt all by myself with the children.

HE (gently): Now I realize that. You know, we haven't even shown Mrs. Freeman their pictures.

By "my" home, he may mean not like father's home. But I let this go, to see how she deals with his criticism.

Not intimidated.

Worker decided to move in on this, and point up their negative interaction.

Clarification by restating the old pattern.

(A photo album was shown. They discussed the children's camping, school work, their friends, and their activities, all of which sounded pretty wholesome. But Mr. Martin's high expectations of the children were questioned by the worker, who pointed out that this can backfire.)

WORKER: To get back to those arguments—

HE: Our fights now aren't so important any more. Before, when we had a row, it was important for me to win. It was important for me to come out on top.

WORKER: And now you feel it's not that important?

HE: No, I don't feel I have to win. But I wouldn't like to think that I'm not trying to get things better. I think we told you at the third meeting, we do love each other. Somewhere we knew this, even though I was ready to separate. You know, when I'm away from home, and I've travelled away from home very often, every night I sent her a letter. Not to say that the weather is fine, but to say how much I loved her, how much I needed her, how much I missed her. It was a lot easier for me to do this; I could never—I still really can't—talk to her the way I can write her from away from home. I don't know why. I'd love to be able to talk to her like that, and I think she would like it.

WORKER: Maybe you're a little shy about showing her you need her and can even lean a little on her, and still be a man. You know, we adults never stop needing people—that's why a man needs a woman, and a woman needs a man. That's what interdependence is all about.

HE: Maybe.

SHE: I still have those letters, and I still think they're wonderful.

HE: I think our companionship is growing every month, and I think my wife has a lot more confidence in herself now. She even went by herself to buy lamps. To me, this was a party. She comes home, she tells me what she bought, and *I* have to ask *her* the price! Mrs. Freeman, this gives me a lot of pleasure.

SHE: And you liked the new end tables I bought last month. I came home and I said, "This is what I really wanted."

HE: And this you have never done before. I said I can't meet you; you went by yourself. And now, we're going to go shop-

Voluntary change on his part is still under *his* control.

Note how his dependency needs come out at a safe distance.

Taking a chance here—dependence is Okay and then I relabel it as interdependence and adult behavior.

Evidence of her growing confidence.

ping together next Saturday. It makes me feel that I'm not working for nothing.

SHE: And I felt that I didn't want to go out and buy it on my own—maybe, maybe it would cause an argument.

WORKER: Are you still afraid of an argument?

SHE: At times, yes, because I don't like to argue.

HE: This is true.

SHE: I don't like to argue.

HE: I can read my wife like a book—if it's pitch black outside and I say it's light, she'd apologize and say she was looking out the window the wrong way. But this annoys me, Mrs. Freeman.

WORKER (to her): Why are you frightened of an argument?

SHE: I don't know, maybe because I never heard it at home. And I'm afraid of it. Maybe I don't know how to argue. I'll argue with myself.

Clarification.

WORKER: You're arguing with Mr. Martin quite a bit tonight.

HE: It's only because you're here.

SHE: No—

HE: Oh, yes. My wife will contradict me—I think this is wrong —in company. But not if we're alone.

Helping her to face her fear of anger.

WORKER: What do you think would happen if he got mad?

SHE: In front of people?

WORKER: No, in front of people he wouldn't do anything; maybe that's why you're not afraid. But what would happen if you were alone? I'm not trying to say you've got to start a fight, but if he tells you he's going to phone and he doesn't, there's no reason why you shouldn't get angry.

SHE: I do, and he knows it. Do you recall one Friday night? I spoke to you from the toy store, and you said you'd be home at 10:30 sharp and you walked in at 3:00 in the morning?

HE (excitedly): Where was I? Where was I?

SHE: You were with a customer. You were trying to collect money, and you got involved in conversation, and you thought I was sleeping—

HE: I was at the customer's home, you know the person, and you knew where I was—

SHE: No, I didn't know at the time. You explained it to me when you came home; you apologized, but I let you know that I was mad.

HE: And I enjoyed the fact that you let me know that you were mad—you acted like a person.

WORKER (to her): You just said before that you were afraid to get mad. Now you say, "When I'm mad, I let him have it."

HE: Yes, she lets me have it, but good.

WORKER: Then you're not that afraid. It's inconsistent—I don't understand.

SHE: Well, I don't like arguments around me—

He helps me out, by explaining the game!

HE: Let's put it this way, Mrs. Freeman. When I came in late that night, I apologized. Although I apologized, she let me have it. But if I came in and said, "What are you doing up?" or if I said, "If you're up, why aren't you doing something?" there'd have been no argument. The fact that I came in and apologized, made it very easy for her. I came in on the defensive, so she spoke up.

SHE: You pick on me when I know that I should be mad at you.

HE: She won't get mad then, and I know this.

SHE: So I can't win, even though I know I'm right.

WORKER: You can't get your point across.

SHE: Even when I'm right.

WORKER (to him): You say you want your wife to express her feelings more openly. Then why play games with her by browbeating her?

HE: But (to her) you talk as if I still do this.

Interesting to note how clients work on material not responded to in the interviews—a form of hindsight learning takes place.

SHE: I know, but I'm still not that sure. (To worker) When you told me, when you said that I must have been dominated by someone growing up, I couldn't see it then; as a matter of fact, last week, two weeks ago, my mother did something that I didn't like, and I gave her an argument about it, and I was sorry for it, but I felt I'm not keeping it in. I tried to phone her, and she hung up on me, and I said, "Well, I'm not phoning her back—let her call me," and she did.

Worker gives Mrs. M. recognition for her efforts to modify her behavior.

WORKER: That wasn't easy. It seems you're learning to stand up for yourself.

In effect, he says: "I'll carry the main responsibility. I'll lead, but I want a follower who can stand up, not just fold up."

HE: This is what I want. I want my wife to be an individual. I don't want her to be just part of me. I want her to have her own thoughts, her own mind, her own opinions. Not that I have to go with her to buy a dress, or do I like this color? Do I like this? Do I like that?

WORKER: At the same time you were highly critical. Can you see how this would discourage some of the independence you want in her?

HE (thoughtfully): I guess it was a way of getting back at her. Anyhow, I'm glad now she's doing more by herself, like going to the hairdresser every week, and dressing better.

He is less critical now, but she is asking for positive reinforcement. Worker decides to pursue this with him.

SHE: But you never say, "Gee, your hair looks nice" when you come home.

HE: Well, I don't comment any more that I *don't* like your hair, so you should know I like it. I do like it. The same way I don't have to tell you, at least I thought I didn't have to tell you, every night that I love you. Mrs. Freeman surely would be the first to agree that this is important, that I tell you. It may not be so important to me, but I consider your feelings, and I think I've told you quite a few times.

WORKER: But you don't tell her when she looks nice?

HE: I'll tell her when she really looks nice. If she looks the way that I feel she should look, average, normal, then it's like praising a child for being honest. It's a principle of mine, Mrs. Freeman, it should be taken for granted. I think good behavior should be accepted, bad behavior should be chastized. I don't want my children growing up thinking they're going to be rewarded every time they act like a normal child.

I note he backs his position with "a principle," but I let it ride here.

WORKER: I think children as well as adults want recognition.

HE: When my children do better than average, my children get the recognition. When my wife dresses out of the ordinary, or really looks stunning, she gets the recognition. Am I going to praise my wife because she's got on a dress and not a bathrobe when I come home, or because she put on some lipstick? I don't see that at all. I may be all wet. If I am, I need another three sessions!

Technique of persistence.

WORKER: Would it take so much? Would it be so hard for you to do that, if it pleased her?

HE: This was something that was drummed into me as a child, very young, that I get no praise for doing what's right.

WORKER: Think about it, Mr. Martin. Your children do have a different set of parents than you had. Must they repeat your experience?

Again spontaneously, he brings up his past. We see it operating inappropriately

HE: That I don't want, but still, unless it's something exceptional, out of the ordinary, I don't want praise, and I don't think my wife should expect it either.

in the present. He never got praise, so his wife and children don't need it.

WORKER: Why out of the ordinary? Even if a woman bakes a cake, she likes to hear that it looks nice or tastes good—not every bite, or every meal, but occasionally.

HE: With my wife, it's every bite and every meal. Let's put it this way—I won't praise my wife because she wears a dress or puts on lipstick.

Discussion is becoming circular. Worker persists, now deciding to draw on his own concept of "principles."

WORKER: Well, this is something. If you want to encourage change, you've got to, it's just a simple learning *principle*, you've got to reinforce it by noticing it at the time.

Technique of using client's own key words is often effective.

It would mean a lot to Mrs. Martin, and help her to maintain the improvement that you wanted so much.

He is encouraged to help the partner, in his own best interest.

HE: You've done it again, Mrs. Freeman, you've just thrown another little switch.

WORKER: I hope I haven't put you in the electric chair!

HE (laughingly): No, you've just thrown another little switch, because I just realized now that if I enjoy her wearing lipstick and putting on a dress instead of slacks or a duster, and I want her to keep doing it, then I've got to think of my own principle. I'd better think what I want, so I have to praise her in order that she'll continue to do it.

At last, it works!

SHE: That would be swell.

WORKER: You don't have to be too parsimonious in recognizing your children, either, if they do reasonably well.

Worker includes the children.

HE: Well, it should be above average.

SHE: An average report card is pretty good.

HE (laughingly): Okay, I'll only say "It's pretty good" then. Look, the point I want to make is, if my daughter found a dollar bill anywhere in this house, and she came up and said, "Here, Daddy, here's a dollar bill I found," I don't have to say, "You're an honest child." Or if my wife makes my lunch, I'm not going to say, "Isn't that nice of you!"

Worker now lets him win, to save face.

WORKER: No, you're right, let's not carry it too far (laughter).

(Here, Mrs. Martin served coffee.)

Note Mrs. M. brings up this important material. Her past also was brought into the marriage. Counselors are often concerned about missing something; if it's important, the client will raise it again.

SHE (to worker): When you first told me that I must have been dominated while I was growing up, by my mother or someone else in the family, I just couldn't see it. I couldn't understand it. And then slowly I got to realize that my mother *did* dominate me, up until the time we got married. I used to come home Friday nights, after I got paid, and she used to sit down at the kitchen table with me and work it out for me—so much for the bank, and so much for clothes, and so much for carfare and spending money.

HE: And this went on until you were twenty-four! I never knew that.

SHE: Yes, till I got married.

WORKER: In other words, you didn't have a chance to act too independently before you got married.

SHE: That's right, that's right.

Useful to note that sharing a growing-up problem often brings out an empathetic response from the spouse.

HE: And I didn't help you along, because I just took it for granted that you should know these things.

SHE: That's true, and I was afraid to try.

WORKER: You know, we all have some unfinished growing up to do, and you, Mrs. Martin, are realizing this. I think, Mr. Martin, you could give a little assist here. I mean, with the kind of understanding you showed your wife just now. You know, Mrs. Martin, I think you still want your husband to be the leader.

Directing his leadership to more constructive use.

SHE: Yes, I really do.

WORKER: But you've also shown you want to be more independent, less dominated, and more confident, which means your project is not to scare off so easily. Mr. Martin will get more satisfaction if he leads you in that direction instead of feeling just weighed down.

If tapes are used in counseling, sometimes playing part of a past interview is a helpful learning technique for clients.

A week later, Mr. Martin brought me the finished tape, with names deleted. He said, "You'll be interested to hear we've listened back to this tape, and had some good discussions and got a lot out of it."

CLOSING COMMENTS

The follow-up interview, nearly a year after the three sessions, reveals that positive changes have taken place. Mrs. Martin is more confident, and Mr. Martin is less tense and critical. He is still the more dominant partner, and Mrs. Martin the submissive one. This leader-follower style of traditional marriage appears to fit the needs of both.

There is still more "unfinished business" left than could be dealt with, or even identified, in so few sessions. The worker had taken the practical position that to enlist Mr. Martin, only a very brief service would be acceptable to him. Now too, at this time, there is no motivation for further help. As the couples in Chapter 2, they have done well on their own, and one should respect their right to consolidate, to reach for further help should this become indicated. The positive, nonthreatening counseling experience that they had should make this possible. In general, the atmosphere within the family has improved, and the children, particularly the older son, have benefited from the lessened tension between the parents.

We see in the Martin case the interaction of the family subsystems—marital, parental and child. With the advent of the third child we see the reality of Mr. Martin's increased financial responsibilities become intensified by his fear of repeating the family drama of his own early life. With his powerful need to be different from his father, he overdoes it so that, in effect, he too acts as his father did—also neglecting his family, but in a different way, by overworking as opposed to underworking. In other words, going to the other extreme is really the reverse side of the same coin. The worker, however, deals only with the surface aspects of Mr. Martin's unconscious defense against anxiety (Anna Freud, 1950).

Mrs. Martin had been brought up in a controlled dependency relationship to her mother and appears to have sought a mate of the same domineering type. Overburdened in recent years with the additional responsibilities of child rearing and decision making, with lessened support from both her husband and her mother, we see Mrs. Martin reacting to her husband with passive hostility. This was not interpreted as such during the sessions. The worker only pointed out the ineffectiveness of this behavior as a form of fighting. Over the ten-month interval that followed, however, Mrs. Martin gained some insight into her hostile behavior on her own. She herself also linked her insecurity to her mother's early domination. This capacity for client self-learning should not be underestimated.

We see a bright child failing in school, in his role of student. He may be reacting with anxiety to the tensions between his parents; he may even feel responsible for their problems. He may be identifying with his mother's passivity or her difficulty in doing the accounts, or he may be upset by the change of school and the loss of former friends. Now, in the role of the oldest, he may feel that more is expected of him. His symptom could be a plea for paternal attention. It may be a combination of these factors.

As already noted, the worker must also take the family's value system into account. For example, school failure in the son of a rural farmer may be of little consequence to the father, but in an urban and upwardly mobile family such as the Martins, it is a serious blow to the father's self-image.

With the Martins, while an eclectic approach was used in treatment, more emphasis was placed on utilizing role theory concepts and less on the behavior modification techniques which proved particularly useful with the Victors, with their clearly defined sexual problem. For example, removing Mrs. Martin from her inept tutor role and introducing an outsider to this role, along with the improved home atmosphere, brought about better student-role functioning for Michael. The case demonstrates that, in marital counseling, a child's difficulties may dissolve when the parental conflict is reduced, even without the therapist having to see the child.

This brief case focuses mainly on the here and now. I made little effort to explore the past. As clients so frequently do, the Martins themselves brought up significant aspects of past material that were clouding and interfering with present functioning. Such information was safely put to use by the worker; that is, deep and unresolved conflicts were not stirred up.

One can also learn, however, to speculate about and even empathize with the client's past without going into it extensively. For example, Mr. Martin brought out the disgrace and financial insecurity with which his family lived. One can speculate further that Mr. Martin's parents, harrassed by the consequences of irresponsibility and financial failures, would hardly tend to give their children praise for small successes. Also, though he himself lacked praise in his growing up, Mr. Martin must have somehow received love and affection, as he is able to give them. Beneath his blunt, often contentious manner, he is warm, kind, and giving.

In terms of psychodynamic theory, we see how an inner conflict can be eased by a change in its outer or surface manifestations. Mr. Martin is now less obsessed with past parental control and so too, to a lesser extent, is Mrs. Martin. It would appear that their basic defenses have become part of their character structure, which only intensive and extensive treatment might change—an impractical goal for the Martins and their children.

The limited use of history will again be noted in the Fisher, Brown, and other cases which follow. This is characteristic of short-term treatment, as discussed in Chapter 1.

4

The Middle Phase

We come now to couples with teen-age children. The child-rearing tasks of earlier years are receding. The picture changes dramatically. There is a spurt in the children's physical growth. They seem all arms and legs—dresses and trousers suddenly shrink. The psychological, emotional, and sexual changes that accompany puberty complicate the scene and add to the tasks the parents face as the children begin to move on to adulthood. There is a drive for autonomy and separation in the youngsters' search for identity. At the same time there is a pull backward to the shelter and security of former years. The adolescent conflict of independence/dependence is under way.

At this stage the task of the parents is to let go gradually, to relinquish those tight emotional ties that may interfere with the maturational process of the teen-agers. This may be a bewildering time for the parents, in what seems to be an ongoing tug of war. The teen-ager blows hot and cold, alternating between a loving and dependent attitude and a rebellious and fiercely independent one. At these times, when criticism, even disdain, is coming hard and fast, the best of parents tend to feel discouraged, even defeated. Many wonder what is going on and cannot help but feel sorry for themselves —all those nights they nursed the children through measles and whooping cough, those annual treks to the circus, the birthday parties, the P.T.A. meetings—all now are as nothing. Such thoughts may even bring to mind the plaint of King Lear:

> *How sharper than a serpent's tooth it is*
> *To have a thankless child.*

It is essential, however, that teen-agers struggle in this way if they are to become adults in their own right and not just carbon copies of the parents. Over the years, as the youngster resolves the conflict, a more adult-to-adult relationship should develop.

Meanwhile the parents have to face the reality that the power of the peer group may take precedence over their own influence during this period. This may involve well-known and increasing hazards, the drug scene, delinquency, and too many others to list here. Outside the home the teen-ager is exposed to positive as well as negative models—a school teacher, a club leader, an older cousin, and so on.

The parents, approaching or already into their forties, are now confronted with the mid-life transition, the halfway mark of the life span. Their sense of receding youth will affect their view of themselves, of their mates, and also of their adolescent children. In our youth-oriented culture, the passage of time is marked all too clearly. Witness the emphasis on youth in advertising, entertainment, clothing, and cosmetics. A premium is put on being young and on looking and acting youthful, regardless of age.

For the marital partners this is a time for looking back and looking forward. It is a time for reappraisal. For the man and for the woman at this stage, it's a time for questioning. What have I achieved? Could I have done better? What have I missed? What lies ahead?

For the father of teen-agers, this may be a difficult time. He is no longer a young adult raising small children. He is a man entering middle age, "seeking new ways of relating to his adolescent offspring. If he continues to treat them as if they were still small children they may submit and fail to develop their own autonomy, or they may move away in defiance and contempt" (Levinson, 1978, p. 254). In the case that follows, we shall see how Dr. Fisher's discomfort with his teen-age boys creates tension that is reflected in the marital relationship.

The mother at this time, relieved of some of her domestic responsibilities, will put her energy and free time toward seeking new satisfactions outside the home. Today an increasing number of women between the ages of thirty-five and fifty-four—over twelve million—are now reaching for work or career opportunities which they were not free to develop during the childrearing phase (Rubin, 1979). This growing trend can often become a source of conflict between the partners if the husband feels threatened in his role of provider. Mrs. Fisher is characteristic of the women in this group in that she has recently returned to the work force, and her increased independence threatens and upsets her husband.

Contributing to the sometimes stormy scene is the couple's reactivation of their own feelings and conflicts when they were teen-agers themselves.

Then too, there is the possibility that they may be facing the climacteric, with concerns about their own sexuality.

Parents are generally encouraged by the counselor's interpretation of much of their youngsters' behavior as part of the normal and healthy transition to maturity. They often need support in the task of reducing controls without abandoning them. While the goal of parenthood is to make oneself progressively unnecessary, at this phase the parents still have an important role to play as guides, mentors, and friends to their children. Whether the youngster accepts or rejects his parents' views, he has the right to know where they stand on important issues, and the parents have the obligation to make their positions explicit.

Parents who are in conflict with each other during this phase tend to try to draw the children in as allies. In the case of the Fishers, we see the mother and sons forming a coalition against the father. He is the intellectual authority from whom the teen-age sons have turned away. His aloof and inflexible parental stance does not meet the requirements of living with teen-agers today. The boys seek and seem to find friends and wholesome activities outside the home, and line up with the mother in the home. While the focus of marriage counseling is on the marital interaction, Mrs. Fisher's coalition with her sons must of necessity be a target for intervention.

Later, in Chapter 7, we will observe the Greens, a remarriage, where the problem of the rebellious teen-ager is salient and becomes the focus of marital treatment.

Every family of course is unique, as is the manner in which it deals with adolescent and mid-life crises, both individual and familial. In fact, many couples ride the ups and downs of this phase without coming to grief; in time, the troubled waters settle down.

DR. AND MRS. FISHER

Dr. Fred Fisher, age 48
Mrs. Anna Fisher, age 44

Married 19 years

Children:　Bill, age 15
　　　　　　Peter, age 16
　　　　　　John, age 18

Referral, October 18

It is important to note the implications of the referral. Dr. F. is at this point motivated to maintain the marriage. He fears the separation is inevitable.

Dr. Fisher telephoned for an appointment to discuss a marital separation for a period of several months. He quickly added that he himself would very much like to keep the marriage together but believed the separation was probably necessary. Yes, he had spoken to his wife, and she was willing to come to one session.

First Interview, October 19

Dr. Fisher arrived promptly. He said his wife was coming separately. He is a tall, dignified, meticulously dressed, middle-aged man. He spoke in a subdued but authoritative and confident manner. I had the feeling that he was both proud and shy. While we were waiting for his wife, I suggested that he briefly give me some background information.

Beginning with one partner before the other arrives is not in line with standard practice. Dr. F., however, seemed so tense and self-conscious, I decided to start in this way.

They met in Poland and were married there nineteen years ago. She was then director of nursing in a hospital where he was heading a research project. Both are Catholic, but neither is particularly religious. They have three sons, aged fifteen, sixteen, and eighteen. They are all healthy boys and "quite good" students. The oldest boy had begun college but recently dropped out. Here Dr. Fisher volunteered that he himself was an only child. He was brought up by and lived with adults. He added, "Perhaps that's why I'm not able to communicate with my children as well as my wife can."

The couple came to Canada by way of France fourteen years ago. Dr. Fisher left a good university position there, as he had been offered an attractive research opportunity in his field (biochemistry) with a large organization in Canada.

Within a year of their arrival, they brought their parents to Canada from France and took responsibility for caring for them. Mrs. Fisher's father, now eighty-five, is her only living parent; her mother died when she was sixteen. Dr. Fisher said her father is a brilliant and remarkable man. He now lives with Dr. Fisher's parents in a nearby apartment. His father is now eighty-two, and very frail. His mother is in her late seventies and in fairly good health. His wife made all the arrangements, hired a competent housekeeper, and is in contact with them regularly. The three old people manage quite well.

At this point Mrs. Fisher arrived, ten minutes late. She is a thin, plain-looking woman, not wearing make-up. Her long hair was pulled back in a bun. She was tight lipped and seemed angry. I shook hands with her, and as she walked into the office, I mentioned that her husband and I had discussed their family size, length of marriage, and some other factual information while waiting for her, but we had not discussed their marital problems.

With this kind of resistance, Mrs. F. is not a client. In

She gave me an appraising look, pulled her chair away from where it had been placed, ignored her husband, and turned her

this first interview she will need help to be inducted into the client role, if the couple are to return.

back to him. She was only partially facing me. This struck me as a loud nonverbal message of what she thought of the whole procedure.

Despite this, Dr. Fisher began to talk about his "impressions" of the impending separation. "Excuse me," I said, stopping him. "I should like to know how Mrs. Fisher feels about being in this interview. After all, Mrs. Fisher, you did not initiate this meeting, and I wonder how you feel about being here."

More resistance, and testing. I avoid being drawn into this.

She gave me another hard, searching look. "I came to see how you work," she said bluntly. I nodded agreement and waited, and then she went on, "I made up my mind I would like to have a separation, although I'm willing to discuss it with a third person."

I said I would try to help them sort out some of their difficulties so that the three of us could decide if this was an appropriate resource for them. I described our short-term service which involves one to approximately ten sessions.

Note that the question is addressed to either partner to promote interaction in problem identification

I then asked if they could tell me what had precipitated Mrs. Fisher's decision to separate.

Dr. Fisher was a bit nonplussed at my cutting him off and was quiet at this point. Mrs. Fisher, however, looking down, began to speak, softly and flatly at first, but soon quite freely. "Look here, I broke down twelve years ago and spent over three months in the hospital with a bad depression; I don't want another to happen."

She is angry and frightened, warning me to "go easy."

My response is supportive, and then I refocus my question as to the current precipitating problem.

I said I could understand her fears and agreed this was to be avoided. I commented that she looked hurt and upset and repeated my question as to what was troubling her to bring the plan of separation to a head at this time.

A role change. He has been upgraded; she feels downgraded.

She answered that her husband had been promoted a few months ago to an even more important position; now he's the "boss" in the home as well.

A precipitating factor—an important diagnostic clue. The move up the economic ladder can upset the former equilibrium.

She went on: "He orders everyone around. He ignores the children. He can't make decisions, and he won't let me make them, so I am forced to go ahead on my own, and against his wishes." Then she went on quickly, "I've tried all ways—arguing, nagging, fighting—and nothing has ever reached him. I've even tried to prepare him ahead of time in writing when I wanted something done, but nothing has worked." She said, bitterly and with defiance, "Now I do just what I want, and

I've given up on him. Besides,'' she said, ''we're too old to change. It's hopeless.'' She added, ''There's nothing between us,'' and almost snarling, she said, ''He takes a stand, then rationalizes it, and makes a list of excuses for himself by way of a long speech.''

I asked whether something specific had happened recently to upset her. She said the real crisis had occurred in August because she had bought a car with her own money. About two years ago, she took on work as a part-time hospital lab technician. When he objected to her buying the car, he cut her housekeeping allowance by $100 a month. ''I just threw the money back at him and told him he could do the shopping for the family himself. So for the past three months he's been doing the household shopping and buying food for the family, which the boys often don't like and refuse to eat.'' Dr. Fisher sat impassive through all this.

Diagnostic comment at this point

Possible psychopathology—Mrs. Fisher looks sad and depressed, which concerns me, but with this outburst has demonstrated that she is able to express anger freely. The depression and hospitalization of so many years back need not be focused on. It may well have been a situational reaction to coming to a new country, caring for small children, and setting up three parents. In assessing Mrs. Fisher's current functioning, it is obvious that despite her upset, she manages to hold a half-time job, to run one household and supervise another, and apparently carries on her mother role effectively. In not pursuing the past breakdown, I show confidence in her and her present functioning.

I decided, however, to move away from the marital relationship, as the situation is so ominously heated at this point, Dr. Fisher having been subjected to such a thorough lambasting. I have at least temporarily engaged Mrs. Fisher in participating in the interview. Moving from the head-on conflict to a related area—that of child management—might be more productive and would, no doubt, again head into the marital conflict. In any case, in the first interview, this related area should be explored, however briefly.

I asked them how they managed with their sons. Here he came in and said, ''My wife has the relationship. She has the facilities.'' He added, pompously, ''In my opinion she is somewhat easy with the children, and I am the more orderly and con-

---

With so much wrong, it is necessary to single out something specific to deal with.

Acquiring the car with her own money so soon after his new promotion has been a further precipitating factor. It appears that she "promoted" herself in competition with him, so that attack and counterattack followed. It seems a sharp power struggle has been under way for the past three months.

At this early point in the interview I decided to move from this hot instrumental issue, to get some picture of their parental goals.

Technique of clarification.

servative one." Mrs. Fisher sat stiff and silent. I asked them whether this was a way of saying that one is more authoritarian and the other perhaps more permissive.

"No," she said, "he is not that way. He is just detached. He is just not present." She went on to say, "He just makes speeches, about how important education is, and how lucky they are." She described herself as being interested and concerned about the boys, but not permissive by American standards.

I turned to Dr. Fisher to ask what he thought of her view of this. He said that by using the word "conservative," he didn't mean he was detached. In fact, he was not detached, and he began to move into a discussion of his work and how actively he is involved with his colleagues. He went on about the complexities of a new project, which prevent him giving much time to his family. It became difficult for me to follow just what he was trying to do or say.

Technique of using one's own reactions to point up unclear communication.

I said, "Dr. Fisher, I find this rather confusing. I would like to know how you manage with the boys." But he went on talking about his work and bypassing the issue. He didn't exactly mean "conservative"; he didn't exactly mean she was "permissive." Here she put in, "That's the philosophizing, and the not understanding." I said, "It sure sounds as though you two are on separate tracks, and on separate trains." She nodded emphatically.

I asked, "How was it when the boys were younger?" "Yes," she conceded, "he noticed them more when they were in grade school. Then, they didn't answer him back."

I cut in, "Dr. Fisher, teen-agers give you a hard time? They usually do." He denied this. "They're really not difficult. They're good boys—just too sports minded." She pushed her chair back impatiently. "No doubt he'd prefer them to study all night—in his opinion," she added sarcastically, "time spent with friends is not really that constructive."

I think Mrs. F. is sufficiently engaged for me to try a confrontation. It is supportive, however, to respond to her anger as "hurt."

Here I remarked, "Mrs. Fisher, you seem to find it hard to look at your husband when he talks. I noticed too you talked for him, just now. You must feel very hurt to act like this. I have the impression you don't even want to listen."

She answered more quietly, "I'll listen, but I don't believe him. I know his pattern."

The possibility of hope is introduced.

I indicated that if we were to decide to carry on and work together, it was just possible that the pattern might change, even though right now she feels there's no hope.

She muttered, "He's always making those long complicated speeches; never really answers us or listens." He moved in to say that he wanted to try and would like to be given a chance.

More resistance and competition with me. Important not to react defensively but to respect her right to take or leave the service.

She snapped, "I don't believe you. It's taken me years to catch on to your way of doing things. How can anyone understand this in a few sessions?" I responded, "Not easily or fully, and it will be important for you to assess if this is helpful or not, before too long."

This seemed to calm her, so I ventured to ask why she had carried on in this unsatisfactory marriage for so long. She indicated, self-righteously, that she had a strong sense of duty. She had carried the responsibility, as a young girl, of raising her three brothers after her mother died. I commented that it seemed she was conditioned to carry a heavy burden; perhaps she took on more than she should? She agreed, but sarcastically added that she certainly wouldn't have refused her husband's help, "if only he had offered any."

Technique of linking past to present.

I felt Mrs. F. was a skilled fencer, and that I should let this go so as not to get caught up in their pattern of arguing.

I needed to know whether she had come here just to show she had "tried everything." They were hitting each other, he by acquiescing and she by threatening.

I wondered whether she had been to a lawyer, if she had thought of a divorce. She said she had talked to a friend about separation. Dr. Fisher hurriedly agreed that perhaps a few months of separation would be necessary. She put in sharply, however, "A *minimum* would be six months, or even a year."

Note that clients will reraise significant issues.

She went back to her husband's reluctance to let her spend her own money. Here he interrupted, "Look, my money is shared, why not yours? Last summer, when you bought the car with your money, I thought it was justified to cut down your allowance, and that you should contribute more to our living expenses." He went on: "When you gave back the food money, I had no alternative but to do the shopping." I said, "Perhaps some alternative could still be considered." They just stared, however, and I left this.

Technique of linking past to present is tried again, with support.

I commented that she probably had greater expectations from marriage because of her especially hard growing-up years; instead, she felt she had received less. She gave me a long look

I test her motivation and capacity to participate in the counseling process.

and said she knew she didn't let her needs come out directly. I then ventured to say, "It usually takes two for things to get so out of line." She nodded, but retorted that what percentage went where she would not say—this with heavy sarcasm. I agreed, and let this go. At this point in the interview, she began to relax.

I gave them a choice about the next interview, indicating they would both have to contribute to the solution of the immediate issues—that is, whether to separate and, if so, how to do this with the least pain to themselves and to their sons, or whether to work together with me on a short-term basis to try to improve their relationship. I thought this decision would involve another two sessions, and said we would then evaluate together whether an additional three or four sessions would be useful. If so, each would have to contribute, as I could not do this alone. I added that they did not have to decide anything today, even about the next interview, but that I would like *Mrs. Fisher* to telephone and let me know. She then gave way a little, saying, "If something, even a little, can improve, and if he will do this sincerely, not just with promises or speeches, then maybe it's worth trying."

Mrs. F. doesn't really want to break up the family but feels lost and hopeless.

Problem identification—an aspect is focused on, and a related task meaningful to the couple is selected.

While this is an instrumental task, it is one that is also very loaded emotionally and seems symbolic of their power struggle, currently affecting the whole family system.

By assigning this task to Dr. F., he is in a sense being kept in a leadership role, which is important in terms of his male status. In any case, Mrs. F. would certainly not make a move at this point.

Around this point, I again raised the shopping plan. Did either of them really like it? They agreed that they did not. I remarked, "Obviously, it's not working. Should this unworkable plan of grocery buying continue?" There was an awkward silence. I turned to Dr. Fisher and said, "You've indicated your wish to carry on with this marriage; you took the lead in calling this meeting. It may be necessary for you to take that first difficult step of changing something, for example, the unworkable grocery plan, something you both can see is contributing to daily tension."

I told Dr. Fisher I was sorry that it seemed he was the one on the hot seat at this point, although we had agreed today that their problems were not created wholly by either partner, that each one is affecting the other negatively. I added, for Mrs. Fisher's benefit, "to different degrees."

This technique of offering and holding a definite appointment indicates the worker's interest—a form of "reaching out."

I set up the next appointment tentatively and indicated that I would hold the time for them in any case, till I heard from Mrs. Fisher. She then said 'it would be useful to get together again, just to talk about separating with the least pain to the children. I noted that Mrs. Fisher wrote down the appointment time.

Worker's comment at close of first interview

One of the main tasks of a first interview is to enable the couple to return. It is sometimes necessary therefore to form a temporary alliance with the less motivated partner. Thus, I lined up with Mrs. Fisher. I didn't feel she would accept any more confrontation until Dr. Fisher made the first move. I hope he will be able to bear with this, as it's necessary to involve Mrs. Fisher in the marital counseling process.

In view of his senior status, however, he may well resent my direct suggestion that he return the household shopping to his wife. I need to anticipate that he, as the authority figure, will resent my putting the onus on him initially. He does, however, get some support and recognition for his initiative in seeking help in this interview.

The marital crisis was used to press for a quick shift from their negative interaction, before the potential rigidity of this pattern set in.

Second Interview, October 25

Today the Fishers arrived together. Dr. Fisher again sat on the sofa, close to my chair. Mrs. Fisher turned her seat so that it faced me and partly her husband. He opened the interview.

Resistance from Dr. F. He takes refuge in "the larger problems," but is also saying "You were wrong." I accept his right to differ, without agreeing.

"It's my impression that we did nothing." He added, "*I* did nothing." He went on ponderously, "I thought about changing the money situation but after consideration, in my opinion, it is only a symptom; what is necessary is to deal with the larger problems."

"Last week, Dr. Fisher, you probably felt I didn't understand what a hard time you are going through. I think it's only natural for you to resent my putting the onus on you to make the first change."

He denied this politely and was moving in pretty strongly about the many more important problems that needed to be tackled quickly—discipline of the boys, budgeting, social life, and so on. It was necessary to deal with these matters if his new work responsibilities were to get under way effectively.

I interrupted him to challenge this. "Dr. Fisher, I understand and agree with you that money is often a symptom, as you say, of much more, but tackling those big general problems at this stage will not be practical. You know that an army does not move forward on all fronts at once." He listened quietly and said, "You have a point." I went on, "In fact, tackling all those difficulties at once would be one way of impeding or even halting the counseling. Is that what you want, Dr. Fisher?"

"No, but," he persisted, "I thought the money was not that important." Had he discussed this with his wife? "Not really," he said. I suggested that he ask her now how she felt about this.

She then said, "He's doing the same thing to you that he does to me—making an argument and rationalizing his way out of it. Of course, handling the money has been a very sore problem with me for three months now, and it's upsetting the whole family." She went on, "He'll never change. He's always got to be right. Just tell Mrs. Freeman what you told me after the last session."

Dr. Fisher looked blank at first, but with prodding from her, he went on, "Well, I did mention to you that I didn't express myself quite well enough to get my point across in last week's interview." Mrs. Fisher, self-righteously, said, "This *proves* that you picked up *nothing* here, although at the time you appeared to do so."

I pointed out it is not always that easy to implement change, but it did seem to me that Dr. Fisher had just done something very constructive in exposing what he had said about not getting his point of view across last week. Furthermore, he had not expressed unwillingness to reopen the issue of handling the money. I asked them to rediscuss this now and try to work it out.

At this point, he told her he would gladly give way about the money. He just didn't think it was that significant. She responded, bitingly, "Why not months ago? Why did you leave it until now?"

I cut in here, "I feel a fencing match is coming up, which you both do with great skill, probably typical of what goes on at home."

This confrontation fails, and I then move the issues to involve Mrs. F. This technique is a more productive intervention.

She had Dr. F. cornered again, and I feel he needs support at this point. As well, this pattern of attack should be extinguished and ignored.

I responded with positive reinforcement to Dr. Fisher's open sharing.

Support for Mrs. F.'s concern and a refocus on problem solving.

She too may resent my authority. Here I ignore it.

Worker instead puts some controls around Mrs. F.'s rage and on their fencing pattern of communicating.

It was important for them
to know I am not afraid to
do this.

They stared at me. "Look, Mrs. Fisher, I understand your anger, but we can't retrace the past three months completely. What about the shopping problem?" He repeated that he was willing to retract and give her back the shopping money, since she thought it was so important. She sniffed somewhat skeptically, but quieted down.

Dr. Fisher, having lost that round, quickly moved on to the car issue. He said she had really bought the car for John, their eighteen-year-old. She wanted him to have access to the car in case it would help him to get back to college and finish the year. She burst in angrily, "That's ridiculous! It's really *my* car!" Here he snapped back, "The boy should work for his own car."

Is John rebelling against his
intellectual father by drop-
ping out of school?

With much heat she responded, "It's *not* his car," and he sharply countered, "If he has the use of it, it's almost as though it were his car." She went on, caustically, "I've been planning and hoping to have a car for years, you know that. And I knew you would never agree, so I bought it on my own." Dr. Fisher said, "That's why I refuse to ride in it."

The fencing match was well under way. I could see it running away from me, so I broke in to ask whether he felt that her getting a car downgraded him as head of the house, and served to draw the boys away from him. Interestingly enough, he became a bit protective of her here, saying that he had to agree with his wife. If she had asked him about the car, it's true, he would not have given his consent. He then went on to tell her that he would give her back the housekeeping money and the shopping job, and that he would even tell the boys he thought it wasn't working out so well anyhow. I commended him for this decision and for the fact that he planned to share his thinking with the boys.

They know how to fight
and don't need any help in
this. This intervention is an
attempt at insight.

Positive reinforcement for
him, but I wonder whether
he'll carry it out.

Note that client himself
brings back the car issue.

Dr. Fisher, however, then went back to the car: "I think we should discuss if some *limits* can be put on the way our son uses the car." In response, she said she would be willing to put down some limits if he would accept the car as a *family* car, and would be willing to ride with them in it instead of refusing even to get into it. To this, too, he agreed. I said again that it seemed

Use of *quid pro quo* (Jackson, 1965, p. 589). If you do this for me, I'll do that for you.

to me Dr. Fisher was expressing willingness to try and help a good deal. I wondered what he would get from her if he did manage this or even some of it?

Again, Mrs. Fisher merely shrugged and said, "He made the problems, let him fix them."

Technique of encouraging behavioral change in client's own interest.

I said to her, quite briskly, "Look, if Dr. Fisher has to make efforts without a little encouragement and some recognition from you, you know the going will be too tough for him. I'm concerned that you may find yourself becoming more and more frustrated." Mrs. Fisher took this in thoughtfully. As she is so quick to protest, I let it go.

Since the couple had not raised anything about the "impending separation," I simply set up a third interview, which they accepted without question.

Third Interview, November 3

Does Dr. F. use this approach to protect himself from criticism and indirectly from any obligation to change?

Again he is vague and global. I focus on one of the instrumental tasks.

Again they arrived together. Dr. Fisher again took the lead. "It's my impression that my wife is right. It's hopeless, we just can't communicate." As I looked at Mrs. Fisher, I thought she seemed less depressed. Today she sat facing him, although she still wore a somewhat guarded expression.

I pointed out that Dr. Fisher had begun by saying there had been no change in general. Can we get to something specific? What happened to the money plan?

Usually, I persist that the partner needs to verbalize positively as reinforcement in the immediate situation. However, Mrs. F. has just given way a little, and I think it best at this point to

Then Mrs. Fisher spoke up, slightly sarcastic. "Oh, he made his little speech before the boys and gave up handling the money." And what did she do when he did this? "Nothing," she replied. I sat quietly and waited. Then she added, "The boys liked it. Well, we all laughed." I turned to Dr. Fisher and asked how he felt when the boys and his wife had laughed at his "little speech." Matter of factly, he said, "It was okay." Now Mrs. Fisher moved in more gently and explained they were not laughing *at* him; they did not intend to hurt him; actually, it was more a release of tension. He seemed to accept this easily. I asked what else she had done beyond releasing tension at this point. She said calmly she felt he understood that she approved of what he had said. I commented that it was a difficult step for him to have taken, and asked how the boys had reacted.

move on to the boys' reaction.

This intervention is productive.

Confronting Mrs. F. with her contribution to their problem.

I bypass historical implications which could develop into another fencing match. I move away from her backlog of accumulated anger and frustration to focus on the present. It doesn't work.

I turn the issue over to Dr. F. This intervention seems more effective.

She then brought out that Peter, the sixteen-year old, had said to her later, "Gee, Mom, he's really trying." At this, Dr. Fisher smiled and said to her, "I didn't know Peter responded like that; I'm very glad to hear it." I pointed out that she had just made a positive remark and in return received positive feedback from her husband.

Why had he opened the interview sounding so discouraged? He had asked her to go out a few times, and she told him she was too tired. She said, "That was just the situation—I was really tired." After a little silence, she went on, "My psychiatrist used to suggest that we get out more often and I never saw any point to it. It's just that there's no way to get a relationship going." Here I told her it sounded as though she was doing just what he does—going in for the big, the general, implying that unless everything is changed almost immediately, nothing counts. "You do work hard at making it hopeless."

I recalled that last week he had refused to return the housekeeping money because he thought it "unimportant," and she had insisted it *was* important. It seemed that working on this specific problem had turned out to their mutual advantage. Here she looked at me quietly and said she supposed she was being a bit difficult. Then she added, "But I am so fed up, and for so long."

I said I knew she felt there was a great deal to be unhappy about. Still, could she tell him what she wants of him *now*? "Nothing—it's no use, really. Although he says he wants to try, I think it's all just theoretical."

I turned to him and asked, "Do you still want to try in the face of this discouragement?" "Well," he answered after a long pause, "yes, I want to keep my wife." "Why?" I asked pointedly. "Well," he replied, "she's a beautiful woman, she's intelligent and has good judgment, a good way of getting through to the children," and with some reservation he added, "and to some adults." Before he could say more, she jumped in, "Why, if my judgment is so good, do you always disagree with me?"

Now he began to slide into a somewhat philosophical discourse, but she pinned him down. "Be definite. Take, for example, the boys," she snapped. "*You* want me to be the disciplinarian and do it all. Why don't *you* deal with them?" She continued, "As far as the after-dinner dishes are concerned, you just mention to the boys that each should take a turn, then you let it go—so the boys go out and just ignore you." He responded, "I suppose I trust them too easily."

"You know," I interjected, "maybe you feel too out of it to persist, as if the cards are stacked against you—"

I decided to try here to give him some help and possibly to involve her too, so as to induct him into a new father role.

Ignoring this, she said again, "You just let it go." He replied a bit sheepishly, "Well, next week I'll get at it again." But he really looked pretty uncertain. So I asked them to discuss at home how they would handle this together. I said Mrs. Fisher's backing was important here in establishing his authority with the boys.

Keeping the focus on the instrumental problem-solving issue of the dishes.

I asked, "Are there other day-to-day chores, besides the dishes, that cause trouble?" "Everything," she said peevishly. "The faucets drip, the plumbing will get done only if I attend to it." He interrupted weightily, "Look here, I take exception to the implication that I never attend to the plumbing. I've taken responsibility for it time and again over nineteen years." Here, I said to him, "That could well be, but right now your wife is raising a current concern and you go sliding back to nineteen years ago! Ask her what she thinks can be done about it now." When he did this, she said rather blandly, "You could fix it yourself or get the boys to do it with you, or," sarcastically, "just call a plumber." On his dignity now, he said, "I prefer to get the boys to do it with me, the way I've done it over these past years."

The focus is still on household management. I'm hoping to get some "easy" problem solving going, but it isn't so easy!

"Hold it," I interrupted, "I think you're going into that slide again." This was more supportive of Mrs. Fisher, so I then turned to her and asked why she was so reluctant to credit Dr. Fisher with anything he does or wants to try. She thinks he may believe she is easily bought off. "This is what upsets and frightens me." Then he slowly and shyly said to her, "I realize I

A touch of humor to break up the fencing match.

can't take you for granted, but if there's even a small change in your attitude toward me, I still want to try." Here his eyes began to fill up; she, not looking at him, sniffingly said, "Theoretical again."

I stopped her. "No, Mrs. Fisher, your husband is showing you some real feeling right now. If you look at him, I think you will see he is on the verge of tears." He nodded silently and she looked at him and stopped. She even became a little sympathetic.

I went on, "You know, you both do a good sliding job. You should get on a toboggan together." Here she smiled at him, and they both laughed a little.

I commented, "Dr. Fisher has just now shown and shared his own pain," and that Mrs. Fisher had noticed. Also, she had encouraged him earlier by telling how their son had made a constructive and interested response to his father. This had not been easy for her in view of her hurt and anger. I asked whether she felt any real effort in him today to work for her, and with her, for the marriage and the family. She said, slowly but thoughtfully, "Maybe." I replied, "Maybe is just fine. I know it isn't easy for you to say that." Dr. Fisher said he too realized this.

I told them today we should decide on further meetings. In my view they had both made a good beginning in these sessions. I added, they knew I was only helping them with the ABCs of building a better understanding between them, but they themselves would have to continue with the EFGs. They both agreed to carry on, and accepted my suggestion of three or possibly four more sessions. We would then consider together whether they would go on by themselves. They left in a pleasant mood.

Fourth Interview, November 10

Again Dr. Fisher opened the interview with a negative: "I didn't do the plumbing." Mrs. Fisher smiled, looked at him and said, "Well, no, the double windows did need doing." Here he said, "That's what I did with the boys." She laughed and seemed less tense and angry. She added to me, "We had a present, actually, the first trip together with my husband in the car." They had gone for an outing in the country, to see the leaves change color.

Margin notes:

Dr. F. is really involved emotionally.

Mrs. F. is now moving in.

The use of humor to release tension.

Three-way planning for further sessions.

This pattern of Dr. F.'s is now clear. "If I criticize myself first, no one will criticize me."

When the parents have located the problem in *their relationship*, it is easier to relieve the children of the guilt they often feel.

She continued that they had told their sons they were coming here for counseling. They were pleased; the youngest was particularly relieved. Dr. Fisher expressed surprise that Bill had even worried that he might be causing some of the trouble. We discussed the need for the parents to assure their sons that they, the parents, had something to work out between themselves, and that responsibility for their relationship rested with them, the parents.

Encouraged by small success, he is freer to go ahead.

Dr. Fisher went on to say that he thought they needed to get out a little more, and to see people they both liked; he'd like to try this, when she's ready. Although still a little hesitant, she seemed less hopeless about this today.

Another precipitating factor contributing to the current marital discord—her full-time job threatens him.

The interview had gone along in a fairly even exchange when he suddenly brought out his resentment about her working full time at the lab. He said, "When you took on the new job at the lab, two months ago, I think it was a mistake." She became angry. "You've always resented me being a person." He said, "There's less time for the family, less time for us." She countered, "I neglect nothing. Why should I refuse a senior technician's job that seldom comes up?" "But I think you work too hard." "Well, then, you could help me more at home."

She fought on, by saying, "You resent the boys buying their own clothes by using credit cards."

He, now on the defensive, said, "They should ask permission."

She responded, "That's silly. I'm their mother, and I know roughly the amount they'll spend."

He answered, "And I as the father should know exactly how much they're going to spend. It should be discussed with me."

Taut and angry, she snapped, "That's ridiculous. They never overspend. In any case, why all this fuss about credit cards?"

He said, "They do overspend—those ragged jeans look second-hand to me."

She, unlike Dr. F., accepts and understands the peer group influence.

Mrs. Fisher, becoming more heated, said, "That's what their friends all wear."

It is now becoming very clear that Dr. F. uses in-

"Excuse me," I interrupted, "I wonder whether Dr. Fisher's concern about the way money is spent and his need to

strumental issues repetitively. These are used symbolically by him in the power struggle between the couple. He feels himself an outsider and feels there is a coalition between his wife and sons to keep him out.

Here Mrs. F. is challenged sharply to find other ways of problem solving. Dr. F. has made important concessions; she too must contribute, or this pattern will not shift and the counseling will break down.

It works. She wants some limits to her anger.

This is repetitive material, therefore important, and will need further working on.

Dr. F. needs help to implement his new father role. I reinforce Mrs. F.'s competence by assigning her the assisting role in this task, which has relevance for her. I hope she will help him, in her own interest.

control this is not in fact a way of desperately hanging on to his family.'' There was silence. I went on to note that the car was an important factor. Here he certainly felt that he was literally and figuratively ''out of it.'' He'd given way about the housekeeping money and how it should be spent, and now he is raising the clothing issue and her working full time. Does Mrs. Fisher's earning more money make him feel less necessary?

He said, ''I do really 'feel out of it'—I never realized how much.'' I responded, ''It seems that the position you are taking today is like a last-ditch stand in a struggle to find your way back into the family circle.''

''You know,'' I added, ''this isn't a fight about money at all.'' This seemed to strike home with both of them. ''Well,'' she said, ''refusing to let me work and hanging on to the money won't buy me back.'' He said, ''I agree.'' I asked her how he could get back into the family. Here she turned to him and with some of her freely expressed anger, said, ''It's *your* doing, and you'll have to do it on your own.''

''You know,'' I said solemnly, ''Dr. Fisher, if you are really on your own, with this line-up against you, I just don't see how you can make it.''

This really threw Mrs. Fisher, and she backed down quickly, ''I mean he has to find his way back to the boys.'' She added she would be willing to work with him on improving their own relationship. He responded quickly that this sounded okay; he thought he could have an effect on the boys. But I said that with this he would need Mrs. Fisher as a partner, because young people pick up messages astutely, such as what Mrs. Fisher thought of her husband and what his position in the family was. When she was confronted here, he again came to her rescue and said he realized he had kept to himself a lot, but now wanted to give them more time and interest.

I said I thought this was something they could discuss together, apart from me. I thought Mrs. Fisher had good ideas as to how they could get the boys to assist with the household tasks, which are giving her so much difficulty. Mrs. Fisher said ''I'm willing to try, if you're willing to listen.''

An attempt at insight. Mrs. F. is quick, and capable of making connections. It is worth a try.

I pointed out that Mrs. Fisher had been conditioned from age sixteen to carry extra burdens, and this in a way had made it easier for Dr. Fisher to stay out of these matters. She nodded slowly, and seemed to accept this. I added, "Neither of you can be held responsible for the excessive pressures Mrs. Fisher experienced as a young girl."

An acceptable interpreta tion of the power struggle.

By way of clarification I went on to explain that their basic conflict now seemed clear, that what was going on between them was not a fight about money, cars, shopping, or credit cards at all, but was a struggle between two frightened people—a war without winners and with two losers—his fear of losing her as she became more independent, her growing loneliness, frustration, and fear for the future. He said, "I can see that." Mrs. Fisher simply nodded.

In sharing this, Mrs. F. now really trusts me; the disclosure, however, caught me off guard and I decided it would be best not to explore this too much. As well, it was near the end of the interview. I also thought it might revive too much pain for him, and too much for her, at this point.

She then abruptly said, "I think you should know that when I came to this country I came out of duty. I had almost given up thought of my marriage then. I had fallen in love with another man, and our marriage hasn't been the same since." I said that this must have been a real and added barrier between them. Yes, he knew about it, and he felt sorry. She said, "I thought I should come to this country and try to make my marriage work." I pointed out a lot of past hurt and disappointment was involved in this present struggle between them.

He is saying "I am able to support us all." I permit him to change the painful subject. He needs to show his adequacy.

He said, "The trouble between us does seem to have been centered around money. I only want you to realize I can manage to take care of my family on my own, that it wasn't absolutely necessary for you to work."

She answered, "I want to be a person too. I need to work. The boys will be needing me less and less." I pointed out that Dr. Fisher had been clear in the second interview that money was only a symbol of their struggle. But as a way of problem solving, it had not worked for either of them. He agreed readily and she said it might be true—from her, a real concession. I suggested they talk together during the week about her need to work, quite apart from the extra income.

Behavioral change—Dr. F. risks a partially positive comment.

Fifth Interview, November 17

Dr. Fisher opened the interview, and this time he said, "I have the impression things are much better, though I haven't done much changing." I looked at Mrs. Fisher, and she said, "Yes, the homework hasn't been that impressive, but the feeling is much better and the atmosphere is better." I said, "This is really more important." She went on, "He listens better. We talk together more." He added that they had gone out to dinner together with another couple, a good change. She agreed, and added that the boys seemed more contented. They had had another talk with the boys about their coming here. I commented that Mrs. Fisher looked more relaxed. Yes, she feels that way too.

The couple seemed to have loosened up following the last session, where the problem between them had been restated and the interactional pattern of their competitive struggle had been spelled out. It appears they have been able now to do some work on their own.

Turning to him, she went on, "We talk at the table now. The boys didn't even know what work you do. Now we can have a discussion, say about scientific matters, something you know much more about than any of us. It's good when you talk more."

This change in behavior indicates that the process can go on without the worker, and that short-term contact may well be appropriate. Note that the other family members benefit from the improved interaction between the parents.

Reinforcement of Mrs. F.'s new pattern of giving him recognition.

I said, "I see you give him an assist here." Since we had all been watching the recent Canadian-Russian hockey games, I said I had only just learned how important an "assist" was, and how it helps in order to get the goal. She laughed quite heartily here, and he did too. I said, "It seems that you are both dealing with the issue of how to bring the family together." I added this sounded great and seemed to be helpful to the boys too.

Positive reinforcement.

She said that the straight talk we had had in the last session was very useful, "I am amazed that our daily life has improved so much." Here he said he could now accept her need to work as an individual and no longer felt that this was going to affect his status at home. Mrs. Fisher commented, "*That* is the big change."

Mrs. F. indicates that she can take "straight talk" and even wants it.

I felt the time was now appropriate to ask whether there was ever any affection between them. He answered, "Well, the boys are around the house, so it's not all that convenient. Secondly," he added, "I don't show feelings easily." Here I smiled at him and responded, "Maybe that order should be reversed." Mrs. Fisher agreed. "I don't see how the children affect this. You used to walk around nude when they were small, just to be

This is a gentle confrontation. Dr. F. does tend to cling to status quo.

natural for their benefit. Those were the days when we enjoyed sex, and we haven't for a long time now. You were affectionate in those days.''

This indirectly re-raised the issue of the former lover, and at this point I deal with it more openly. But it is still not probed. Rather, it seems more useful to link this to ways in which affection is given or withheld between them in the present. I felt that for Dr. F. this level is more tolerable.

In response to my question, she said they do have sex, but she's not that much interested in it. She has rarely had an orgasm *since they came to this country*.

I asked if she still had in mind the other man she spoke of last week.

Note use of clarification here.

I encouraged her to discuss this a little more, and it emerged that she had never really had an affair with him. She said, ''Maybe I should have. Then maybe this marriage would either be mended or broken.'' I commented that they had both been fighting a phantom, and that this was a tough one to put to rest. She must have constantly compared her husband with an imaginary lover, an impossible role for him to fill. She was quiet and thoughtful here.

Technique of linking past to present.

He said that although he knew about it, he had not talked about it with her since they had come to Canada. We talked further about how this could have affected her and inhibited him in giving her sexual satisfaction.

Although the fantasy is brought out into the open, the emphasis is on its reality implications.

Worker gives permission to have some fun and lightness in their daily living.

I again raised the question of affection, which Mrs. Fisher related to her sexual responses, and asked, for example, what had happened that morning—how did they part? Oh, they just said ''goodbye''—that is, if they happened to see each other. And in the evening? Well, she's working in the kitchen; he may come in and say ''Hello.'' ''Good gracious,'' I said, ''What could happen if he planted a peck on your neck?'' She was smiling. ''Would you collapse and drop to the floor?'' Here they both laughed heartily. I said, ''Of course, Dr. Fisher, you'll have to use your ingenuity. You might even find a spot on her ear, or her arm.'' Again she laughed and admitted that she wouldn't mind. In fact, it would be really fun for the boys. I said I liked the fact that she could see it in this light vein, and he nodded. I mentioned that how they withheld or showed affection, with more of this lightness between them, could in time be reflected in their sex relationship, particularly as they had both enjoyed this in the past.

Both again said they were amazed at how things had eased up at home. Although they had taken such small steps, both said they felt the other was really reaching out. He said, "I feel it when you are responding," and added, "I want to continue to see you happier." He cautiously said that he didn't know how far he could go, as he does have his limitations. She said, "I have mine too. I can't change much, either." He responded, "I don't want that. I don't want you to be too different." At this she smiled. I said it seemed they understood each other and themselves better and could tolerate their differences better.

I indicated they had both made a real move forward, but should also be aware that ups and downs are part of the process of an improving relationship. They would probably never move back to quite the same low level as when they had first come to see me. Mrs. Fisher said she realized that everything would not always be smooth sailing.

I added, "With a little more fun coming into your lives, some of the heaviness might move out of your relationship." "Yes," she said, "we are beginning to bring in a lighter note," and to him she gently added, "Maybe you're more ready now." He nodded, and she even added brightly she knew she had more "facilities" to explore and enjoy but if he wants to continue trying, she would give him that "assist."

We agreed that there would be another two sessions at intervals of two weeks and that we would then discuss breaking off for a period of time.

Sixth Interview, December 4

Dr. and Mrs. Fisher arrived promptly for their appointment. She was wearing a bright-colored blouse and looked at ease. He, too, seemed less tense. He again opened the interview: "The impression I have is that things are better." Here, though, he turned to his wife for a response. She said, "Yes, things are better, more friendly." The most upset son, the youngest, was more relaxed, too.

She went on that she had a birthday a week ago, and her husband had brought her a gift. Yes, it was very nice. Had she told him so? Yes, she had. I said she sounded rather half-

Marginal notes:

It is significant to note that they only want to reestablish the meshing of emotional needs that drew them together originally. It is essential to watch for clients' goals.

It is important to prepare couples for the fact that an up period may be followed by something less high. Not doing so may cause a great deal of discouragement and make them feel nothing has happened.

Worker is checking for immediate positive reinforcement, then comments on the discrepancy between content and affect—what she says and how she sounds.

Still I use the small incident to confront her mildly with her nonfunctional pattern of holding back complaints.

Now *his* pattern of protecting her needs to be discussed.

I point out his fear of her anger is excessive. Also, it creates frustration in her and increases her upset feelings toward him.

I continue the effort to help him with his fear of her anger, which he likely equates with rejection.

This discussion was on a more intellectual level, but is one which this couple responds to, in that they perceive themselves as intellectuals, and feel respected when they are dealt with accordingly.

Worker shares how an overreaction can be a clue which they themselves can use to separate past from present upsets.

hearted about this. "Well, I would have liked to be asked out to dinner. We so rarely do anything of that kind." Dr. Fisher said to her, "I never really thought of it." She responded a bit coyly, "You even asked, 'What's for dessert?' I had made the dinner, and I thought that was a bit much."

I wondered why she had not said anything to him before now. Silence. Could she even have suggested that she would have liked to go out for dinner? Here he replied quietly, "Well, it was really up to me; I should have been the one."

"Yes," I agreed, "but again it seems you are protecting Mrs. Fisher from my questions. Are you afraid she will become angry?" He protested, "I don't like to see my wife upset."

I suggested he ask Mrs. Fisher how she felt about my questioning. She said to him, "It didn't make me angry. In fact," she added, "I think I could have told you, 'Let's eat out.' " Dr. Fisher looked surprised and I pointed out, "You're really surprised that your wife didn't get angry with me. You know, it appears that Mrs. Fisher *can* take a little challenge. I think your fear of getting her angry or allowing her to be upset isn't really justified." Here Mrs. Fisher nodded and said, "It only makes me feel I have no one to talk to, or to understand me."

I asked Mrs. Fisher what would happen if he were to differ from her on a current and clear issue. She said, "At least I would feel he was listening." She turned to her husband and said, "I wish you'd realize I'm not really that dangerous."

We went on to discuss a little the difference between current and immediate irritations and old hangovers, the appropriateness of sharing upset feelings around current situations, the value of letting off steam and quickly clearing the air. He said it was a useful way to view things, and she agreed. I suggested that if a small issue became intensely overheated, as if a volcano were going to erupt, then surely there was more going on than the present situation warranted. This kind of reaction in the future could be a clue to the fact that an accumulation of *past* hurt, anger, and frustration was being tossed into the arena. Mrs. Fisher said she thought they were beginning to realize this, and that was why there was less tension at home. I said this would be an ongoing project for them on their own.

I asked about their physical relationship. I gathered there had been a little more sexual activity which he more or less initiates, but she still feels she is accommodating him rather than being an active participant. Though obviously reluctant to discuss this, she indicated that, for her, sex was part of the total relationship. She volunteered that they hadn't yet changed their form of parting from and greeting each other in the morning and evening, which I had suggested. He calls out, "Hello" when he comes in, and she comes out of the kitchen to respond. He said, "But it is a bit of a change." I added, "It's a move in the right direction!" They chuckled a little at this.

It is useful to help a couple see how one can sometimes retrieve a situation, and this is pointed out to them.

We were close to the end of the interview. I asked if there was anything to be done about that missed birthday dinner the week before. Dr. Fisher smiled and said, "Some form of delayed celebration?" She responded by looking at him quite warmly, and he said, "Well, maybe I can still ask you out to dinner." I put in enthusiastically, "Well, now, how about that?" She said, "It would be nice rather than going home now to prepare dinner." I wondered if there was a special place they would go to, and she said, "We haven't been out for so long." I mentioned a couple of places that were on their route home. One of them, she said, she had often noticed and thought it looked nice. Dr. Fisher said, "Well, let's try that one." They left in a cheerful mood. The next interview was set for two weeks hence, with the option of one more after that.

Seventh Interview, December 16
The Fishers arrived promptly. Dr. Fisher opened with his usual, "I have the impression that things are better between us." She said, "I agree. We had a lovely dinner out the last time we came. However, I'm worried that we will just stand still or slip back into the old way of doing things."

At this, Dr. Fisher began to make one of his long speeches, talking at her, saying he thought there was a better attitude in the home on the whole, that things would continue to improve in the future. Although she's afraid things will slip back, he himself does not have that impression, and so on. While this global and general speech was going on, Mrs. Fisher began to put her head down, leaned on her hand and looked really "out of it."

I asked Dr. Fisher to note the expression on his wife's face. How would he describe it? He looked, as he had not done while he was speechmaking, and said he wasn't sure. Did he think he

(margin notes, left column)

Note that small behavioral changes are occurring.

It is useful to help a couple see how one can sometimes retrieve a situation, and this is pointed out to them.

Worker actively encourages pleasure outings and at an indication of interest, makes concrete suggestions.

Mrs. F.'s fear of slipping back can precipitate just that. In addition, she may be worried about termination from me.

We have planned only one more session. I decided, however, at this early phase of the interview, to hold off discussing separation from worker and see how the interview develops.

Mrs. F. is held responsible for her behavior.

In the ending phase of short-term work, the beginning problems often recur, but less intensely. I touch some of the feelings around termination, but still do not dwell on these at this point.

Again enlisting client to change in her own interest.

Dr. F. equates being "right" with being loved.

I cut through her attack to show that his behavior is linked to his need of her, but then point its nonfunctional nature out to him.

This broad question is ineffective.

I try another approach related to the current discussion.

I ask them to talk to each other *now*, to teach them

was getting through to her? Again he looked uncertain. I said, "Why not ask her?" He did so and she said, "Look, I'm really turned off. It's all so vague and theoretical."

"Well, Mrs. Fisher, I noticed that you did not comment or interrupt Dr. Fisher to tell him so."

She answered sharply, "I've tried for so long to do so much." Here I offered, "I guess, too, you feel disappointed with me at leaving so much still for you to do." There was a silence. Finally, Mrs. Fisher said, "I know. I know I just withdraw." To this I said, "Not *just*. You really take cover. This makes it hard for your husband to reach you. Yet this is what you really want."

Again there was a silence, which Mrs. Fisher broke by saying, "Perhaps I should be a little more patient." But he said quickly, "You *are* being more patient." I intervened with, "Whoa, you're doing it again, Dr. Fisher, you're afraid to annoy your wife or even let me do so. Instead, you rush to the rescue to cover up what's wrong, and slide away from the issue. I think this is why you talk for her and give the answers for her that you *want* to hear."

She broke in, "Yes, he's very touchy. He won't let anyone disagree with him."

I moved in to ask Dr. Fisher if this fear of being wrong was a fear of losing his wife, so that he too has built a wall around himself against criticism or disagreement. He nodded here and said, "I think this is probably so." Could he see how this had actually worked against him? He said, "I believe I do." "Then what would happen if you risked coming out from behind that wall?" He just looked lost.

I said, "Let's go back. A few minutes ago Mrs. Fisher told you how annoyed she was that you were so theoretical and vague, and she has just complained about your touchiness and sensitivity, all of which sounded pretty vague to me." Here Mrs. Fisher agreed without prompting that she had been vague.

I suggested that he ask her now to be more definite and tell him what happened recently that she didn't like. "Well, I

to get some clear communication going.

The interaction here is constructive. I let them carry it through.

Pointing out the negative effect of the unclear message, where assumption and thinking for the partner go on.

They are now involved in clarifying communication.

Positive reinforcement.

Repetition is used to emphasize their pattern of

wanted you to consider us taking up bridge." Here he insisted that he didn't think bridge was a good idea, though it might be something for the future, but right now it would be much too time-consuming. Mrs. Fisher said, "It's only a means of keeping us involved with other couples and doing something together, which we haven't done for so long." "Well," said Dr. Fisher, "we've just agreed to do some cross-country skiing. This is something for the whole family, and it will be a nice activity." Here she argued with him, pointing out this might happen only ten or twelve times during the winter but really wasn't going to involve that much time. What was wrong with taking a look at learning bridge with a couple they hadn't seen for some time and used to enjoy? "Well," he insisted," that is something for the future, but right now it would certainly take up too much time."

They seemed to be bogging down on the time issue, so I asked if they had discussed how much time might be involved. Here he turned to her and asked exactly how many hours she thought would be involved. This got her angry. She said it wasn't a question of settling on numbers of hours or adding them up. He should know that what she had in mind would be reasonable, that she wouldn't hold him to a rigid schedule he couldn't manage. She knows that he is busy, and so on.

Here I said it seemed that he anticipated being boxed into a tight corner with unmanageable demands, yet it really didn't sound that way to me. Mrs. Fisher looked pleased. But I pointed out that earlier *she* had been vague about what was expected of him, and her vagueness brings out this negative response from him.

Mrs. Fisher then told him, "As a matter of fact, it might be only once or twice a week, or it may be we won't even like bridge. I just thought we should explore it." He said, "Well, if it's just a matter of exploring something, I would be willing to do that." This pleased Mrs. Fisher, who said, "We may even decide to drop it and try something else." He said he'd go along with that too. I pointed out that they had just managed a piece of clearer communication and a constructive step in problem-solving instead of using a sort of crystal ball, where each assumed what the other thought.

The rest of the session focused a little on summarizing their particular patterns of dealing with each other—his style of get-

negative interaction.

Use of analogy—a technique that sharpens the point being made and facilitates understanding.

I thought it would be useful to demonstrate my flexibility and offer them another session. Also, spacing the interviews at two-week intervals would be helpful in diluting feelings of separation from the worker.

ting into a broad intellectual discussion for fear of facing her annoyance or anger, her reluctance to tell him that she's annoyed, followed by withdrawal, anger, and her feeling that all is hopeless. This arouses his fear of losing her, then comes more withdrawal from her, and so the negative pattern escalates.

I pointed out that Mrs. Fisher had built a wall to protect herself against being hurt, just as he had, and it seemed to me that the walls were equally thick. Perhaps they could both risk getting out from behind their barricades—a joint project—as part of their ongoing work.

This was toward the end of the session and I asked them what they thought about another session, as we had more or less arranged for only seven. He began by saying, "It's my impression that it would be a good idea," and then turned to her and said, "What do you think?" She smiled at his direct question to her, and said to me, "Look, I really think he's learned a lesson!" She meant his new understanding that he couldn't talk for her or at her but could directly involve her in planning ahead. He said he was pleased she had noticed this. They both thought it would be a good idea to come back in two weeks. I said, "We are getting to the point of separation, which is often difficult. It's natural to feel let down when there's still ongoing work to do. You both have shown the ability to do this, and of course the door here is never closed."

We set up the appointment, and I said we could then discuss whether any further sessions were indicated.

Eighth Interview, December 28
Two weeks later the couple arrived together, promptly.

He opened the interview by turning to her, knowing he is usually the one to begin, and waited. She said, somewhat blandly, "Well, there's very little going on now. We don't seem to be having as bad a time; I think it's a sort of plateau. I think it's going to stay that way. I wonder if there will be any vital relationship developing. He gets so global when anything is raised with him." I responded that right now *she* was sounding pretty global in her expectations.

Confronting Mrs. F. with her contribution to their difficulties.

Here Mrs. Fisher said, "Well, if I sometimes feel hopeless, it's because we haven't developed any common interests." I suggested that she now raise with him a specific interest which they could have in common. "Well," she said, "take retirement, for example."

Mrs. Fisher went on, "Retirement is something necessary for us eventually. I would like a house, and to have our home fixed up. I would like to have a garden, so that we have this as an interest in common, but you don't care. You're just as pleased to live in an apartment and travel." He said, "That's true. But you sound as though you want to stay put and have a quiet life." He added, "On what basis do you feel this will suit you, since you've lived so differently up to now?" Mrs. Fisher replied that she doesn't really know.

They are actually far from retirement, but are about to "retire" from me. The original problems are returning, as they did in the last session.

Here I interjected, "You are discussing retirement, and at your ages this is rather remote. It is closer to reality that you are about to 'retire' from me. I wonder how you feel about that?"

Mrs. Fisher said, "Well, we both realize how helpful you've been." I replied, "Yes, I know, but it is also natural in ending a helpful relationship to be concerned about what lies ahead." I went on to explain that most couples have mixed feelings at these endings.

I raise the issue of termination, giving permission to be ambivalent. Generalization in this as a technique is helpful.

Dr. Fisher turned to his wife and said, "You know, Anna, we never really talked about finishing up here." She said, "That's true."

I then said, "This makes me think it wasn't a retirement plan that concerned you just now, or the house you wanted, rather a place where the two of you could be more friendly and closer." She nodded and commented, "Yes, I suppose that's what I really want."

After a quiet interval, I repeated, "My leaving you to face the unfinished work that is ahead must be somewhat of a letdown." She didn't pick this up, however, but went on, "I know I've been out of sorts lately. I think it's because of my new job. Not that it is a *new* job, but there is a new pathologist at the head of the team, and I have trouble working with him, and bending to his ways. I know I get upset, and take it out on my husband." Dr. Fisher spoke up here and said, "You know you don't really have to work." She flared up: "You just don't care. You want me home. You resent my working anyhow." Dr. Fisher responded firmly, "No, I do go along with it, now that I realize you need outside activity. The boys are growing up, and it's really okay with me."

Here, too, this problem can so easily be linked, that is, the implications of the new boss to her husband. I deliberately avoid making this interpretation. If it can be linked to their reality and current problems, that would seem more profitable.

I pointed out that his attitude does seem to have changed, and that she finds this difficult to believe. "Yes," said Mrs. Fisher, "I'm afraid, afraid of being trapped."

I asked how he felt, hearing his wife express her fear. Looking at her, he said gently, "I know you're disappointed, and I would like to do more to make you happy." Her voice had a soft pleasant quality as she said, "That's a change."

Again engaging them in problem solving.

I returned to Mrs. Fisher's earlier frank remark that her tension on the job was being taken out on her husband. As her job affected them both, what could they do about it? She answered, "There's nothing else I'm trained for. Besides, I earn good money. What can I do? If I leave, there's only a few hospitals I can work in, and senior lab openings are rare."

When Mrs. F. got angry, Dr. F. was now able to respond without withdrawing or getting defensive. He was able to focus on the problem at hand in a calm and straightforward manner.

Here he suggested she go back to her original profession, nursing. This got her angry. "You know I would hate that. There've been so many changes, I would just be doing menial work in this country."

He responded, "That's true, but then you did get into this by accident." "Yes, it was accidental. I got into the lab and then was trained on the job itself, and now I train others." "Well," he replied, "maybe there's something else you could do. Perhaps you should think of some different training that could broaden your chances to find other interesting work." He even added that he could easily look into this for her, as he is close to a variety of training programs. This pleased her, and she said, "That's a good idea—I never thought of it." Encouraged, he went on, "It might even be a very good move, for you to make a change."

Note that because Mrs. F. is feeling understood by Dr. F., she is less tense about the new team head. Thus, there is no need to uncover her transfer of feelings from her husband to the new boss.

After this discussion, Mrs. Fisher, more relaxed, said that maybe she would try to carry on with her new chief, for the present anyhow.

The couple are again given positive reinforcement for effective problem solving, at least for their attempt at it.

I pointed out that they had talked over a problem just now, and although they had not come to a firm decision, talking the problem over together was in itself important in demonstrating improved communication between them. I pointed out that Mrs. Fisher had felt understood and responded positively. She agreed it was good and that he had been helpful, and he said he was pleased to hear her say that.

I pointed out that today Dr. Fisher helped clarify the issue of retirement, and that he had not been thrown by her anger in discussing her job. Instead, he clearly expressed his point of view and focused on her needs. This is exactly the change in understanding that pleased her and gave her, and Dr. Fisher too, a measure of hope.

We were now moving to the end of the interview. I asked if there had been any change in how they greet each other when they return home in the evening. "Not really," he said. He would like to do more, but she still seems to push him off. I asked him why he gives in so easily. He said, "Well, maybe I do," and she looked up at this a little quizzically.

At this point, since he had been sitting on the sofa by himself, she on the chair, somewhat removed though facing him, I suggested that they sit together, as they had not yet done in an interview here. Neither moved. I said lightly, "That's another problem I've given you. How are you going to handle it?" Again there was silence and we all just sat. Finally, he got up rather clumsily, took her arm, and got her to take a few steps to the sofa and sit down. I commented that this was difficult for him to do; he seemed uncomfortable when he first stood up, but the rest seemed to come without much difficulty.

They were still a foot and a half apart. I smiled and commented gently, "You could move an inch closer." She moved over. "He can't—it's his Victorian upbringing," she said, and added, "He never saw his father kiss his mother." Dr. Fisher shyly put in, "Well, only on special occasions." "Look," I said, "if you're held down by these old family styles, who needs them? You and your wife are lonely for affection and tenderness. It's safe here to move closer." Dr. Fisher said, "What? In public?" "What's public here?" I asked. By now she had moved quite close, even leaned on his arm, and he took her hand.

I then changed my seat and sat facing the two of them quite closely. I asked what they thought of my changing seats, and he said, "I appreciate that. Now she won't move off." She laughed a little, and said it would be nicer, however, if it had been more spontaneous.

Worker's positive recognition of Dr. F's asserting himself is also reinforced by Mrs. F.

Dr. F., having stood his ground earlier in the session, is encouraged to do so in this situation too.

I used bridging the physical distance to help break into their emotional distance and reserve.

Counselor gives permission to discard the outmoded parental model.

Worker's nonverbal communication reinforces more physical closeness.

I agreed, but drew the analogy of learning to drive a car. One is very self-conscious about every move until it becomes an automatic response. There was a little good-natured fooling around all of this. I said it seemed that Mrs. Fisher enjoyed the fact that he could be less frightened of her, and she nodded.

As they left, she said she thought another session in a month or two would be useful. I agreed that she should call me. Meanwhile she thought they could now manage on their own. He said he'd like that.

As they were leaving, I wondered if they had plans for New Year's Eve, and she said, "Well, we never do celebrate." I said, "There's another chance for you two to do some gear shifting"! He said, "I'll get busy on that tomorrow." I looked at her. She was smiling. I said enthusiastically, "That's terrific."

They left in a light mood. We made an appointment for two months later.

Follow-up Interview, Two Months Later
Both arrived on time. Today she was again wearing a bright-colored blouse. *She* opened the interview by saying they had talked a good deal about these sessions with me and were managing better now on their own. She said, "We had some pretty strong arguments, but when he gets into one of those long speeches, I just tell him about it, and he's even thanked me for doing this!" She added, "I've told him he doesn't have to push his wares so hard." He grinned and added, "I find I don't have to work so hard at home to be heard." I commented that they were sitting together on the sofa today, and that I enjoyed seeing them this way. He said, "Best of all, she is not so angry." I said it sounded as though good work was going on, and I was delighted.

I asked about her job. She is still in the same situation, but finds that the new chief is not so difficult as when he first came. Dr. Fisher said he had explored training for her in other areas. She said his interest is encouraging and a change might be a good idea. Most important for her, she emphasized, was having him accept and understand her need to work. I asked if she believes this now, and she said she really does. Also, she added, "The boys are more friendly and table talk is lively."

Use of concept from learning theory—learning does not take place in a straight upward line, but in a zig-zag fashion, with "plateaus" between, for consolidation.

I pointed out that there might be other "plateaus," and that there will also be "down" periods ahead. I repeated that change comes slowly, with its ups and downs. Mrs. Fisher said she did understand this, and she understands too that the door has been left open for another session or more if the need arises. I indicated that this would not be seen as a failure, nor need they wait for a serious crisis in order to call. He said it was good to know this.

Earlier, he had volunteered that they had gone to one of his conferences together for a weekend, and Mrs. Fisher said she thought there could be more of this, especially now that the boys, all keen athletes, have so many interests apart from them, though they still do things together as a family.

Dr. Fisher said he regrets that John has left the university, but he went along with his wife in this. John wanted a year out of school. He found himself a job. They told him they hoped he will return to complete his degree, as he is a top student. I said they had done well to permit this and to make their position known.

Some discussion of the normal maturation process. Intellectually they are well aware of this.

I brought out that it was important for John and for their other sons to see that their parents can differ and still remain friendly. We talked a little here about teen-agers today and the need to differ from parents in their struggle to find themselves as individuals in their own right.

I did not explore other areas in the marriage. I felt that a better balance had been achieved between them, and that "pushing my wares" was not indicated for this couple. We shook hands, and the parting was pleasant.

It is now seven months since the last interview, and I have heard nothing further from the Fishers. The case is therefore closed.

CLOSING COMMENTS

Many different approaches could have been tried with this couple. Practically no use was made of their past conflicts and struggles except what was offered spontaneously by Mrs. Fisher. The treatment focused on reality issues and conflicts in their present situation and problems of day-to-day living which they themselves brought to the counselor. A more cognitive style of working was utilized with this intellectually sophisticated couple. Problem solving, support, clarification, confrontation, and insight were all involved. In addition, techniques from learning theory such as the immediacy of positive reinforcement, information sharing, repetition, and imitation or modeling, were applied. In more traditional terms, one could say a positive identification with the worker took place.

In terms of ego psychology, Dr. Fisher uses denial and intellectualization as defenses against anxiety. As he became less anxious, he became more companionable and able to be a bit more assertive with his wife and sons. It was necessary not to threaten the emotionally constricted Dr. Fisher too deeply and to respect his defenses. (I recall the late Dr. Ackerman saying at a workshop, "One can tickle the defenses but need not puncture them.")

The emphasis therefore on concrete change affecting day-to-day living was significant. The change in behavior and thinking brought about a modification in feeling and served to get a wedge into the vicious circle of the couple's negative interaction. Derivatives of past conflicts are operating in the present. In brief counseling, as noted in the Introduction and in the closing comments on the Martin case (p. 100), one counts on some reduction or easing of the underlying conflict when the present surface disturbance settles down or improves.

The focus on the present was equally important to Mrs. Fisher. Her early deprivation was only touched on. To dwell on the conflicts of her early years or to reopen the pressures prior to her hospitalization would have been unwise, even risky. When the healthy defense mechanism of repression (Anna Freud, 1950) has taken hold, the notion that old problems can be "talked out" should be questioned. This may in fact open old wounds which have to some extent healed. In some situations, that is, it is wise to avoid too much uncovering of the past, particularly where no benefit may result from probing.

Dr. Fisher's gradual acceptance of his wife's right to a career outside the home was of prime importance to their relationship. With the home atmosphere improved, Dr. Fisher was better able to relate to his sons. This should help the teen-agers as they move ahead to adulthood. The counselor does not reach for further problems in connection with the teen-agers, as this is not now indicated. None was stressed by either parent, and these particular parents would have brought out any serious concerns about the boys.

For people of intelligence, pride, and inexperience turning to outsiders for help, the limited counseling seemed important, particularly in view of their own goals. As already noted, experiencing this much help, with trust in the worker and in the services of the agency, the couple are free to return for future help should the need arise.

A NOTE ON TERMINATION

As discussed in Chapter 1, in short-term counseling feelings around separation from the worker are present, though less intense than in a long-term relationship. With the Fishers we saw a brief return of the old problems, a stirring-up of anxiety, and a fear of carrying on by themselves.

It is often sufficient, in order to free the clients, simply to recognize that such feelings are natural at termination, to encourage expression of these feelings, and to reassure them that they can return for further help if necessary. In the case of the Fishers an extra session was offered. Spacing the last two sessions at two-week intervals also helped to dilute the relationship.

Workers who are accustomed to psychoanalytic terms will think of transference reactions occurring in the relationship (Garrett, 1950), unconscious feelings from past significant figures placed by the client onto the worker. In brief therapy these can be dealt with at termination on the reality level of the relationship. It is not necessary to interpret the transference.

Sometimes the worker has difficulty releasing the client and may need to consider if countertransference is operating. The worker may be transferring feelings related to significant past figures in his or her life to the client. The worker's clue to possible unconscious reactions could be his feeling too strongly negative or unduly positive toward the client. It is of course understood that liking or disliking a client need not be unconscious and can occur realistically at any point in the helping process. Consultation with a colleague or supervisor should help keep the worker in control, able to deal with his or her own feelings as well as those of the client, on a reality basis.

5

The Child Leaving Phase

Time moves on, and we come full circle. The children begin to leave, and before long the couple are once again on their own.

Ready or not, most young people leave home by their early twenties, to study, to work, to marry, or just to be on their own. Along with their possessions many carry with them a good portion of the unfinished business of growing up. Others, however, seem unable to leave. Is the home too comfortable, too sheltering? Or is one of the parents holding on, even clinging to the young person? In counseling we often see both sides contributing to the inability to cope with separation at this stage of family life.

As the "empty nest" becomes a reality, two interacting tasks, among others, face the marital pair: dealing with the heightened issue of separation from their children and the likelihood of increasing closeness to each other, involving the risk of excessive expectations from the partner.

With the children absent, the parents now sit at the dinner table alone. They take a fresh look at each other and sometimes do not like what they see. Have their interest in and concern for the children crowded out the closeness they may have had in former years? What lies ahead?

Many couples do achieve more intimacy and closer companionship when the young people have left, but often a feeling of loneliness and distance develops. In these cases they may turn to each other with excessive expectations and demands, reviving and intensifying conflicts which were less active when the tasks of child rearing were a major preoccupation.

In any case the mother, who has probably borne the major nurturing role and homemaking responsibilities, is likely to find the period of readjustment more difficult than the father, who continues, as formerly, to spend his days outside the home.

The feminist movement, accelerated in the past decade, is bringing about new ideas and changed attitudes. Lillian Rubin's research (1979) and other recent studies reflect these changes in the current scene. *Women of a Certain Age* reports Rubin's finding that a surprising proportion of women expressed relief on having their nest emptied. They indicated that the sense of loss had passed easily, although they hesitated to express the pleasure they experienced at the thought, "Now there is time for me, before it's too late." When her children are gone, the woman of today can consider her own needs in a manner she was not able to for many years.

In this time of high inflation, rising costs of living, and increasing difficulty in finding employment, practitioners are now also seeing that some young people who left home are returning when the going gets too rough. The so-called empty nest then becomes filled again, even if only temporarily. The next parting will be less painful and even welcome.

A further task facing both the man and the woman during this phase is dealing with the implications of the climacteric. Myths about loss of sexual adequacy during this period (Schlesinger & Mullen, 1977) often add further stress, particularly in our youth-oriented society.

When the child-bearing period has passed, some women express anxiety about their capacity to enjoy sex. On the contrary, it is well known that the menopause, bringing as it does increased freedom from the risk of pregnancy, can often be, as one client put it, "like walking into the sunshine." A number of studies confirm that sexual satisfaction for women increases with age and the length of the marriage (e.g., Fuchs, 1977).

Men sometimes express concern, as they approach their fifties, that the frequency and strength of the sex drive are weakened. Some seek reassurance in extramarital affairs; others are assured by their wives' reaction to their more patient and skillful, if perhaps less frequent, lovemaking. A surprising number are not aware that sexual activity and enjoyment can continue as long as life itself, although during the sixties and seventies, frequency is generally reduced rather sharply (Rubin & Newman, 1969).

At this phase of the marriage the task of preparation for retirement is highly relevant. This is usually not dealt with adequately. The abrupt relinquishing of lifelong work roles can create havoc in the marriage. The wisdom of cutting competent people off from their work arbitrarily at age sixty-five or earlier is now being seriously challenged. Many studies have shown the disturbing consequences for people forced to make an abrupt and radical change from a productive work role to being put "on the shelf." Left at loose ends for the first time, many men find time heavy on their hands. Their wives, accustomed to a routine that does not include a husband around the house all day, moan, "I married him for life, but not for lunch."

Along with reduced income and lowered self-esteem, some physical deterioration may occur. The sight of rows of spiritless oldsters in our public malls and shopping centers is a painful reminder of the unmet needs and wasted social contributions of many of our senior citizens, the most rapidly growing element in the population.

Taking on new or reviving formerly satisfying roles, activities, or interests will help the couple achieve a new equilibrium during the transitional phase of child leaving. Counseling can help lighten the pressures that tend to arise during this period and later, when retirement becomes a reality.

The new role of grandparent can be a most rewarding experience, particularly when the grandparents can participate in child rearing without the responsibility of parenting. It becomes a stressful task, however, when the young couple resent their "spoiling" the children or "interfering" or when the older couple feel exploited in the babysitting role.

In the two cases that follow—the Browns and the Donaldsons—despite differences in education, culture, and financial status, as well as social and religious differences, each of the women feels a need to broaden her outlook and find gratifying occupations outside the home. Both of the men will probably continue to carry on part-time work as long as they are physically able, a choice not available to the majority. Participation in community activities and other interests will be necessary for both men as they withdraw from their occupational roles.

In each case, again with marked differences, the marriage was disturbed when a son left the nest without his transitional crisis to adulthood adequately resolved. We can recognize in both pairs features which are common in varying degrees to all couples going through the child-leaving phase.

MR. AND MRS. BROWN

Morris Brown, age 57
Deborah Brown, age 54

Married 28 years

Children: David, age 18
             Al, age 23
             Lena, age 25, married 1 year

Referral, January 24
Rabbi X telephoned me to say that Mr. and Mrs. Brown, after twenty-eight years of marriage, were going ahead with a separa-

tion. Mrs. Brown had already seen a lawyer about a month ago. The rabbi, who knew them as regular attenders at his orthodox synagogue, said that he had already given Mr. Brown "a good blast" and urged that I do so too. Said the rabbi, "He neglects her and uses her shamefully." Mrs. Brown was persuaded to telephone for an appointment before going ahead with the lawyer. This was set up for the following evening.

First Interview, January 25

Mr. and Mrs. Brown arrived punctually. She is a good-looking, somewhat buxom woman, neatly dressed. Mr. Brown, in contrast, seemed rather colorless. He is short and slim and seemed to limp slightly. He sat down on the edge of his chair with a frightened furtive expression. Mrs. Brown took a chair as far from him as possible and began to weep softly.

I told them I understood from the rabbi that they were having a difficult time together and asked them what the problem was. Mrs. Brown was now sobbing quite hard and could not answer. I turned inquiringly to Mr. Brown. He shrugged his shoulders, looked helplessly at the floor, and in a low voice said, "There is no problem."

"You say there's no problem, but you look very sad." I went on gently, "It's very strange. Here is your wife, crying her heart out. There must be something wrong."

He said, "She has nothing to cry about." After a short silence, he asked me, "Do you speak Yiddish?"

I said I didn't but that I thought we could manage, and if he didn't understand me, I would try to explain in another way.

I asked, "Why did you come here, Mr. Brown?" and again he insisted there was no problem. After a silence, he said to me, "I don't hear very well." At this, Mrs. Brown picked up her head and through her handkerchief, said, "He hears when he wants to, though he does have trouble with his ears." I said that it would then be better if I just moved closer. I pulled my chair toward him, almost touching his knees. I talked loudly and slowly.

"I see you do have a problem—you two don't talk to each other." Mrs. Brown nodded. He just stared. I added, "Your

---

Margin notes:

Worker notes implications of the referral for possible clues. Mr. B. will expect "a good blast." Mrs. B. may be coming only out of respect for the rabbi.

Note nonverbal messages. He is tense, worried— "What will happen here?" Her crying says, "It's all hopeless."

Technique: if one is crying, turn to the other for a response, an explanation. It doesn't work—he denies any problem. I point out that his words and his feelings are not consistent.

The immediate situation is then used for problem identification. It brings more resistance from Mr. B.: "You won't understand me. You don't speak my language."

More resistance! I won't hear you!

Technique of persistence— repeating a question, even if met by resistance at first try. Worker offers a nonverbal message of interest.

Problem identification, or an aspect of it, is an important part of the first interview.

wife wants to leave you. Do you want her to go?'' Softly, he said, ''No, I want she should stay.'' ''Well, then, Mr. Brown, I'm afraid you have big problems.''

He looked at me sullenly and said, ''She has everything—a good home, what she wants. Why should she go?'' Slowly and distinctly I said, ''She's been to a lawyer for a separation. Did you ask her why?'' Here, he dug his heels in, and sat looking at the wall, offering no response.

Mrs. B. is now in the interview; some background history is spontaneously offered.

By this time, Mrs. Brown, who had had a good cry and felt encouraged, I thought, by my sympathy for her position and my efforts to involve her husband, began to talk. She is very verbal and her English is quite good. She quickly brought out her complaints. She said, ''I've been married to him for twenty-eight years, and I've had it. There is no companionship, no love. I've worked for him in the grocery store all this time. We came from Israel newly married with $50 in our pocket. I built up the business for him; I had more education. He can't read or write English. I raised his three children on my own. I've done everything for him, and now I'm getting on. I want a few years without the aggravation. I'm living on tranquilizers. I've nothing in my life. I'm lonely. I know there's no man out there on a white horse waiting for me, but I'll take my chances.''

Mr. B. is still out of it.

Mr. Brown looked blank at all this. I asked him how he felt hearing it. He whispered, ''I think we should stay as it is.''

I said, ''You have an unhappy wife; you must be unhappy too. Could you ask her what's wrong?'' ''He knows what's wrong,'' she said. ''He takes advantage of me. I even can't sleep at night. He wakes me up twice a night for sex. I'm just a convenience to cook and work and be used.''

Exploring previous efforts at problem solving. She threatened; he used denial.

I asked what she had done about this before coming here. She said she had often talked of leaving but he never believed her. Even now that she's gone to a lawyer, he doesn't want to believe it.

For the past three weeks, she has been sleeping in the room of their eighteen-year-old son to get away from her husband. I asked how they thought this affected their son. He just stared at me. She had told the boy it was not his fault and that he shouldn't worry. I said, very directly, that I was sorry to disagree, but the boy must be worried and must feel very much a party to their separation. Here Mr. Brown added, ''It's not good for the boy.''

When the worker knows that something is harmful, a strong stand should be taken.

Mrs. Brown said she doesn't want her son to be upset. He is a clever and sweet boy and she doesn't like to see him unhappy. I asked whether there was any other way that she could sleep apart from her husband, if this was so important to her. No, she had never thought of twin beds, and yes, there was a daybed in the living room. Mr. Brown didn't like this. He said in his monotonic voice, "You should come back into the bedroom." Mrs. Brown angrily said, "I need my sleep and I will get it. He thinks only of himself. He never even talks to the boys." She went on almost breathlessly with numerous complaints, so that I finally asked her whether there was anything at all about him that was worthwhile. "How about his work?"

"Well," she said, "if the business has been a success, it's due to me." She admitted he worked in the store from eight in the morning to eight or nine at night, but she works there with him; *she* has the personality that people like, and *she* has the better command of the English language, and always puts on a smile in spite of her troubles. She also drives him back and forth, as he has bad feet. His right foot is worse, so he can't drive. At home she cooks and cleans too. I asked whether they had any friends. She pointed to herself: "*My* friends—they like me." I asked, "Do they dislike your husband?" "Well," she conceded, "we have some mutual friends."

"In that case," I said, "some people must like him, or at least tolerate him." I added, "You must be very hurt to find it so hard to see anything good about him at all." She went on belittling him, and I interrupted her to ask: "Must you make such a *schmotte* of him?" (This is a Yiddish word—one of the few I know—meaning an old rag.) "You know," I said, "you do a good job of knocking him down." Here Mr. Brown pricked up his ears and looked a little more animated.

She said, more quietly, "It's true. I suppose I'm so hurt I can't see anything nice about him. The boys do like him although he's very weak with them, and he doesn't have much to do with them. He never disciplines them. I do it all."

Margin notes:

Concrete suggestions are then made to move her out of the boy's room.

Worker feels Mr. B. needs some support and recognition in order to become involved. He needs to know that the worker does not perceive him as utterly worthless. He expects "a good blast."

Mrs. B., however, is too hostile to accept this, and continues to pour out her anger.

I let her "blow," but make a mild effort to support her husband.

A strong confrontation now stops her, or she may just have spent her anger for the time being.

In the parent-child system she is dominant, he is passive. But a positive does emerge: the boys do like him.

We talked a little about their background. During the war in Poland, after his father was conscripted, he went into hiding, often in the woods. This is where he lost some toes, from frostbite. When he was reunited with his family, he worked at night to help his mother, as he was the oldest of nine children. Mrs. Brown had also had a hard time. As a youngster during the war years, she had been sent to Siberia. They had both lost relatives. I said they had had a very painful background and had coped with much stress in growing up. Then to come to a new country and make their way with so little help was a great achievement.

Mrs. Brown said that actually he had had a worse time than she. They weren't so badly treated in Siberia. *She* was sent to school and was properly cared for. *He* never knew what would happen to him from one day to the next. She spoke for him, and I let her do this as he is almost painfully inarticulate, and it moved the conversation away from her self-pity. It also seemed to make her feel adequate to act as interpreter for him. In addition, I noted a kind of tenderness and gentle tone in her voice as she spoke of his difficult early life.

I gave her credit for raising a family and working with her husband as she had done. I asked about their sons. She described the twenty-three-year-old, Al, as lazy. "He doesn't know what he wants; he never finished high school. Our younger son, David, is a darling, a sweet bright boy. *He* is going to college."

The older boy, Al, left home about four months ago for Florida, where he manages by driving a taxi. "He works for two weeks, then takes it easy." He used to work with them in the store but wasn't really a great help.

I had to draw out of her that the older boy was honest and good-natured. Her main complaint was that he had no ambition, that he was just satisfied to drive a taxi. I pointed out that the two boys are growing up. One was already a man and was away from home. "And Lena?" "Lena," she said, "married a year ago. She was a wonderful daughter, more like a good friend, and I miss her." Now she lives in New York. I brought out that their struggle to make a living and raise a family was

---

To ease the tension, worker moves briefly into history. Also necessary for worker to understand something of their past traumatic experiences.

Note that such use of the historical brings out empathy from the partner.

It also helps him to hear her express some understanding and feeling for him.

A glance at the whole family system is necessary for the assessment.

Note that idiosyncratic roles often emerge. Al is the "bad one," David the "good one." Had Al, as the scapegoat, held the family in balance until he left home?

This is a simple interpretation which they may understand—i.e., the change in the family system: one child has left, another is married.

Generalizing and explaining the child-leaving phase, as a stress factor.

over. Now, as a couple, they are left more and more to themselves. Now they look to each other for more than they ever did. For many couples this is a very hard time, when children leave.

Mrs. Brown responded thoughtfully, "I realize I'm getting older and there's nothing to look forward to." I brought out sympathetically that it was important for her to find new satisfactions when old responsibilities are over.

He seems so passive, she so discouraged, I simply take the lead with the decision to keep the marriage, if possible. They can always refuse.

At this point I told them I would like to work with them for another five sessions, to see if some things could be improved between them. They would both, however, have to try to find ways to improve their day-to-day life, and I hoped that this would help them feel better. She would still have the option of continuing or discontinuing the marriage.

He is selected because his motivation is stronger.

Here I turned to Mr. Brown and said clearly that he would have to take some first step to ease his wife's unhappiness and give her some hope.

Worker's tentative marital assessment and treatment plan at this point

The Browns, with twenty-eight years of marriage behind them, have demonstrated ego strength in coping as well as they have against great odds. A cluster of realistic problems has thrown the marriage off balance, in the midst of the child-leaving phase. Mrs. Brown is still mourning separation from her daughter, and Al, probably the "stabilizing scapegoat," has left the system. With the climacteric, Mrs. Brown feels life is passing her by. Mr. Brown, also insecure and fearful for the future, may be seeking reassurance by his increased demands on her.

There is a possibility that they can both be enlisted to work on their marriage, if only to a limited extent.

Re the plan for treatment: in terms of crisis theory, the time-limited service offered could be an opportunity for the couple to improve their coping patterns. Modest goals of behavioral change through the application of learning concepts will be attempted.

These are easy tasks. They can understand this and feel worker's interest in both. A medical check-up is too often neglected by workers.

She agreed to see her doctor, to check on the medication she is using and for a general examination as she may be undergoing menopause. I asked about his health and he said it was good, although he still suffers with his feet as a result of his wartime experiences. I asked whether he had seen a doctor about his hearing. He had never done so. They agreed to contact a specialist about this.

Mrs. Brown seemed greatly relieved by this plan and then brought out that before the interview with me they had been to a second rabbi. The referring rabbi had been so angry with her husband and had yelled at him so much that Mr. Brown's friend told him to go to another rabbi. Mrs. Brown is traditional enough to have gone along with this suggestion but it turned out to be a very upsetting experience for her. The second rabbi told her that she should be ashamed of herself, that her husband made a good living, didn't drink, didn't go with women. He insisted that she sign a paper that she would not proceed with a separation for the next six months, and said that he would work with them during this time.

I am prepared to be her advocate, as she is nowhere near ready to do this for herself.

She said she knew that this rabbi was an important man, but that she couldn't live throught another six months like this. She asked me to phone him and explain so that he wouldn't be angry with her.

I agreed but said that I needed a clear understanding that they were both going to work on the marriage during the next few weeks and not leave it to me to fix it up. They would need to decide, before leaving this session, on some change in their day-to-day life during the coming week. Here I turned to them. "You both agree the sleeping arrangements are a problem and it's not good for the boy. What are you going to do about it?"

Note that her sleeping in the eighteen-year-old son's room can be viewed as the current symptom of the disequilibrium in the marital axis. A mutual problem, identified, to be worked on.

He said, "You should come back to the bedroom." She insisted, however, that she needs more sleep. Again silence.

Technique of restating the issue, and offering a compromise. The direct guidance makes sense to this unsophisticated couple.

I said, clearly and slowly, "Mr. Brown, you want your wife back into the bedroom, but she doesn't want to be awakened twice a night, or even once. Could you let her come back and still sleep apart?" She interjected quickly, "He'll never do it!" I asked whether he kept on his side of the bed during her monthly period and the five days following, as is required by Orthodox Jewish rules. They agreed that he did.

Re task setting—put another way, they are directed to continue sleeping apart, but now to do it differently until the next session, in their own bed. Note that this is supported by drawing on their reli-

I asked them whether they would try sleeping apart in this way until I saw them again. He looked at me so strangely that I said again very slowly and empathetically, "I know that you find this hard, and that you don't like it. However, you don't have a woman in your bed anyhow. Have you got another one to sleep with if this one walks out on you for good?" He whispered, "No"—he had no woman.

gious practice. As well, this task helps to remove the son from involvement in their marital conflict.

Mrs. Brown again indicated her distrust, but I suggested that there was always the living room couch to resort to. I told him that if he were to do as I suggested it would show her that he was willing and able to make a big effort to do something special for her. On this basis she agreed to try.

I also asked whether her hours could be reduced in the store, as I thought she could consider some outside activity. She liked the idea of doing some volunteer work two afternoons a week, and she said that a hospital for the aged would appeal to her. I expressed my approval.

Encouraging the role of hostess could be helpful to Mrs. B. and to Mr. B. too. This technique of re-creating formerly gratifying roles is generally useful, also as preparation for retirement.

I then asked what they could do to ease the situation during the next week for him as well as for her. When had they last visited, or been visited by, those mutual friends? Not for some months now. She reflected how her son used to like it when she had friends in. "And what about you, Mr. Brown?" I asked. He said he liked this too. She thought that Sunday evening would be a good time, that she would ask a few friends in.

Important that client and worker role be made clear.

An element of hope is offered, while they retain control of their situation.

I added firmly that if they couldn't make some efforts, *no matter how small*, to change this situation that was so miserable for them both, and to keep up an effort, that I would have to pull out from the counseling before the six sessions. Without their help and their work, I could do nothing. I told Mrs. Brown that she had invested so much of her life in this marriage, they had struggled together for so long, and with so much to their credit, that an effort now, despite her pain, was worthwhile. I repeated that she could still leave the marriage before the six sessions were ended.

Note "closure" in the ending phase of the interview. Also a little humor is used as a technique to reduce tension.

By this time, as they were both more relaxed and the interview was over, and Mrs. Brown had said she was glad she had come, I said, a little facetiously, would she please not waltz into the bedroom in a fancy see-through negligee but just slip in quietly and keep to her own side of the bed. She laughed and said, "Don't worry." I also asked whether she had occasionally enjoyed sex, and she said, "After all, I'm only human." As he left, Mr. Brown turned to face me, bowed very shyly, and said, "I have for you a big respect."

I said that I knew he was a tryer and that he really was going to help her through the week.

One additional small task was given to both—that in each other's presence, they tell their son that they are coming for help with their marital problems.

Here is a mutual task of common concern. This one they can now understand and accept.

Second Interview, February 2

Mr. and Mrs. Brown again arrived punctually. Mr. Brown meticulously hung up her coat and carefully put her rubbers and his own side by side. He then took his seat solemnly on the sofa, close to my chair. She again sat in a far corner of the room near the door. I asked them how they are managing.

This is a general opening question, leaving it possible for either Mr. or Mrs. B. to respond.

Mrs. Brown took over quickly and said, "He's been a little better; I think he's trying, but I really don't think it will last." To this I asked, "In what way is it better?"

At this early part of the interview, I choose to respond to the positive part of her message, knowing that this may draw Mr. B. into the interview as well. Mrs. B. will likely repeat, as the interview proceeds, her doubt that the improvement will last.

"As far as the bedroom is concerned, he kept it up for only two nights." No, she didn't go into the living room. They had sex on the third night. She paused, and added that she didn't mind too much because "he *is* being more considerate." Here, I turned to Mr. Brown and smiled a nonverbal message of encouragement. Mrs. Brown went on that she had had her period after that, so that took care of the rest of the week. As far as inviting friends in on Sunday night, she said she really was too tired. Instead, her husband took her out one evening and they had dinner out. She paused, and I waited inquiringly. She added, "It was a nice change." I said I was glad to hear this, at which Mr. Brown gave a shy little smile. I commented that her husband appears to have tried to make some changes, and that it seems difficult for her, with so much built-up hurt and frustration, to hope for any lasting improvement.

Mrs. Brown replied, "Exactly," but then went on more brightly to say they did tell the boy they were coming here for help with their marriage and that he'd been very pleased. I said this was an important step, especially if they were together in doing this.

Here, Mrs. Brown went on about her son: "He is such a sweet boy. He has nice friends." She was continuing along this line, but I made no response. Instead I turned to Mr. Brown, to question the ways in which he had been more considerate. She brought out that he sent her home earlier from the store. Instead of having her pick him up at eight o'clock some nights, he offered to come home himself by bus. Again, after a long silence, she added now he always tells her to go home earlier, and even to come to the store later.

I asked Mr. Brown how he feels about leaving the house at 7 A.M. and taking the bus instead of getting a lift. He said he doesn't mind. I remarked that this was quite a change, as she used to drive him to the store and back almost every day. She agreed, but said rather sadly, "He's trying, but I don't think it will last." I said, "I agree. I don't think it will last either, if this is the way you are going to encourage him." This startled her. I explained that her attitude would naturally discourage him, and if he did slip back she would then again be very disappointed.

She said, "I know he has done some good work." Here he nodded and smiled. I asked whether she doesn't tend to get discouraged too easily, and she said, "Yes, I think so, I do." Then she tossed in, "But he didn't want to come here the first time, and again even tonight, he said he didn't want to come." I turned to him and said, "But you did come."

To Mrs. Brown I said, "I know you are hurt, and it seems you still need to knock him down. But if you feel you want to

---

One can expect a skeptical reaction. We saw this also with Mrs. Fisher.

Mrs. B., feeling more accepted and understood, is now able to report on a task carried out.

Worker refocuses on the marital problem for which they came. A technique of extinction used to divert Mrs. B.'s unwanted behavior (to be effective, technique should be systematic and consistent) (Leitenberg, 1972).

At this point I felt sure that Mrs. B. should be confronted with her resistance.

By showing how Mr. B. would like to keep away from me, is she projecting her resistance, or trying to get me to line up with her? Worker, however, responds only to the positive in his behavior—the fact that he did come.

Accepting feelings but not her destructive behavior,

again teaching importance of immediate reinforcement in shaping wanted behavior.

Pointing out that her option to leave is still available.

Inducing interaction. Helping them to discuss an uncomfortable feeling *now*, to test out if they can use this at home.

Support followed by mild confrontation.

Mrs. B. is still not ready to accept consequences of her behavior, and changes the subject, to talk about Mr. B.'s inadequacy with the son. I decide to go along with this topic switch (a frequent diversionary tactic to derail the communication— sometimes deliberate, sometimes unwittingly). If it recurs, however, I shall point out what she is doing.

give him a chance, then you must notice his efforts to make you feel more satisfied.'' This was important for her too as well as for him, and I added it was most important for her to comment on any improvement at the moment it occurred. I added, ''Of course you can still decide to break up your marriage, but I think you would feel better if you let him try, and if you try too, before giving up.'' I knew there was still a great deal that she wasn't happy about, and this was not going to be an easy time. Mrs. Brown was attentive here and said she was frightened that this change in him *really* would not last. I asked whether she could talk with him about this now and explain her fear to him. This she did, and quite gently too, saying that she did not want him to take her for granted again, to think all was well and that she is now content. He replied softly to her, ''I understand.''

I said if they can talk like this here, they can try it at home too; this is an important way of ''working.'' I pointed out to both that it is difficult to see small changes in a situation that has been so hard and disappointing, but the situation itself is now different. In her distress, Mrs. Brown had gone to a lawyer and both have come to a marriage counselor for help.

I noted that Mrs. Brown looked sad and gave her support for the feelings of sorrow and anger she had built up within her. Why had she waited so long to complain? She said she had felt it would be useless to do so. I said I could understand her feelings and the difficulty of noticing his efforts to change, which might help her unhappy situation; ignoring his efforts might well bring about what she fears most—that is, that the situation will continue or even get worse.

She then complained that he doesn't take a stand with David, who expects to be catered to so much. He's such a good, clever boy, but so demanding. She went on to complain that the boy expects her to make him a hot breakfast and to rush home to give him a hot lunch, or at least to leave something tasty ready for him if she can't get home at noon. It seems she gives him many other little services too. I said she was entitled to some free time of her own and turned to Mr. Brown, but he sat passively. After a pause, he said it would be all right if she did less for David. This came out only in response to my question. I said it seems Mrs. Brown does too much for others, then becomes frustrated and feels taken advantage of. ''Yes,'' she said, ''this is so.''

Rechanneling an established pattern of nonproductive behavior into a more satisfying situation. She is encouraged to "give" outside the home, with more rewards forthcoming.

I asked if this was a way of behaving that began even before her marriage and here she thoughtfully agreed. We discussed the need for her to have some time for herself, and an outside interest beyond the home and the store. She again said that she would love to get into some volunteer work, as some of her friends do, and is particularly interested in working with old people. I encouraged her to explore possibilities and suggested that she ask Mr. Brown his reaction. He simply said it would be all right. I also found they had both made doctor's appointments during the week, and this I recognized with them was constructive.

I told them I thought both had contributed during the week in their own way.

Repetition as a teaching technique, also reward by approval, is demonstrated.

She needs permission to find interests for herself. By defining this as also helping the family, she is still "serving the family," and is not just "selfish."

I repeated that she should consider ways to notice and encourage his good efforts to help her, as he had begun to do. I said, too, he had made a beginning in understanding her fear that this would not continue. As to her interest in doing something outside the home and store, I pointed out that this would not only help her but would be good for the family as well. I also added that a little change was a lot in their situation, and they left, I thought, both feeling somewhat encouraged.

Third Interview, February 9

A nonverbal indication of an improved marital interaction.

Mr. and Mrs. Brown were again on time. She came into the room and sat on the sofa next to him for the first time.

Verbalizing his feelings difficult, he says it with Roses!!

She opened the session again, saying, "Things are a little better; he really *is* more considerate." Then she brightened up and said, "Now, you won't believe this, but he sent me red roses and put a nice card in."

I pick up on this topic switch, and direct her to respond to her husband.

I said enthusiastically, "That's terrific." He gave me that little half-smile and said almost coyly, "I'll do more." I looked at her and asked, "How about that?" She began to talk about her son. Here I interrupted, "What about your husband's comment just now, that he wants to do more for you? You're unhappy that he takes you for granted, and just now he said something nice, yet you didn't seem to hear him. You even changed the subject." She looked a little surprised at me and said, "Well, I guess anything can happen, after the roses."

She asked him, "I did tell you I was pleased, didn't I?" "Yes, you did tell me." I said, "That's fine, but it's also important to encourage Mr. Brown right now for his offer to do more. Only by noticing and saying that you are pleased, immediately, when he does something like that, something you like, will you keep these new ways going."

Mrs. Brown said, "You mean, I shouldn't just take it for granted."

There was discussion around disciplining the boy, and her pattern of giving him too much. She said she had thought about my remark that she may have brought this habit into the marriage with her and said that her mother, as an invalid, passed a lot of responsibility on to her as a young girl and yet whatever she did was never enough. She could see that today the situation is so different, but she still feels expected to do too much.

I asked her if there is a point where she begins to feel tired and resentful, and she said, "Yes, there is." I said that when she feels like this, that is the time for her to question whether she is overdoing things, that when she begins to feel tired and resentful she should stop, and tell her husband and son just that. She has a right to this feeling, and her husband and son have a right to know it too, so that they can begin to give her some help rather than assume she has boundless energy to give them. She said she is beginning to see this, and he nodded. I told them that old habits change slowly, and he can help her to work on this when they leave me.

Further to the volunteer work, she has visited two hospitals, and thinks the convalescent geriatric hospital would like her to begin in a few weeks or so. She plans to contribute two afternoons a week. She seemed most pleased about this and is looking forward to it. One of her friends was very helpful in this connection. I praised her for her initiative and for following this up.

She has been to see a gynecologist and he told her she is in good shape physically. Mr. Brown has been to an ear specialist who cleared away masses of wax. He is to return for further hearing tests. She thought he is hearing a little better now, and he thought so too.

Somewhere in this interview Mrs. Brown said about her husband, "Today he wanted to come here." She also offered that he is speaking a little more to her in bed. I said I was demote some behavioral change by verbalizing for the nonverbal client. This gentle nudge to the ego tests his capacity to learn through simple imitation.

It works!

A balanced "push" as Mrs. B. is taught to reinforce with a rewarding response—a small example to illustrate that with her help he does better.

The son is responding to the improved marital relationship—an example of the "absent interaction."

Mrs. B. sees her contribution to the problem. "Doing too much" is a simplification. This is enough for her to act on, and for him to respond to.

This interpretation is likely beyond them both.

lighted to hear this, and added that perhaps I'll have the pleasure of hearing him speak to her a little more in one of our sessions, before the six meetings are over.

He looked at me enquiringly, and I said jokingly, "For instance, it would be nice if next week I could hear you say something like, 'Deborah, I hope we have a better week.' " At this he looked at her shyly, and said slowly, "Deborah, I hope we have a better week." She smiled and responded quickly, "Morris, I hope we do too." I also smiled and said to her, "I bet you can do better than that." At this she bent over and gave him a sound kiss on the mouth. She said quite warmly and tolerantly, "You know, he'll never be much of a talker." I said I realized this, but he seems to be able to do a little more with her help, and she agreed.

Fourth Interview, February 16
Both came in looking more relaxed. She began, "It is really much better, what is going on now. My husband is really trying." She laughed and said, "He sent me a Valentine and a large bottle of perfume for Valentine's Day. You should have heard our son, David. He's so happy he keeps on saying, 'What's going on here?' " Mr. Brown listened carefully and primly to this with that little shy smile of his and when asked how he felt hearing this about himself, he nodded, closed his eyes, semiwinked in agreement. I repeated the question slowly, and he answered softly, "It's good." They were sitting together on the couch, and at this Mrs. Brown put her hand on his arm. I commented that last week she told me he talked more in bed. "Oh yes," she said, "he still does." Here she smiled and looked at him, "He's still considerate, sending me home earlier from the store." She added, "I know a lot is my fault. I never refused to do anything. I was always too ready to do too much. But my husband has really tried, he's more considerate in bed, too. He doesn't wake me up so much."

I said I wondered whether, now that he's getting more recognition from her in other ways, he feels less need to have so much proof of her love in terms of sex. He said softly, "Maybe." But I was not sure he got the point. I asked her, now that

Mr. Brown is given recognition from the worker to encourage him, and Mrs. Brown continues on in the same vein.

he shows interest and concern for her, whether she can enjoy sex more and she accepted this readily. To Mr. Brown I said how pleased I was to hear these "good" things about him. He smiled. She said, "Although he did not want to come here at the beginning, now he told me he likes it." She laughed and said he told her, "I should have gone to school much earlier." She said this encouraged her very much; it showed he was trying to learn how to please her. I said, "It seems now you feel less frightened that your husband will stop understanding, and you can say nice things to him more easily."

This recurrent concern—that is, the parent-child conflict—is now focused on. I have found that movement is quicker in related areas when the marital problem is appropriately dealt with.

She again brought up her concern about their younger son, David. Although he is so good and clever, it seems he still expects and gets those two hot meals a day. As to why she continues to do so much, she explained, "It's up to his father to discipline him, and to get him to do more for himself." No response from Mr. Brown.

Putting a searchlight on a small current incident can be highly productive. It often illuminates a significant interactional pattern. Her expression and tone in telling this is half-accepting. The collusion with her husband to indulge and serve David becomes apparent.

I asked them to give me a recent instance to help me understand what goes on between the parents and David. She gave this example: "This morning was my day off. I felt very tired, and wanted to sleep in, so I told my husband to tell David to get up and make his own breakfast, and to let Mummy sleep. But," she said, "he only woke David up but didn't tell him to let Mummy sleep."

She went on, "As a result, David woke me up to get his breakfast." Here I turned to Mr. Brown, and asked why he had been able to perform only part of his wife's request. "Oh," he said, "I had no time—I had to leave early. I have to leave the house at seven o'clock in the morning." Then Mrs. Brown got excited, jumped in, and said he never helped her discipline the boy in any way.

Worker persists in using this current incident, to cut through their pattern of fearing to discipline the boy, probably a fear of depriving him as they were themselves deprived.

Here I said, "Hold it. Right now we're talking about this morning. It sounds to me as if you're quite accepting of your husband's explanation about this morning and that you took it very casually, and began to talk about discipline in general. How come you let this go on?" She asked me what I meant, and I said, "You seem to accept his reasons for not getting David to make his own breakfast and let you sleep. Why don't you question him about this?'' She said, ''He thinks David needs a good breakfast, too.''

I said, ''Maybe you, too, feel that David needs that good breakfast. Is that why you let it go? If you really wanted your husband to take a stand, as you say, why did you let this go?'' They both lapsed into silence, and I asked how long they thought it would take to finish the sentence and give the boy the whole message that she had asked her husband to give. He stared, and she said, ''Oh, a few seconds.'' I asked him, and he said, ''That's true.'' I repeated, ''I really wonder why you didn't finish the message.'' Again he remained silent, just staring at me. ''You know,'' I said, ''I have an idea, maybe you're afraid of David.'' Mr. Brown replied, ''Oh, no, oh no.''

I then asked him what it was like when he was eighteen, as David is now. Slowly and quietly, he talked a little about himself at David's age. He was a good son, and worked hard. I gathered his family was broken up, and on the move, hiding during the war, but his mother always tried to cook a hot meal for him whenever she could, and this was very important.

He slowly recalled that in his earlier years, his father was the ''big boss'' in the house. He nodded when I asked if he was afraid of his father. Was that why he was such a good obedient boy? Here he shrugged.

I asked if he was afraid to let David be deprived of a hot meal. If David was refused something, did Mr. Brown fear the boy would become angry and dislike him? Here he looked at me intently, and although I could not be sure he understood, I felt he would say, ''No, no,'' as is his custom if he really disagrees. I went on to say, distinctly, ''Look, David is not you.'' ''No,'' said Mr. Brown, ''he has it better than I did.''

''That's right,'' I said, pushing my chair closer to him, ''that's very important. If David misses a hot meal, it's not like those hard times when *you* missed a hot meal. David at eighteen, and you at eighteen, are not the same.'' I talked slowly and carefully, and directly to him. At this, Mrs. Brown excitedly burst out, ''That's psychology!''

I turned to Mr. Brown again, and slowly asked what was it his wife had wanted of him early this morning. Softly and a bit awkwardly, he answered, ''To wake up David and let Mummy

---

Margin notes:

Using my hunch that Mr. B. overidentified with David.

Worker tries to get across how his own unhappy past could affect his attitude as a father, and attempts as simply as possible to separate him from David.

Here I use nonverbal behavior to underline the message that David and he are two different people.

I doubt my attempt at insight will help him. I move back to work on behavioral change. I realize, however, he feels I am pressuring him, and he pulls back.

I retrieve with a supportive comment and an alternative behavioral change is offered. This is easier and more acceptable.

Again, repetition to foster the principle of positive and immediate reinforcement.

Preparation for separation.

Mrs. B. has made good progress in seeing *her* part in their problem.

Again, the use of repetition as a learning tool. Modest expectations make the learning a feasible goal.

sleep.'' This came out with a lot of hesitation but I waited it out, and he did manage it. He stalled on the breakfast bit and I repeated, ''What about the breakfast part?'' Still he didn't answer. I said, ''It's pretty hard for you to do this now. Later on, maybe you could think about it. Meanwhile, how would you like to make a kind of deal with David? It would be good for David to feel that he is working with his Dad, by letting Mummy sleep in.'' He was listening carefully. I added, ''This would help David feel more grown up. You know, he has to grow up anyhow. It would be like two men getting together on this.'' He smiled a little in satisfaction, and I felt he understood what was going on.

Mrs. Brown then told me she was going to New York next week. She said her husband had encouraged her to visit their daughter and Mrs. Brown's sister, who both live there. She's really glad. I said, ''That's great. What did you tell him this time?'' ''Oh,'' she said, ''he knows I appreciate it.'' I said, ''I still think it would be nice if he could hear it.'' She answered, smiling, ''Yes, I know what you mean.''

We arranged to have our fifth session in two weeks. I said they would soon be working on their own, as a team. I playfully suggested that he could be the doctor and she could be the nurse! They both laughed at this. He nodded agreement to do what he could to make her feel appreciated. I was glad she felt she was getting a better deal, and that he was too. She said, ''What helps one, helps the other.'' She added she gets too discouraged; she could understand that a lot of it was her own doing, that she has to watch her tendency to do too much. ''I know what my project is—to stop before I feel too much is building up, but it will take time.'' I agreed it would, and that she couldn't do this in a week or two or three. I thought she had made a good beginning. I also indicated that sometimes there are ups and downs, and that things do not always proceed smoothly, as we would like. I hoped she would enjoy her visit to New York.

Toward the end of the interview, Mrs. Brown volunteered she was not so worried that he was going to slip back. Before coming here, he didn't really believe that she couldn't stand things as they were. Even when she went to see the lawyer for a separation, he didn't believe her. And even when the rabbi yelled at him, he didn't believe it. But now he is kinder, and really wants to please her. I reinforced this, turning to Mr. Brown, "Your wife is not so frightened now, because you're much more thoughtful." He said, "She's treating me much better." I added that they both looked better. He told me he had gone back to the ear specialist and that he may need a hearing aid, but on the whole, the doctor was encouraging. They left in a friendly mood.

Fifth Interview, March 8

Mr. and Mrs. Brown arrived punctually. Today they sat together on the sofa, quite close. Both looked more relaxed, and smiled when they greeted me.

Mrs. Brown began the interview by saying, "You'll never believe what I got for my twenty-eighth anniversary." As a surprise, her husband bought her a new car! He let her choose it herself! He didn't even see it! I responded with enthusiasm, and asked whether this was the first time she had made a big decision and choice in this way. She said she always wanted a new car, yet they had always used a second-hand one. She never thought it right to ask for such things. Mind you, he never refused her, but she really never asked, so getting it this way was very nice indeed. As usual, Mr. Brown sat still and quiet, but looked quite pleased with himself.

Again, he expresses his positive feelings in concrete giving.

They began to speculate together as to how long it had been since they last saw me. He said it was a few weeks; she said, "It was after the fourteenth of February. I remember now, because that was the week of the storm." Then they had missed a week when she had been in New York. She asked him, and he agreed that they had managed very well. She added, "I really think now we'll be able to go on our own."

I expressed my pleasure that they were taking over. I thought they both understood better how to help each other. She added, "Yes, things are much better; not exactly everything I'd like, but much better than I ever thought." More specifically, she's pleased that he has taken a hand with David. It seems that now and for some days he has been waking David, telling him to get up and to make his own breakfast. Here he interjected shyly, "I even told him to wash the dishes." I said, "That's great," and she went on, "This morning I slept in, and

Mr. B. demonstrates he can learn, and can change his behavior with encouragement and modest expectations.

when I saw it was a quarter to nine, I was amazed. 'Oh, my goodness,' I thought, 'What happened? I never slept in like this for such a long time.' " Mrs. Brown is now going to the store much less often.

She then expressed her concern about her husband. She feels he works too hard, twelve hours a day. Then she went on, "I think it's to do with our problem with our older son. Now he's suddenly back from Florida. He got fed up there. He is so lazy, and doesn't work properly in the store. He can't get along with his father. They're not a team. Just get on each other's nerves."

She brings in another problem, the older son, and soon reverts to her pattern of blaming her husband, thus reinforcing his feelings of inadequacy.

She said her husband should try harder to train the boy, and when I turned to Mr. Brown about this, he said, "He doesn't work, he sits and reads the newspaper." Then he added, "He doesn't know the prices."

Here Mrs. Brown flared up. "You should teach the boy the new prices. Instead," she added sharply, "you just scold him."

My relationship with Mrs. B. can support this quick challenge to her nonproductive pattern.

I interrupted, "And you are just scolding Mr. Brown. How will that help?"

This stumped her. "What can I do?" she complained. I responded, "If you see a problem, it might help to encourage your husband to work on it with you."

Her hurt, expressed as anger, is directed at her husband, not her son.

In exasperation she said, "But he never helps." I said, "Before you get so angry with your husband, let me ask how do you both feel, now that your son has returned home?"

Mr. Brown shrugged, and sighed. She said, "We're so disappointed. I'm upset. I was hoping he would make something of himself down there."

Helping them express their negative feelings about Al.

I said, "You two are just beginning to get along better between you. Now your problem son is back on your doorstep. That's hard to take."

"Yes," she agreed, "it was so unexpected." Mr. Brown said, "He didn't write us." She explained with irritation, "He just decided he doesn't like working for somebody else. He wants to own his own taxi, and then he'll go back to Florida."

"No wonder you're both upset at his returning home," I said. To this, Mr. Brown just repeated, "He doesn't work hard enough; he doesn't work hard enough." Showing my interest, I asked him, "What do you think can be done about Al?"

Is Mr. B. not ready to let
Al go on his own?

Is her unwillingness to let
go of Al linked to guilt feelings of failure as a parent?

"I want he should work in the store—there's a lot to do."

Mrs. Brown also wanted Al to take more interest in the store; it would be "better for his future," and she said, "soon we'll have to hire someone full-time."

"You're right, Mrs. Brown. Your husband should get more help now." After a pause, I suggested, "I wonder if you feel Al didn't get as good a start as David?"

They became thoughtful. Then Mrs. Brown said, "When he was growing up, it was hard. We only had a little stall in the market. We were often from hand to mouth. Yes, David had it better."

"Still, you both did the best you could. You even managed to get him into high school."

"Well, we wanted him to better himself."

"But not everyone can be a scholar. There's no shame in driving a taxi." Then I said, "I have an idea you both feel you want to give Al another chance." They agreed.

Worker demonstrates tech-
nique of clarification as part
of a problem-solving exercise, then assigns the resolution to them.

We then clarified what Al would be doing in the store. Most of the canned items have the prices marked, and do not change daily. It's mainly the fruits and vegetables that change. I suggested that the two of them discuss how this could be handled. After a little discussion back and forth, they agreed that Mr. Brown could work out the changed prices for the day for the boy and let his son write them down. While this was going on, Mrs. Brown kept complaining that her son was incompetent, lazy, and spoiled.

Technique of exaggeration
of the boy's negative qualities pushes Mrs. B. to note
some of his good points.
One can always count on
ambivalence in a parent,
and reach for the positive
feelings.

I said, "It sounds pretty bad. I wonder if he also steals, uses drugs, or gets women into trouble."

"Oh, no. He's a good boy in many ways. He's warm-hearted, and has some good ideas."

After further discussion, it emerged in essence that what was wrong with the boy was his stubbornness and unwillingness to listen to either of his parents. Mrs. Brown laid the blame on Mr. Brown's lack of communication, his inability to train and discipline his son. I pointed out that Mr. Brown was again getting the blame. Had she perhaps been overgiving to this boy, too, and made things easy for him, as she had with David?

Use of confrontation. Support here would only serve
to reinforce her ineffective
pattern.

She didn't accept this too readily and attempted to change the subject. Here I pointed out what she was doing, changing the subject, and brought her back to her behavior, reminding her of her tendency to overdo things. "Yes," she conceded. "I know I give too much. Still, I've tried so hard. I've cried so much. A few years ago I even had a social worker come to the house, to try to talk to him, but he walked right out of the house and wouldn't listen to the social worker."

I bypass the implications of this reference to the social worker. This could be self-pity or anger at me, inappropriate to explore at this point, distracting from the current issue.

Keeping the focus on Al, I therefore tried to find out more about him. Apparently he has worked in the store on and off for some years. Whether he works or doesn't, he gets paid. He lives at home, gets his laundry done, his meals prepared, and apparently lives quite a comfortable existence. I asked them why he should change this comfortable way of life, why should he work hard when everything is laid out so nicely for him?

Mrs. Brown said, "What can we do? You can't let the boy go without money; you can't let him go without food."

Raising the parental contribution to son's laziness.

I put in here, "Well, maybe you can't just let him grow up and take some responsibility, either."

She is resistant—guilt feelings are in the way.

She went on to say she did want him to take responsibility in the store, but her husband wouldn't trust him. I pointed out gently, "You do know, Mrs. Brown, when you work so hard and get frustrated, you tend to blame your husband."

Worker tries direct confrontation.

At this point I tried to draw in Mr. Brown. I again asked him what he thought could be done with the boy. It seemed he wanted the boy to do what he himself does, and in the same way. I pointed out that it has taken him nearly twenty-five years to build up his good way of doing things. The boy couldn't do this overnight.

The same pattern. She overserves, complains, and blames Mr. B.

I asked him what he does when the boy sits and reads the newspaper, and he replied, "I tell him, 'You're getting on in years, what's going to become of you? You've got to learn to work.'" Here, Mrs. Brown impatiently jumped in and said, "You see, he doesn't teach him the right way. He doesn't have the patience to talk to him properly." She said she wanted to try to train and talk to Al herself. She'll have to take him into the store and *she'll* teach him and show him.

Mr. B.'s excessive expectations of his son are questioned. This gives Mrs. B. some support.

She is less angry, but persists in blaming Mr. B. for mishandling their son's inefficiency. I therefore include her as a party to the mishandling.

I said, "I now have the feeling you both expect Al suddenly to jump out of his skin and become an efficient manager of the grocery store." With more questioning about the boy, it emerged that he does have some good ideas. For example, it seems he suggested putting in a health food counter. This they had done, and in a small way, it was going very well.

Clarification is useful here.

I said this sounds ingenious and clever, also very practical, not the way they had described the boy. What had they told him about these good ideas? They both looked blank. I pointed out that the boy may possibly have more ability than either of them realized. Although he wants to do things his way, it seems some of his ideas are good and should be given some praise and taken more seriously. Also, I again said I thought they were both try-ing to do too much too quickly with him. And who likes all that criticism, I asked? Here she said, "That is what I've been tell-ing my husband all these years. He doesn't have the patience to talk nicely to him." I replied gently, "And maybe you're too soft with him. You know what I think? When you're fighting about him, you are really fighting with each other." She seemed to take this seriously.

Since Al's inadequacy as a worker and as a son is a blow to their narcissistic pride as parents, it is com-forting to hear that the worker sees some worth and ability in him.

They are indirectly fighting through the boy. His return has stirred them up and really upset them.

Then I said, "Suppose we pretend that the boy is coming in the store tomorrow morning. Let's see how you will deal with him when he picks up the newspaper." I turned to Mr. Brown, and waited. In a somewhat flat, matter-of-fact way, he said, "You're getting on, and you should try to get to work. What will happen to you when your parents go?" I interjected firmly, "No, that's not going to work. That's what you've been doing up to now, and you tell me it hasn't worked, or has it?" He agreed that it had not. I turned to Mrs. Brown and waited for her. She too said it had not worked. Finally, I continued, "There are a few things you can do tomorrow. You can tell him you're glad about the good ideas he brought into the business lately, and that they're working well."

Now, a practical incident is anticipated, to teach them new ways of dealing with Al.

Technique—a form of role playing is used—an adjunct to direct teaching, and to help them rehearse a new way to deal with their son's behavior. Worker acts as a role model.

Involving them in this seri-ous effort should ease their guilt feelings toward Al,

I continued, "A compliment will help him to listen better. You catch more flies with honey than with vinegar." Mrs. Brown laughed, and said, "I know what you mean." He laughed, too. I added, "You can say to him: 'Today, we'd like you to help by

and help them perceive him more as an adult.

Note how the client has now taken hold of the concept of partialization.

Anticipatory guidance and rehearsal are used as preparation for carrying out the task.

Technique of taking the pressure off the boy and themselves; what they have done at such cost to themselves hasn't worked, anyhow.

Mr. Brown's father role has been strengthened, and Mrs. Brown gives him recognition.

marking the new prices, and we hope then you can handle the fruits and vegetables by yourself.' ''

I told them that's their job for the next three days, and not to try to teach him anything more. I repeated, ''You can't teach him too many things all at once. That makes him very stubborn.'' Then Mrs. Brown turned to her husband and said, ''That's good, Morris—one thing at a time.''

I added to Mr. Brown, ''If your son gets behind the paper, and keeps on reading while you're working so hard and feeling angry, could it be that he thinks there's nothing for him to do? Or maybe he's trying to get some notice from you? Why don't you fool him? Go over to him and say, 'So what's in the news?' '' Mr. Brown really laughed at this, and so did Mrs. Brown.

Again I asked Mr. Brown what he's going to do tomorrow and repeated what he might say to Al the next day, that is, ''The health food is going well. I want you to mark the new prices and to handle the fruits and vegetables.'' He rehearsed this slowly, in his usual hesitant way. He actually repeated it once more. At this, Mrs. Brown reached forward, patted him warmly on the cheek, and said, ''It makes me feel good when you do things like that, and try.'' I said I could see how fighting about this boy must have come between them. I thought they already had enough to fight about, apart from him. I explained, ''It's time now for Al to earn his living in the store, or elsewhere if he won't work in the store with this kind of help from you.''

Mrs. Brown said, ''You know, I've really learned something tonight. One step at a time, one step at a time.'' I said that was great, that all anyone could manage was one step at a time; too much too quickly would only turn him off, and this is what had been going on all along. If Al is going to grow up and be a man, he has to worry for himself, not have his parents worry for him. They had done their best, and now they have to leave it to him.

I then asked what goes on in the home these days. Apparently Mr. Brown has no trouble getting David up after one call in the morning. He used to have to call him half a dozen times in a vain effort to get him out of bed. Now, Al also gets up with one call. Mrs. Brown said this is a big improvement and most times they get their own breakfast. I commented that it looks as if Mr. Brown is gaining respect from both his sons, and I added that Mrs. Brown is noticing. "It's good for them when they do more for themselves, and Mrs. Brown is entitled to her sleep."

As to their future relationship, it seems Mrs. Brown feels things are so much better. She's not really worried any more. She feels if they come here once more, that will be enough. She will talk to the rabbi who originally phoned me, and say they are going to stay together. She added, "Now he talks a little more—not as much as I'd like, but he's better, and he is much more kind."

The ending phase, summary of gains made.

Then I asked Mr. Brown about our ending. With his shy smile, he nodded, "Yes, it's better now." I commented that they had both done good work to make things better. Then she put in warmly, "*He* did most of it, and now I know he has his own way of showing he appreciates me." "Yes," I agreed, "some men show more by doing than by talking."

Unfinished business—some tasks for dealing with child-leaving stage identified.

I then raised the subject of both sons moving out before too long, when they would be left on their own. Could they both find some outside interests? She had made a good beginning for herself, and he had helped her. She responded by saying that the synagogue always has something doing, if they have the time. He indicated he would like that. She then asked him about contacting two old friends with whom he had lost touch. Again he nodded agreement. She squeezed his hand, and they left looking pleased and friendly. We arranged for the sixth and final interview to take place in four weeks' time.

Sixth Interview, April 9
This turned out to be a telephone interview which took place about a month later. Mrs. Brown called me to say that they did not feel it necessary to come the next day but wanted me to know that things were going well. She told me that her older son was now working outside the store, driving a taxi. He is living on his own but comes home on Friday nights, and she is satisfied that this is working out well, though he will never be very ambitious. This change in him followed a talk when she told him he must take over more responsibility and earn his way in the store, or he will not get paid. Yes, Morris backed her up in this. Al said he prefers to be out and likes the activity of a taxi.

She feels her husband still works too many hours, but she hopes now, with his plan to increase the part-time help, he can come home earlier.

He certainly pressures her less at night. She thinks he is more relaxed, now that she has told him she intends to stay with him. She realizes that he is loyal and devoted, that he is hard-working and will always stand by her, and this is important to her.

She told me with some pleasure of her volunteer activity. She is giving two half-days a week in a program for the aged and has met some very nice people. She may increase this to a third afternoon in a few weeks when they get more help in the store.

I expressed my satisfaction to Mrs. Brown with the way she and her husband worked together on improving their marriage. I hoped she would not hesitate to call the agency if she felt they needed further sessions, and she did not have to wait for it to be anything serious to do so, nor should she see it as a failure. Mrs. Brown said both she and her husband had learned a good deal from their meetings with me, and she stressed she would not feel at all shy about calling me again if they needed to. I asked her to give my regards to Mr. Brown.

Indicating the door is open is important in short-term counseling, and makes it easier to "let go," both for clients and workers.

Note
It is now ten months and I have heard nothing further from this couple, and assume they are coping adequately.

CLOSING COMMENTS

The mounting pressures of the child leaving phase, with its separation anxiety, are intensified in the case of this immigrant couple by their own sad adolescence, with the loss of family and friends during the Holocaust. It took exceptional effort for them to cope in a strange land without the language and without money, to rear and support their children. In fact, the culture shock which immigrants experience can be compared to a stroke, relearning how to speak and finding new ways to manage.

At long last the Browns have achieved modest financial security and the young people are now more or less launched and on their way out. Mrs. Brown feels less needed and more lonely. She sees little to look forward to in the remaining years. The prospect of spending the rest of her life with an uncommunicative and disappointing partner is unbearable to her.

Mr. Brown reacts to anxiety in his own way. He expresses the need for closeness and reassurance by increased sexual demands. But this only creates greater distance between them. The vicious circle of negative interaction is well under way. Mrs. Brown goes to a lawyer, bringing the marital crisis to a head.

During a treatment period of just two months, the Browns not only achieved their former equilibrium but were enabled to move ahead to an improved balance in their marital relationship. In addition, they learned how to deal more effectively with both their sons, who were not seen in counseling. As the parents became less sheltering, this furthered the maturational development of the sons.

Al, who was vacillating in his coming and going, in and out of the home, with options and choices made clear, moves out of the home and is now more likely to take on adult responsibility. He seems to have borne the "scapegoat" role* rather than that of the older son.

An important aspect of working with couples like the Browns, who have limited education and a background of years of economic deprivation, is that the worker must be able to talk to them in terms and at a level they can understand. Such clients tend to be less verbal, more action-oriented, more concerned with present and concrete issues than are their more advantaged middle-class counterparts. The middle-class counselor often has difficulty understanding and relating to such clients, and needs to learn new ways of communicating and counseling. For some ethnic groups, passivity and a lack of directiveness are interpreted as lack of caring.

With the Browns, the worker again used an eclectic approach but treatment drew heavily on educational principles and direct teaching procedures from learning theory, imitation, repetition, recognition as a reward, positive reinforcement, and extinction. Limited insight learning was attempted, and linking their past to present problems was important.

Most of all, it was necessary to get across the counselor's genuine interest and respect for the Browns, for their courage and stamina in managing against great odds to do as well as they have done, and to have confidence in their potential to cope with their situation.

---

*The term "scapegoat" usually refers to a child who is labeled "bad" or "sick," onto whom the heat of marital conflict is diverted. Instead of quarrelling directly, parents fight through the child. Parents tend to project their anxiety and hostility onto this member of the family, thus avoiding their own interpersonal difficulties. In family as opposed to marital therapy, the "scapegoat" is usually presented as the problem, often known as "the identified patient."

A comment on why I offered this couple a six-session contract: in terms of crisis theory, I considered Mrs. Brown's seeking a legal separation a hazardous event for the family. It has been found that the resulting crisis settles down, one way or another, over a six-week period. With Mrs. Brown so upset, Mr. Brown so resistant and nonverbal, and two rabbis involved, I thought the usual three assessment sessions would be insufficient. I also thought that I could later extend the treatment to, say, ten sessions, if necessary.

To add a note of interest: at his request, and of course with the clients' knowledge and consent, a tape of the fifth interview was sent to one of my former students, now working in Israel. He wrote me that he found the use of simple teaching techniques, the modified role playing, the direct advice, repetition, and modest goals very helpful in his work with immigrant and low-income families who had limited education; he also mentioned it was useful in teaching his supervisees.

THE LONG-TERM CASE THAT TURNED SHORT

The case of Mr. and Mrs. Donaldson follows. All three children have been out of the home for several years, and the couple are at the empty-nest stage of the family life cycle.

With the tragic death of their only son, the marriage has come to grief. The impact of this final separation has stirred up overwhelming feelings of guilt and inadequacy as parents.

The case is also offered because it shows that despite the bleak outlook at the point of referral—raising doubts that brief conjoint marriage counseling was suitable for this couple—the outcome was for me an exciting example that the scope and potential of this service is greater than even I had anticipated.

MR. AND MRS. DONALDSON

Ronald Donaldson, age 62
Lenore Donaldson, age 56

Married 35 years

Children: Mariane, age 33, with two children
Grace, age 32, with one child
Bill, deceased at age 25, four years ago

Implications of the referral.
A professional social work

Referral, September 10
The Donaldsons were referred by a social worker friend, who expressed a good deal of concern about them. For four years now, they seem to have grown further and further apart. Their

friend reported serious problems of long duration, coupled with weak motivation.

friends rarely see them and when they do, they cannot help but wonder whether they are still together. They don't talk to each other, and barely look at each other. They are living under the same roof but for all intents and purposes they seem to be separated. It appears that their only son committed suicide at age twenty-five, about four years ago. Mr. Donaldson found him dead one night in their garage, at the wheel of their car. Terrified and fearful of his wife's reactions, he ran to a neighbor to ask for help and advice on how to tell her what had happened.

The social worker friend added that Mr. Donaldson retired about a year ago. He had been a successful executive in a large shoe manufacturing company, and has since become a consultant in this field. Mrs. Donaldson seems to keep very much to herself. Her friend thinks she may be alcoholic; she stays indoors a great deal although she did do some part-time teaching for one or two years after the girls were married. This friend keeps in touch with Mrs. Donaldson and believes that things are now so tense between them that they would accept a referral on her recommendation. She has tried unsuccessfully in the past to make a psychiatric referral.

I expressed some doubt that their situation would yield to a short-term conjoint treatment program. I agreed, however, to see them for an assessment, and if I thought a referral was indicated, I would work with them to facilitate this.

First Interview
The Donaldsons arrived promptly. He is tall and dignified, she an attractive, somewhat plump woman, who looks younger than her fifty-six years. Both were solemn as I shook hands and took them into the office. They sat apart from each other, she closer to me.

This nonverbal clue to their emotional closeness or distance is frequently confirmed.

I told them I knew a little of their difficulties from their friend, who had told me how they tragically lost their son. I said this must have shaken them terribly, both as parents and as a couple. I wondered what help they had had with such extreme pain. Mr. Donaldson sat rigidly, and Mrs. Donaldson responded in a shaky voice that they had not really had any help, but at the time, they had talked to their family doctor who had known their son well and who had been of some comfort to them.

With tears falling, she said, "It might have been avoided if I had known about my son's involvement with drugs, and his heavy debts." Mr. Donaldson was looking down. She continued that although she hadn't liked some of the boy's friends, she learned only later that her husband had been paying his debts from time to time.

Now very excited and angry, she went on, if her husband had only told her of this, if he had shared with her, maybe she could have done something, maybe they could have done something to prevent the boy from doing away with himself. Now she began to sob uncontrollably, and Mr. Donaldson, who had sat immobile, obviously tense and pained throughout this recounting, said quietly that he had kept a lot to himself, to spare his wife from what was going on. Here he added, in a flat voice, that they had both learned later from their clergyman that Bill had been posing as a salesman for a large drug company, that this had been found out, and the clergyman thought a jail term threatened.

This rage has probably protected her from a serious depression. The technique of quiet listening was important, and I did not wish to interrupt her blaming Mr. D. at this very early point.

The next half-hour or more was spent listening sympathetically, and allowing Mrs. Donaldson to release a lot of the anger she felt toward her husband who, she insisted, had been at fault by not telling her what was happening. I wondered whether this would have made any difference. To this she replied she now realized, after all this time, that there wasn't much they could have done. I tried to comfort them, that they had done their best as parents, but once their son became trapped in the drug scene with shady characters, all sorts of dishonest practices and frightening experiences would have followed.

I brought out that many young people from good homes and families had been caught up with the use of drugs, with dreadful consequences. My purpose was to ease their guilt, and allow them to express their pain. Here I included Mr. Donaldson, commenting that while he had not expressed much, he was obviously close to tears, and must have kept his hurt inside for a very long time.

Worker can express feelings for the client who is unable to do so himself.

The counselor must experience enough of the couple's pain, anger, and iso-

I said that much time had gone by, that they had each suffered and mourned enough, and the time had now come for them to look ahead, not back. I said they still had a lot of living

lation to understand the reality of their present relationship. But to allow the old feelings to continue too long in this new situation, without useful intervention, is not therapeutic.

Had the second room not been available, the worker would simply indicate that the time had now come for us to make a fresh start.

It helps to turn to factual material when great emotion has been generated, particularly in a first interview.

The assessment—strengths in the individuals, and in the marriage emerge.

During the first three years after their move, they weathered the crises of a change of locale, of two daughters leaving the family system, and of their only son and remaining child moving out to live on his own. These successive stresses, however, could leave the couple vulnerable and unable to cope with further blows, particularly that of death by suicide.

to do, that their misery must somehow be put behind them, although it would always leave scars.

I then took them into another office which was available, telling them I wanted to change the scene, that I wanted to talk with them about what was going on now. When we had settled down, he still away from the two of us, I explained that I would like to meet with them a few times, when the three of us would make a decision whether I was the best resource for them, as our policy was to give service on a time-limited basis. In response to a question from Mrs. Donaldson, I told her this would probably involve ten to twelve sessions.

I now asked them for some factual information. This helped Mrs. Donaldson to quiet down, and enabled Mr. Donaldson to tell me about their marital past. He told me how they had moved eight years ago from a small town, where they had both been raised, to a large city. He had needed to better himself financially, and had had the opportunity, and he has really done very well. He went on: he knew that his wife had felt lost and uprooted. Here she explained that in her home town she had been an active and respected leader in the community. She was a member of several welfare boards, had many childhood friends nearby, and they had enjoyed a good social life.

After the move, they bought a large home in a good suburban area, but the adjustment was not an easy one, particularly for her. Having been a respected leader in her old community, she felt unwanted even as a volunteer in her present milieu. Still, they were busy with the marriages of their two daughters, which took place in close succession, and she did make a small circle of good friends in a year or two.

Mr. Donaldson had done well in business and had been in contact with key members of his new community, who drew him into a number of communal activities. He became a board member of several welfare organizations, and of the local YMCA.

At the child-leaving phase, Mrs. D. felt the need to revive a former role outside the home.

She withdrew from outside activities after the death of her son.

Important to establish the spouse's autonomy and responsibility. He can and should speak for himself.

Worker is empathetic.

For the assessment, former strengths in the family and in the marriage are noted.

After their two daughters had married and moved away, with Bill at college, Mrs. Donaldson was lonely but managed to get back to part-time teaching. She continued, however, to miss the warmth and status of her home town. Bill moved out to his own apartment about five years ago. He had been working on his master's degree but was not sure of a career direction. He continued to come home occasionally but seemed to be pretty self-sufficient. The big new home seemed to be empty without the three children.

When I asked what was going on between them now, she again took over, saying she was the one with high blood pressure; he has high blood pressure too, but his is more under control. She went on to say that "he's the lucky one; he has his work and all those lunch meetings and board meetings." She went on that he enjoys all these outside activities, while she is left feeling lonely and abandoned.

During this part of the session, he seemed really turned off. I commented that she appeared to talk for him, and that he permitted this.

He said there was little communication between them. To this she said bitterly that there was none. When I asked what had kept them together during this painful period, there was silence. Then he spoke stiffly, "I guess I love my wife, but I don't like her." He is weary of the constant criticism, of the constant "nattering." How does he deal with this? He simply walks out of the room. Mrs. Donaldson had quieted down. She said, "I know it sounds silly, but somewhere I still love him too."

I asked about the other children. The two married daughters are both doing very well. One has two children, boys, and the other has a little girl. They both live out of town; they telephone regularly and visit the parents from time to time, bringing their children. Mrs. Donaldson put in sarcastically, "They don't stay long, because the atmosphere is too unpleasant." I commented that this must be hurtful to her and Mr. Donaldson.

I asked what the atmosphere had been like before Bill's death. Mrs. Donaldson said sadly that it had been very good,

Under their grief, the unac-
knowledged feelings of anger toward their son have
been turned against each
other. I relabel this affect as
abandonment.

Their sex life had been
good, a plus for the mar-
riage.

It is important for the worker to bring this into the
open.

and her husband agreed. I said they must have felt abandoned
by their son as a consequence of this terrible event. At a time
when they most needed each other, they had actually turned
away from one another, both feeling alone and in need of affection.

Mrs. Donaldson was weeping again, and said, "Affection?
He hasn't put a hand on me for eight months now." She
couldn't recall when he had last approached her for sex. Yes, it
used to be very good, and she does miss it.

Mr. Donaldson said that whenever he tried to approach her,
she would begin to weep and wail, so that he gradually withdrew. He thought she just couldn't bear him near her. No, they
don't discuss this at all. I asked her what she thought and felt,
when he approached her. She replied she would think of Bill,
and how he had been conceived, and then she just went to
pieces. I said it seemed that all the bottled-up hurt and unshared
pain had come out in the intimacy of sex, quite irrationally.
This had caused more distress to Mrs. Donaldson, and of
course to Mr. Donaldson also.

This type of response indicates insight learning.

They were both listening closely. After a silence, I went on
emphatically, "Mrs. Donaldson, conception just isn't part of
sex any more. You do know you're well over the child-bearing
age, and sex is not now the same at all." Quietly and slowly,
Mrs. Donaldson responded, "I never really separated it like
that in my head." I saw him soften. "I thought it was just me,"
he said, "I didn't realize what was going on."

It is essential to confront
them with their feelings
and show them the worker
is unafraid. In such an impasse with the clients now
feeling accepted, the worker must be clear and directive. Mr. D. was selected
to carry out the first step,
as he is the more able to
do so.

I went on, that the loneliness between them must be awful,
particularly when there had been such a loving relationship before. I said, "It's painfully clear to me that each of you is in
desperate need of comfort. This can't go on. In fact, Mr. Donaldson," I added firmly, "I'm not letting you out of this room
until you give your wife a shoulder to lean on." I motioned
with my arms, directing them to move toward each other.

He slowly moved to the sofa, and sat down close to her. She
hesitantly put her head on his shoulder, and he put his arm

around her. They both cried, he with quiet sobs, but she freely and heavily. He patted her, and she clung to him. For me, it was a most moving sight. I remarked that he had given her comfort, and she had shown her need of him.

After a while, I asked him how he felt having her in his arms like this, and he said, "I never thought this would happen. I can't believe it. It's as if you've broken through a wall of ice."

The remainder of the interview was more relaxed, and they continued to hold each other. I said it was wonderful to see this, and a great start had been made today, that they really loved each other, and needed each other.

After some discussion we decided to set up a series of six to nine weekly interviews.

Until next week, I told them, I would like each of them to take on the job of pointing out when the other seemed to be operating on an assumption. The object was, I explained, to get some clear and open communication going. Instead of thinking for each other, as they had been doing, he could ask her what's wrong when she looked troubled, instead of assuming that he's at fault. I also suggested they they continue to show some affection to each other, at least at parting and when he returns home in the evening.

As they were leaving, both in a much lighter mood, I lightly tossed in, "Remember now, don't start any sex during the week; just stay with a little affection." With a twinkle in her eye, she responded, "What would happen if we did?" He was smiling. "Well then," I said, "you'd have to come to confession!"

Second Interview
They came in greeting me in a friendly and easy manner. Mrs. Donaldson said, "We asked each other, what are we going to talk about?" The whole week had been so very different. He too said they could hardly believe how much tension has been cleared away. I said I was delighted to hear this. I did have to tell them, however, that everything had not been cleared away so quickly, that there was plenty of work still to be done in repairing a relationship that had been as badly broken down as theirs, and for so long.

Margin notes:

The contract now can be set up at the first session.

Task assignment.

Workers should keep in mind that a light touch, and a little humor, where appropriate, can be very useful and indicates that life is not all grim and earnest, even if we do have problems.

Worker should respond with encouragement, but not get carried away by the clients' report of dramatic improvement at such an early stage.

It is essential that the worker retain control of the interview.

In this session I concentrated on their pattern of communication. I pointed out how Mrs. Donaldson tends to answer for him, and how he seems ready to let her do this. She took umbrage at this suggestion, that she interrupted and takes over for him. I pointed out, however, that she tends to do this with me too. She took this quietly, even nodded agreement. I asked him to note this, and to discuss his resentment at not being able to put his position forward before she cuts him off. He seemed to be reluctant to do so, and I remarked that he appeared to be afraid to upset her, and to put any brakes on her. I added I thought she really needed some of that, at which she again agreed, saying, "I know I do." She went on: "At least I'd know you were listening and taking notice of me."

This theme—of her taking over and keeping him out of the conversation, and resenting his lack of getting into it, and his part in keeping the pattern going—was worked on for the next two sessions or so as it recurred. Several times I encouraged him to stop her doing this, by directing him to say to her, "Just hold it." I said that as a successful businessman, he knew when a deal was not at risk, and his wife wasn't going to fire him as a husband. They smiled at this, and I went on to say that it would help them both for him to press his point with her. I explained to them that much of her anger was really a plea for help. When he walked away from her without responding, he left her feeling abandoned and neglected.

Technique of using an analogy which makes sense to the client; also useful to link an area of competence to one of incompetence. Indicate she has accepted limit-setting from me, although he has been reluctant to do this.

In subsequent sessions it was interesting to note how Mr. Donaldson's attitude changed. From being detached and hardly taking part in the interview, he began to speak up a good deal, and continued to sit close to his wife.

Fourth Interview

Mrs. Donaldson brought out how she hated the apartment they now lived in. She said he had sold their house and had not even discussed it with her. He had selected the apartment they now live in, and had even signed the lease without telling her. I turned to him, and said in a shocked voice, "You did that? I just can't believe it." I asked them to discuss it now. She said to him, "I didn't care, and I didn't want to tell you, but I really hated the apartment, and I hate it now. I'll never like it. Why did you do it?"

Inducing direct communication between the couple.

He said, "I had several good reasons. First of all, I sold the house to get away from the garage, and thoughts of Bill. I also thought you'd make new friends here, and get out more when you met people in the elevator, or something like that." She said softly, "You mean you thought it would help our marriage?" She put an affectionate hand on his arm. He said, "Yes. Also, it was a big help financially. I was able to make a good investment with the money." In a few more years, he explained, he would have a nice nest egg. He was hoping they would then go back to the country town from where they had come, and be happy there. She responded warmly, "That would be wonderful."

She went on to say that she had no idea he had such feelings about the garage after all this time. She said their present rooms were so small, after the house, and she was nowhere near settled. He said he would like to help her with shelves and closets, and he hoped that she would get to like it when they were more settled. His consulting hours now are very flexible and he can get to it soon.

At the fifth session, she spoke enthusiastically of buying two new dresses and that at long last he has bought a new suit. "Oh, that dreadful green one you bought three years ago—it was ghastly. It make you look sallow and old." He cut in, "Why did you drag that up?" I gave him the victory sign, indicating my approval, but she put up a struggle here, saying, "Can't I even make a comment?" and asked me, resentfully, "Must I watch every word?" I said, "Of course not. One can't live like that!" I continued, however, to say that Mr. Donaldson had a right to resent these old criticisms, and to say so. Actually, in doing this he was helping her as well as himself.

Then she said, "I know I still get all wound up too quickly," but he said supportively, "You really are so much better." To this I said, "True, but all the more reason for you not to back off, which is what you've been doing. If something annoys you, come out with it."

Sixth Interview

In the next session, he began by saying he really got fed up with her this week. He thought they had "reverted." She thought so

---

Note how their manner of communication has changed for the better.

His new self-assertion must be reinforced.

Important to disrupt over-support from one just when the other is ready to face his or her contribution to their difficulties.

A backward step is to be expected before the new

interactional pattern gets going.

too. I asked them for an example. They were watching a television program. She had said to him, "I want to talk to you—about me." Although he had said okay, she explained, he had soon left the room. The show finished, and another one came on. She began to get heated up, angry with him for not coming back to talk to her. She added, "It was nearly an hour." She was so upset she didn't speak to him until the next night.

She had wanted to talk to him about taking on a part-time job again, and to discuss teacher counseling courses. No, she had not told him at the time what she wanted to talk about. When he walked off like that she felt slighted and hurt. He said, "I was just writing a few letters, and thought you'd come out when the show ended." She interjected pleasantly, "Anyhow, Ron got us back on an even keel. He came home the next night, cheerful and friendly, and kissed me affectionately, which he's been doing since we've been coming here."

Worker acknowledges the positive change, but restates the need for further work on this pattern.

I remarked that this change was to the good, but they hadn't actually dealt with the upset, just letting it go. "In a way," I said, "it seemed both of you were doing what you used to do—one feeling ignored and not listened to, the other just walking off to avoid unpleasantness."

Counselor gives them the opportunity to rehearse a similar situation.

I asked them how they would handle something like this if it happened again. He said, "I really could have told you, 'Let's talk now, turn off the T.V., or if you want the T.V. on, call me when it's over.'" She said, "That would have helped. I see now I overreacted. I could have come out of the room, and said, 'Can we talk now, Ron?'"

Establishing mutual responsibility for the ongoing work; unfinished business identified.

I said it didn't matter which of them broke in before tension built up between them. Each had the responsibility to do this, to break up this outworn pattern when assumptions and misunderstandings had taken over. I said this was something for them to work on in the future as they had done just now. I indicated there would be plenty of steps backwards and forwards, but they would never reach the same "low" they had got to before coming here. At this Mrs. Donaldson put in an enthusiastic "No way," to which Mr. Donaldson heartily agreed.

Such final comments are often highly significant, sometimes known as "Doorknob Therapy," if the interview is then reopened.

As they were leaving, with an air of having achieved something special, she remarked: "You'll be pleased to know we've had sex lately, and very good too!" I smiled, and said enthusiastically, "That's great!"

With the relationship improved, sex can be dealt with in a more relaxed way. The worker is aware that this has been a satisfactory area in the marriage, and to deal with it at this point is a sort of frosting on the cake.

Seventh Interview

During the next session, I suggested we talk further about sex, as I was so pleased to learn last week they were again enjoying this part of their marriage.

They then told me they had both been virgins when they had married and how they had gradually learned together how to arouse her, and she usually reached orgasm. I said they deserved credit for their youthful idealism and their success in learning how to enjoy physical intimacy.

He said: "We never discussed sex in detail, although we expressed our pleasure affectionately when it was over."

I asked them whether or not Mrs. Donaldson ever took the initiative. "No," he replied, "I always do this—I just take it for granted." Did Mr. Donaldson sometimes wish his wife would approach him? Yes, he would have liked this. Mrs. Donaldson now said she didn't know he felt that way. I remained quiet, and they got into a discussion in which Mr. Donaldson was quite active, speaking to her directly, asking questions. It came out again that he often felt it would be nice if she took the lead sometimes and after a pause added, perhaps even to fondle him occasionally, though he had never raised this. She responded softly, "It's silly, Ron, but I guess I'm still a bit shy." Here I commented supportively that this was understandable.

I went on to suggest they might like to bring some novelty into their present sex life. I suggested some pleasuring exercises they could experiment with, each one taking a turn leisurely to receive and then give the other sensuous pleasure. They agreed it would be fun to try out something like this, wihout having intercourse as a goal.

During our talk he asked about sex as one gets older, "Although I don't feel I'll soon be 63." Here she commented how pleased this made her feel, "I would never have expected you to talk this way, especially with an outside person present." I told them sex can be a source of mutual pleasure throughout their lives, although frequency may be reduced and arousal may take longer. The quality, however, endures.

The rest of this interview dealt with a forthcoming reunion of both daughters, with husbands and children, for a weekend visit. They told me how they looked forward to this with pleasure, rather than with the tension this would have caused in the past. I said this was an encouraging sign of the progress they had made.

Eighth Interview

In the eighth session it came out that they had planned an out-of-town weekend and that they were more relaxed with sex. She approaches him sometimes, which in the past she did not do. He said, "It's sure a lot better in bed these days, or rather, nights." She giggled. Mrs. Donaldson reported that she is going out a good deal more, and has lined up a part-time teaching job. Their apartment is taking shape; they have had friends in two or three times. Their friends had commented on the change in them, and so have their daughters. "Due to you, Lenore," he said. She said, "Yes, I feel better. In fact, we're like two different people." I said that they were probably more like their old selves and added that *they* had done good work, but then they did have some good qualities and strengths on which to build. Without these, I couldn't have helped.

It was at the final session that she raised her old drinking problem, which had begun after Bill's death, saying that Ron also used to drink too much. She wondered whether this had affected their sex life over the past years. She volunteered she had been to AA for quite a period, and that this had helped her during the time she stayed home so much. He acknowledged that in the past he would often drink at bedtime, just to get to sleep. They both agreed that the drinking problem was well in hand now; in fact, they still enjoy two drinks before dinner, "and that's it!"

We discussed how a little alcohol can be a stimulant sexually, but that too much just makes one ineffective. Sex is a lot better, but she brought out that she doesn't always feel like it when he does, and there are times when she doesn't have an orgasm. But she always enjoys having him make love to her. I said that was natural and, in fact, I added, "What's wrong if he sometimes has a 'quickie' if she doesn't feel sexy, as long as she is well lubricated?" She found this somewhat hilarious, and he grinned broadly. They both seemed to enjoy the notion that she could then wake him up later for her "party," if she felt like it.

As we stood up at the close of the last session, I told them I would be available for a review session, if they thought this was

> Counselor should freely acknowledge that the credit rightfully goes to them.

indicated. In any case, I would call them in two months to see how they were doing. After that, I would be away for a couple of months, part holiday, part work as I wanted to complete a book I've been working on.

"Oh," said Mrs. Donaldson, with interest. "Will we be in it?" I said no, I hadn't thought of this; as they had suffered so greatly from the death of their son, I thought it might be too much for them to have it written up. "On the contrary," she said, "I would be very proud." He added, "If it would help others in any way, we would indeed be proud." She went on, "You'll be pleased to know that in unpacking books the other day, I came across Bill's 'Baby Book,' and I was able to look through it without crying."

He took her arm, and just before leaving, he put in, "Just one thing, Mrs. Freeman—if you do write us up, please give me a full head of hair!"

Follow-Up Contact, two months later
When I telephoned, Mr. Donaldson got on the extension. Both said things were going very well between them. They had "reverted" a few times but nothing that serious. Both daughters have made visits recently and the grandchildren were a treat too. Mrs. Donaldson said she was glad to be working again. If they feel the need, they will call me.

Mr. Donaldson asked about my book, and if they would be in it. I said I had thought about using their situation, but wondered whether they had changed their minds. No, in fact they had written up some notes together about what they had gained from counseling, in case this would be helpful to me. I thanked them and assured them their identity would not be disclosed, although they insisted that they didn't mind.

I explained to them how their situation might be used, as "The Long-Term Case that Turned Short." Both expressed enthusiasm at this idea.

The following are a few extracts from the notes sent me a week later, over both their signatures:

> "listening, opposed to just 'hearing' one another."
> "when one partner goes off track, the other should step in right then and say 'Hold it' and settle."

"the need to accept what is past, don't go back, build on the good things of which we have so many."

"we started to regain our great joy in physically loving one another, step by step."

"don't expect miracles—it takes time to rebuild. We may 're-vert' but don't panic."

CLOSING COMMENTS

This couple had left family and lifelong friends to move as strangers to a new city. This created added stress for them during the child leaving phase. They had managed, however, to come through the transitional crisis of this phase, coping adequately with the two daughters' leaving to get married and releasing their youngest, a son, to live on his own.

Devastated for several years by the tragedy of Bill's death (Bowen, 1976; Paul, 1967), at the stage in life where there is need for increasing closeness, they had turned away from each other in confusion and anger. Before the first session ended, the counselor moved in to cut through their escalating misery, using support, absolution from guilt, learning, and insight, to which firm and direct guidance was added.

This was possible as a rapid assessment indicated good ego strength in each of them, with intelligence, past achievements, and effective patterns of coping. In addition, the former marital relationship appeared to have had many assets. It was almost as though a dying marriage needed mouth-to-mouth resuscitation.

In subsequent interviews the worker was able to move ahead to focus on improving their pattern of communication, which had become distorted in recent years. This case also points up the serious consequences that ensue when unresolved grief and mourning have not been dealt with, and when the help urgently needed during the crisis period is not forthcoming. One wonders about the medical doctor, kind and comforting though he was, when he first learned of the tragedy. Was he aware that the couple should be referred for more specialized care than he has either the time or likely the training to provide? Medical doctors are in a key position to effect such referrals, which in this case could have averted several years of their emotional distress, possibly leading to separation.

Giving the Donaldsons permission to develop and enjoy more sexual satisfaction was an important feature of their treatment. Unlike the Donaldsons, for the Browns sex per se was not a real problem, and for them work in this area was neither indicated nor appropriate. This raises the necessity for the counselor to be sensitive to where older couples stand regarding their sexuality, "so that we can honestly appreciate their individual needs in this area, and leave them to their privacy or help them with their sexuality" (Schlesinger, 1977, p. 69).

Mrs. Donaldson, like Mrs. Brown, was encouraged to broaden her horizons and to find individual outside interests. This reduced the excessive expectations to which troubled partners are subject at the child-leaving phase. The brief therapy also took into account their plans for eventual retirement, which is implicitly linked to the inevitable conclusion of the family life cycle when time intervenes finally to separate the marital pair.

PART TWO
Further Considerations

6

The Use of the Telephone in Acute Marital Crisis *

The traditional one-to-one interview in marital treatment has been utilized less and less in recent years. It is of course generally recognized that in the case of separated or divorced couples and unmarried people, the joint interview may be impractical or not possible.

Apart from these categories, the one-to-one interview is still occasionally a necessity even when conjoint marital counseling is under way. We see this, for example, in the single interview with Mrs. Victor (Chapter 2) and again in the single interviews with the adolescent boy in the Green case (Chapter 7, below).

The joint interview, as it quickly highlights the interactional pattern, has rightly come to be favored by most therapists. At the same time, the one-to-one interview, whether face to face or ear to ear, has certain advantages. The worker can empathize more fully with the client and can confront the client less threateningly with his or her contribution to the problem. The technique of using the telephone as a professional adaptation of the face-to-face interview sometimes provides an invaluable opportunity to get the helping process under way.

*Some of the material in this section is drawn from an article by the author published in *Intervention*, Summer 1972, no. 38, the Bulletin of The Corporation of Professional Social Workers, Quebec.

It is one hundred years since the telephone was invented. This extension of the human ear has revolutionized communication between people. While the telephone is not yet able, for practical purposes, to provide the intimacy of visual contact, it does provide immediate verbal contact, which is so vital at points of crisis.

There is a growing development in urban and rural centers to provide telephone service and valuable referral information to people in acute distress. These programs are usually manned by volunteers with some brief training from professional counselors.

For the most part, professionals tend to confine the first telephone call to arranging a formal office appointment. It seems to me, however, that the potential for use of the telephone in marital crisis is not sufficiently recognized. In fact, a telephone interview, regardless of its efficacy, is at present not administratively equated with an office interview. Yet, as noted earlier, the telephone call for an appointment in a case of marital disturbance may be an urgent cry for help. The initial telephone contact may be the very means of engaging the client and facilitating the helping process.

Social workers are familiar with the woman who telephones for an individual appointment to discuss a marital problem (it is usually the woman who initiates the request for help). She may indicate that her husband does not know she is calling, as ''he would be much against the plan to see a social worker.'' Sometimes workers go along with such a request, but this may well be colluding with the core problem in the marriage—that is, the woman's difficulty in sharing her concerns with her husband.

She may wish to win the worker's sympathy or to gain an ally against her husband; she may wish to punish the husband and use the worker as a threat to bring him to heel, or she may have a genuine fear of his negative reaction. A brief interview on the telephone of, say, fifteen or twenty minutes may be productive in bringing the couple together into the beginning phase of treatment.

The woman's fear of being criticized, her feelings of hurt and anger, can be supportively recognized and empathetically related to on the telephone. The worker's tone of voice is as important as the words. Relieved and encouraged by the worker's understanding and interest, the woman then usually agrees to tell her husband that she approached the worker for help.

The worker should then explore the manner in which the woman will explain this to him, expecting some ambivalence. How she deals with this first task of involving her husband is often very revealing. For instance, she may say something like, ''I have spoken to a marriage counselor who wants to see you too. You know how fed up I am, and I'm hoping this will get you to straighten out.''

The worker then asks, "Do you really think this will help?" In response to this mild confrontation, the woman has to concede that it will not. The worker then offers her an alternative: "If your husband is to come here and help with your troubles, you will need to say something like this: 'I spoke to a counselor. She wants to see us both at least once and says there are two sides to every story. Your side should be heard too, and you should know what is being said about you.' " This direct guidance is offered to enlist the positive side of her ambivalence. I supportively explain that this will not be easy for her, knowing how she feels. A little rehearsal may even be necessary to help the woman over the hurdle of her negative or ineffective approach. In my experience, such preparation rarely fails to bring in the partner and is a good investment of the worker's time.

There is a different order of situations when the marital crisis is so acute that it is essential to assess the level of anxiety and how hazardous the situation may be then and there, on the telephone.

The following three "interviews" illustrate how more comprehensive intervention with one partner on the telephone is sometimes a necessity. The advantage this provides, compared with a deferred conjoint office interview, will be apparent.

THE ALCOHOLIC AND THE LONG-SUFFERING PARTNER

An interactional pattern frequently found in marriages with alcoholism in one partner.

Facing an acute marital crisis, Mrs. B. needs and seeks immediate help.

Mrs. Butler telephoned the worker in an excited state. Could she see someone that evening about her marital problem? As this was not possible, the worker explored the current situation with her on the telephone. It emerged that her husband had come home late two nights before, very drunk, had resented her questioning, and had beaten her up. The two sleeping children, ages five and seven, woke up crying and frightened. When he fell asleep, she managed to bundle them up and take them to the home of her uncle, who had always been kind and understanding. She was in fact telephoning from her uncle's house. Earlier in the day her husband had contacted her and offered to see a psychiatrist if only she would return home. In fact, he had already made an appointment to see a psychiatrist the following morning at nine o'clock, and had told her she was expected to attend as well.

Here Mrs. Butler became quite agitated, and wanted to know what to do. Since his call, she had been turning it over for hours, trying to figure it out. If her husband would really undertake treatment, should she not agree to go home and encourage this? When I asked what she felt like doing, she said she would like to stay away from him as long as possible. On the other hand, she did not want to discourage his efforts to do something constructive.

Sufficient clarification of the problem to relate to the crisis situation.

I asked whether he had been to a psychiatrist before. Yes, on and off over the years, but it had never stuck, and he had never stayed in treatment more than a few weeks. His drinking pattern had persisted over the nine years of their marriage. I asked whether she had ever before picked up like this and left him.

The ambivalence of the wife of the alcoholic, her repetitive pattern, the need to forgive, to "rescue," or to collude with his weak motivation to take help are sufficiently well known for the worker to recognize the current crisis as potentially an important turning point for Mrs. B. and for the family. It is only by being faced with serious consequences, such as loss of family, loss of job, or of health that the alcoholic may agree to take help.

No, this was the first time, and she had tried everything else. Her great fear, and particularly the repeated exposure of her children to his behavior, were more than she could stand. She felt sorry for her husband but wondered whether she had the strength to carry on with him.

Worker faces client with her reality, and points out the possible hope in the step she has taken.

The worker pointed out to Mrs. Butler that the pattern of her husband's drinking had not changed over the years, nor apparently had her previous methods of coping been effective in sustaining him in treatment. The worker restated the conflict Mrs. Butler had expressed, pointing out both her wish to leave her husband and her desire to stay with him. There were a few moments of silence, and then she softly agreed that this was so.

The worker further discussed Mrs. Butler's feelings of loyalty, mixed with her anxiety for her children and the realistic

It is important to reinforce the new method of responding. The worker then helps to assuage her guilt, at the same time still permitting her to "rescue" her husband, by letting him face the consequences of his behavior.

fear for herself, and then told Mrs. Butler quite emphatically that she had just now taken an important step, a new and courageous step, to deal with an old problem. This could not only be to her advantage and that of her children, but could possibly prove helpful to her husband as well.

As she is vague and fearful, worker must be clear and firm, confronting her with fact that her indecision is a decision.

I said it was difficult for her to avoid repeating the pattern of the past nine years. I added, however, that there was no doubt in my mind that if she went to the interview the following morning without having made up her mind as to whether to go home to her husband or to separate from him, *she had in fact made the decision.*

Mrs. Butler was upset by this, and said she could not follow me. I repeated: "If you go with your husband to the interview with the psychiatrist tomorrow without your mind being definitely made up as to the stand you intend to take, your husband is going to ask you to come back. The chances are that the psychiatrist will either encourage you to take him back or, more likely, will take no stand at all and leave you to face your husband's pathetic pleas on your own." She said she was afraid of that. I added that if she returned to her husband at this point, the chance of a repeat performance in their marriage and family life was strong indeed, since she had said this had gone on, over and over, in the past. Here too, she sadly agreed.

I said that if she decided to take her husband back, she would have to make the best of her unhappy situation. Alternatively, she could make a firm decision to proceed with the separation until he had demonstrated that his drinking pattern had in fact consistently changed. This was her choice. I added that it often helped men like her husband to take hold of their problem when they knew clearly and firmly just what was at stake.

She responded slowly that she didn't realize that leaving him might be helpful to him, and would not just hurt him when he was down. She would certainly try to go to the psychiatrist's office with that decision, and she hoped she would be able to do so. I said I knew it would not be easy for her to do this, and asked her to telephone me the next morning to let me know what happened.

This method of expressing ongoing interest is important and security giving. It also leaves the door open for further help.

Actively "tipping the scales" at the crossroads in such a way that the worker reinforces a new coping method, which often arises at the peak of crisis, may be frowned upon as being "too directive." It was apparent, however, that Mrs. B. was really looking for support and permission to carry out a plan she had not had the fortitude to undertake before.

She did call the following morning, and said she had talked things over with her uncle. He reminded her that he had often encouraged her over the years to get out of this situation. His attitude and my talk decided her. The psychiatrist readily accepted her decision to proceed with a legal separation, and her husband had then been forced to deal with a new reality.

I then offered an appointment to Mrs. Butler. In this face-to-face meeting, I helped her confront the implications of her decision. She accepted a referral for ongoing service to the family agency, where, I explained, she would have legal and psychiatric consultation available, should the worker there consider this indicated.

A "PARENT-CHILD" MARRIAGE

The Referral

Implications of the referral are important. Here I should have requested more information about Mr. Davis's emotional state. Workers are often hesitant to question the referral source, particularly the psychiatrist. The referral may not be appropriate for the client and this should be considered.

In this highly sensitive situation, separate interviews were indicated.

A useful technique to see who takes the lead.

Mr. and Mrs. Davis were referred to the center by a psychiatrist, who reported that Mr. Davis, age thirty-nine, had telephoned when he learned that his wife, age twenty-four, was carrying on an extramarital affair. His first reaction had been that she must be completely out of her mind to behave in this way, and he had forced her to see the psychiatrist. The psychiatrist had told him she was not motivated for therapy, nor was she "crazy," and he had suggested marriage counseling.

I could see at the first joint interview that Mr. Davis was terribly upset by the referral. I decided to confine the conjoint interview to explaining briefly the service and our short-term method of working, and then to see each partner separately. When I asked who would like to see me first, Mrs. Davis quickly suggested that her husband should go ahead, as she had already had an interview with the psychiatrist.

Mr. Davis expressed his anxiety to me. If his wife was not "crazy," then he certainly was inadequate as a husband. He indicated that he desperately wanted to keep his wife, but at the same time he found it hard to insist that she give up her boy-

His insecurity and fragility were apparent.

friend. Actually, he was afraid that putting his foot down would cause her to leave.

When I saw Mrs. Davis, she said she was fond of her husband, as he was generous and tolerant, but she found him dull and boring. As she put it, "two years of marriage seemed like ten." It came out that she still resented her strict upbringing.

Was she seeking a permissive parent in her husband?

Her father, in particular, had held a tight rein; when she was in her teens they fought constantly. Every date caused a scene. Her admiration for and attachment to her boyfriend were apparent. She gave me permission to share her background problems with her husband.

The couple were each seen separately for another session, Mrs. Davis to express her feelings about her boyfriend and to clarify the meaning her marriage held for her. She had been involved with the other man for nearly a year. They shared an interest in the theatre, and he was sexually attractive to her. She was so deeply involved emotionally with the other man that it was hard to engage her in any serious consideration about her marriage. It became apparent that she would give up her marriage rather than break up this extramarital affair. She was convinced, however, that her husband would tolerate the affair.

In his session, Mr. Davis expressed his apprehension and fears of being abandoned by his wife and of being left alone. It emerged that seven years previously he had been hospitalized with a psychotic breakdown. He had subsequently received supportive psychotherapy for a number of years.

He was a brilliant man, intellectually highly endowed, emotionally very constricted, and tightly defended. The present blow to his ego was drastic. Gentle and soft-spoken, he needed a great deal of support and recognition for the success he had achieved in his field (radio and advertising). He found it helpful to understand from me that his wife's resentment and her unsuccessful rebellion against her father were now being directed

Worker attempts to strengthen his ego—that is, to emphasize that it's not *his* inadequacy.

against him. It helped his self-respect to see that her unrealistic expectations of him, indeed of *any* husband, would have been brought into any marriage from her own unhappy adolescence.

The Telephone Interview

On a Saturday night, two days after my last interview with them, I received a telephone call from Mrs. Davis. Her voice

It seemed to me that if she

was quaking. She frantically told me that her husband had

had somehow managed to get to the telephone and to the bed, at least her back was not broken. If at this point I were to give her the names of any doctors, I would reinforce an already explosive situation when her husband returned. Obviously for him to behave in this manner indicated that his defenses had broken down.

Clients at times tend to defend such provocative disclosures as "honesty." Laying it all out on the table, however, may do nothing but hurt the partner. It should be pointed out to such clients that there are times when honesty is destructive and should be used with discretion. For instance, past love affairs should be shared sensitively, if at all, by the man or woman.

Direct guidance was essential, with rehearsal to avoid possible violence.

Calling in a doctor, unless really necessary, would agitate Mr. Davis further. If it were *my* recommendation, it would impair my ability

flown into a terrible rage, had thrown her across the room, and had then stormed out of the house. She felt that he must have done some serious damage to her back and asked me to give her the name of a doctor.

Instead I asked her where she was. She said she had managed to get to the phone, which was by the side of her bed, and called a neighbor, who had been with her for the past fifteen minutes.

I told her I was sorry she was in so much pain and asked her what had happened to bring all this about.

She told me that in pleading with her husband for a divorce, she had been discussing her feelings for her boyfriend, and acknowledged going into detail about his physical attractiveness, the "chemical pull" she felt toward him, and his lovemaking abilities. I pointed out that she had obviously provoked and enraged her husband, and that this behavior was very unlike him.

To this she agreed, and said she was terrified of what might happen when he came back. She had urged her neighbor to stay with her for the rest of the evening.

I emphasized that the situation was dangerous, and told her firmly that if her husband should return, it was important to tell him immediately that she had spoken with me and that I had stressed her own excessively provocative behavior and told her *she* had in fact precipitated this outburst of anger, which was not typical of him. I thought this was so important that I even asked her to repeat to me, twice, exactly what she would say to him. I made it clear that unless she accepted responsibility for what had happened, I was frightened for her, as he might react in a very destructive way.

We then discussed the issue of the doctor. I pointed out that she probably knew a doctor. Mrs. Davis said somewhat sheepishly that she could call a doctor she had seen a year ago and also that her neighbor knew a doctor. She then said she would rest for half an hour, perhaps with a heating pad, and I encouraged her to call the doctor if the pain persisted or became worse. I also told her to tell her husband I was concerned about this turn of events and wanted to see them both the following morning. Would she please tell him when he came in that I expected them both at ten A.M. tomorrow at my home, as the office is closed on Sunday? To this she agreed, with obvious relief.

They both duly appeared the following morning. I had a brief joint interview, primarily to put a firm brake on any possible future violence, and then saw them separately. Mr. Davis agreed to a temporary separation at this point, as a cooling-off period.

To summarize the several supportive sessions which followed with Mr. Davis, he decided to break the marriage. He maintained his work role and sense of adequacy as a person. He himself told me that the telephone "interview" with his wife was crucial in averting a possible disaster. When he walked out that night he was blind with rage, and had she continued in the same vein when he returned, he might have had no control.

THE STRAYING SPOUSE AND THE VIRTUOUS CONSORT

Mrs. Winters telephoned me one afternoon to say that she wanted some advice, but was not sure whether to seek it from a marriage counselor or from her lawyer. Her medical doctor, whom she had known for many years, had told her to call me. A little exploration revealed that her husband had gone off to Austria with his secretary for a three-week holiday. Before he left, she had agreed to give him a divorce and her lawyer had told her this could be arranged.

She had just received a cable, however, in which he said he was coming back by plane the next evening and hoped very much that she would meet him. She added she had also received a letter a few days ago in which he expressed regret for his behavior. She read part of the letter to me on the phone. It was obvious that he wanted to rethink the divorce and possibly retain his marriage, if his wife would permit it.

Facing her with the alternatives.

As I was unable to meet her the following day, I asked Mrs. Winters at this point whether she really wanted to keep her husband or had decided she was ready to use the evidence she had for a divorce, in which case the lawyer was definitely indicated. She responded that actually she wanted to keep her husband, but that she felt discarded and terribly hurt. I said she also sounded very angry, and understandably so. She said she was angry with both of them, but particularly the woman. I said that with so much bitterness and anger, she probably felt like punishing her husband. "He certainly deserves it," she said.

I bring out her angry feelings, apart from her helpless ones.

Worker then offers her a clear choice.

I then pointed out to her that if she wanted to keep her husband and her marriage, she would have to make a choice—either to cling to her hurt and her legal position, or to fight for her right to hold her husband if she could. She responded softly that she wanted her husband. It sounded, I said, as though she was not ready to step aside and hand him over to the other woman. I asked her pointedly what this woman had that she didn't have. She responded, "She's a flashy dresser, a dyed blonde, selfish."

Support is now followed by confrontation.

Mrs. Winters went on to emphasize that she had always been careful about spending her husband's hard-earned money and continued self-righteously that she hadn't bought a new dress in years, and *she* didn't run up bills in beauty parlors. After a pause, I said, "I wonder—perhaps you should have done these things." There was a long silence.

Further support, then use of generalization to suggest she has played a part in this situation.

I explained that it seemed to me that Mr. Winters could well afford clothes and hairstyling for her and that they would be good for her morale. "It's true," she replied slowly, "I don't think enough of myself." I went on to indicate that sometimes the "injured party" contributes to the situation which may culminate in the kind of behavior her husband had displayed. Mrs. Winters muttered again that she had neglected herself too much.

Direct advice is given and three "easy" tasks assigned. These may seem superficial but could symbolically represent a beginning breakthrough in her poor self-image.

She asked me what she could do now. Here I gave her some direct advice; in fact, I gave her three specific recommendations or tasks. First, I suggested, she should buy herself a new dress. Then I advised her to go to the hairdresser and splurge. Third, I suggested that she meet her husband and tell him she wanted to continue the marriage, and that she hoped he would come with her to a marriage counselor, to improve their relationship. She agreed, and I asked her to phone me the following day to let me know what happened.

Note that some behavior
change occurs.

She did call, and in a rather coy way told me that she had followed only two of my recommendations. She couldn't quite bring herself to buy a new dress, but she found something she had saved in her wardrobe and had not used except on rare occasions. She wore that, and did have her hair done.

She didn't feel so angry with her husband when she met him. He complimented her, saying he had not seen her looking so lovely in years. At this she was very surprised and pleased, and they went together for coffee at the airport. He agreed to undertake marriage counseling with her.

I told her she had done well and deserved credit for her efforts. She asked for an appointment, which was arranged with a colleague, as I was leaving on holiday shortly. I learned when I returned that they were coming regularly and were doing well.

CLOSING COMMENTS

In all three of these telephone interviews, two operational principles, drawn from crisis theory, were implemented: quick intervention and the setting of tasks. It will be noted, as in the previous cases presented, that the tasks were not only relevant to the crisis situation but were manageable, so that the client could meet with some positive results. As already indicated, it is less important that these tasks be carried out specifically than that the client's ego strength be mobilized, to facilitate clearer thinking and action.

For those colleagues who may still consider guidance and directiveness suspect, it should be noted that the client can disagree and can literally "get off the hook" on the telephone. The client can hang up and turn off more easily than can be done in a face-to-face interview. Further, it is highly unlikely that a telephone plan which is not acceptable will be carried out, nor will one which is inconsistent with the client's needs. Action and direction are essential in an acute crisis. We don't help people with a soft-headed message in an emergency. This has been emphasized by crisis theorists. To quote Florence Hollis (1964, p. 91), "The very anxious client is sometimes in need of direction, and it may be appropriate for the worker to provide this in the initial contact or throughout a period of crisis."

By drawing on basic social work treatment principles (Hollis, 1964), it was possible in these telephone interviews to isolate the current problem, to relate it to the feelings associated with the crisis, to restate the conflict, and to clarify some alternative outcomes. The client was given support but was also confronted with his or her contribution to the problem. The worker then actively helped the client to reach a decision, reinforcing adaptive responses and prescribing specific tasks so as to facilitate carrying out the decisions more effectively. A follow-up contact from the client was encouraged, so that further help could be offered.

It would seem that experimentation and follow-up studies are indicated to validate much freer use of this mode of intervention by professionals in their encounters with acute marital crisis.

7

Divorce, Remarriage, and Short-Term Counseling

Better to light one candle than to curse the darkness

Marriage, the basic institution of our society, is in a state of upheaval, rocked by many changes in the aftermath of two world wars. When women moved into the assembly line during World War I, the seeds of drastic change in the roles of men and women had taken root. They were sent back to the kitchen after the war but have come out periodically over the years, and today the women's movement has gathered great strength. Women now have options and rights which were unknown to their grandmothers.

The impact of numerous technological and scientific developments has made inroads into the traditional family. The massive mobility of modern life has removed those family supports that were formerly provided by the smaller, more closely knit and more stable community. Apart from nearby relatives and friends, there was support even from the corner grocer, who asked how Johnny's birthday party went, and from the local doctor, who had brought "Mom" herself into the world. Many interacting economic, social, and psychological factors have also contributed to the great increase in marital breakdown and divorce.

In the United States today, divorce takes place half as frequently as does marriage; that is, in 1978 there were over two million marriages and over one million divorces.*

When a couple have decided on divorce and each side is in contact with a lawyer, they are not seen by the short-term marriage counselor unless referral has been made as a legal requirement (Barrier & Freeman, 1969).

When troubled couples come, with all their distress and doubts, for marriage counseling service, one partner, if not both, has at least a faint hope that the marriage can be helped. But the fear and the threat of divorce are never remote, and the short-term marriage counselor must realistically face the possibility that divorce may and sometimes does ensue.

What are the attitudes and values the marriage counselor holds in regard to divorce? These may be crucial to the couple seeking help. Counselors will frequently say that they take a neutral position on divorce, or they will indicate that they do not have a bias. We've often heard, "It's entirely up to the couple."

For me this is an unreal position. Our attitudes and values do affect our performance. We do have values, and if we don't make them explicit, a negative value is implicit. So-called lack of bias carries an implicit message not only of acceptance but even of permissiveness, which may prematurely move the couple in the direction of divorce.

In a first session I freely acknowledge my bias to clients, that the goal will be to help them maintain their marriage if possible, particularly where children are involved or where the marriage has endured for many years. I may say, "You have invested twelve years of your lives and three children in this relationship. This investment should be salvaged if it is at all possible." I do add, "If, however, divorce is inevitable, you will at least feel better for having made a serious effort to work things out."

When a couple are involved with lawyers and the adversary roles are already under way, hurt and anger have probably mounted to a point where short-term marriage counseling is unlikely to be effective. If one partner has in fact made a firm decision to break the marriage, usually with a third-party commitment, the couple cannot be worked with. There are times, however, when one partner has had a preliminary contact with a lawyer but is ambivalent, and it may still be possible to reconstruct the marriage. Unfortunately, sometimes such couples get caught in the machinery of the law, and once the wheels start turning, it is often too late to halt the process.

Occasionally one partner appears in the first interview to be so disinter-

*According to data compiled by the National Center for Health Statistics. Quoted in the *Newsletter of the American Association for Marriage and Family Therapy*, July 1980, **11**, (4).

ested in the counseling that the worker may wonder whether such a decision has not already secretly been made. Cues are a lack of involvement in the interview or a lack of interest in the partner (she may say, "Let him go to other women for sex," or he may say to the counselor, "I'll come back if *you* think it will really help"). What is going on is simply a ploy with which to beat the partner, to be able to say, "We even tried marriage counseling, and it didn't work."

I carefully point out in such a situation that marriage counseling has *not* been tried. I make it plain that if a firm decision to break the marriage has been reached by one of the partners, this is an adult right and responsibility, and there is no need for permission from me to proceed.

Short-term counseling cannot restore a dead marriage, but it can and should offer a service to an ailing one. Although a legal contact has been initiated, there may be something to work on if even a vague doubt exists. Actually, when patience has been strained and tensions are high, the offer of time-limited service has strong appeal as opposed to open-ended counseling.

On this basis, the counselor is usually able to enlist the reluctant partner to a contract for at least three interviews. With the prospect of relief in a short period of time, the effort may seem worthwhile, whatever the outcome. The more motivated partner is encouraged, and the notion of brief service is welcomed by both.

We saw this happening in the Martin case, with the Fishers, and again with the Browns—the counselor actively enlisting them, tipping the scale toward retaining the marriage. In the process of searching for what's right as well as bringing out their notion of what's wrong with each of them and with their marriage, enabling each to see his and her contribution to their upset state, tensions were reduced. Also, when the impact of pressures outside the home as well as inside is better understood, they are able to work at, to halt, and to reverse to some extent their spiraling negative interaction. We saw that marital conflict can actually provide an opportunity for individual and mutual growth.

Knowing the many pressures and stresses the couple will face as a broken family and the gravity of the issues involved in divorce, the responsible marriage counselor is justified, even required, to be biased in the direction of restoring and rebuilding the family.

Now let us turn to the exceptions, for it must be made clear that this bias does not imply that all couples must stay glued together indefinitely. In a destructive relationship divorce may well be the best solution. As we also know, there are couples who need lengthy and individual help to become separated from a damaging relationship.

Again, in families where misery and hate, with or without violence, permeate the home atmosphere, for couples to stay together "for the sake of the children" makes no sense at all. As Louise Despert has brought out in *Children of Divorce* (1962), divorce is not automatically destructive to children. On the contrary, the ending of a bad marriage may bring great relief to a child. Relaxation and warmth may replace the tensions of a chronically disturbed marriage.

Also, we saw in the case of the Victors, the counselor's position, far from holding the couple together, encouraged consideration of divorce if the marriage did not have the potential for a satisfying balance, and *before* children complicated the scene.

Today divorce is no longer regarded as unusual or shocking, although there may be curiosity as to "what happened." As Hunt pointed out back in 1966, divorce is regarded as "more normal" than never having been married at all. This statement sounds old-fashioned today, now that nonmarrieds have also become more accepted. This is indicative of the rapidly changing attitudes in our world.

The broadening of legal grounds for divorce reflects the new realities. Not only is divorce more socially acceptable but it has become legally easier. Also, many women today are no longer completely dependent on their husbands for financial support.

Still the nagging question arises—is divorce too readily resorted to as a solution for marital conflict? How many of those million couples in 1978 really *tried* marriage? Do couples throw in the towel too easily? Is this sufficiently challenged by the counselor?

Factors that have contributed to undermining the stability of the modern family are far too complex to be considered here. Still, as marriage counselors, we must be concerned with the stance we adopt. The counselor with specialized knowledge and expertise may sometimes be able at least to encourage the deferring of a drastic solution and to enlist the couple in the search for a better and more satisfying marriage.

From my experience, however, when the initial sessions show a static or deadlocked position, the couple are likely to be moving toward divorce. One of them may be privately determined to pursue this course. I tell such couples at the outset that I reserve the right to see them separately and confidentially. I now suggest this, adding, "I do not consider that our joint sessions are being helpful." I then ask, "Who would like to see me first?" Such responses as, "You go first—you have all the beefs," or "It makes no difference to me" are revealing.

In the subsequent individual interviews, of say twenty minutes' duration, it may emerge that one partner is afraid to share the decision to break the marriage. He or she is fearful that the spouse may show violence or may react with a "nervous breakdown." Sometimes a lawyer has already been contacted and a commitment to a third party is involved.

When the second partner is seen alone, it usually becomes clear that he or she knows the marriage is likely to fall apart but is reluctant, even unwilling to face this fact. The reaction of denial has been referred to as the first stage of divorce (Golan, 1978, p. 173).

When we resume the three-way session, I cannot share the "secret," but I point out they each realize that short-term marriage counseling has not been effective and that alternative plans for their marriage should be considered. They can continue as they are, or they can try separation, or consider divorce. I make it plain that if they decide on separation or divorce, further sessions are available to them to discuss the issues involved for them and for their children. Either partner may call the agency at a later date for an appointment or for referral to other resources.

A different situation arises where divorce is openly recognized in the assessment period as the inevitable solution. I then raise the issue of the children, pointing out that this part of their marriage will always be with them and that counseling, with the worker as mediator, apart from legal services, will help them to separate their marital hurt and anger from their parental function.

A series of conjoint interviews is offered, to help them deal with the emotional reactions and practical needs of the children in the period ahead. Some couples are able to use this service well. With the counselor's help, they may be able to negotiate such issues as custody, visitation rights, and even financial and property aspects in a civilized and nonadversarial manner.

Haynes outlines the social work skills which can be used in the role of divorce mediator, and adds, "Attorneys will continue to be responsible for drafting the final agreement and obtaining the court decree. However, they will be freed from dealing with the couple's emotional conflicts, for which they are not trained" (Haynes, 1978, p.8). The social worker, too, would be enlightened and helped by earlier and closer teamwork with the lawyer (Steinberg, 1980).

I try to convey to the couple that the children need their mutual love and help, so as not to feel that they are responsible for the break-up of the family. Divorcing parents are frequently unaware that children tend to blame themselves and are troubled by thoughts that some misdeed of theirs may have caused the divorce. There is often a persisting fantasy that the parents will come together again.

The risk that parents will downgrade each other to the children is also raised. Sometimes they are encouraged to use a family service or individual therapy to get them through the difficult and lengthy adjustment when the divorce becomes a reality.

In addition, I indicate that remarriage is a real possibility as the majority of divorced people do remarry, and that premarriage counseling with the new partner would help them to face and deal more effectively with the complexities of the second marriage.

As indicated, with the decision to dissolve the marriage, further conjoint interviews are sometimes no longer practical. There are times when it is necessary for the short-term marriage counselor to continue with one partner, and without a time limit. When a good relationship has been established and the client has a strong need for continued support, an outside referral may be perceived as another rejection. This is illustrated by the following case— Mr. and Mrs. Gray, a short-term case that became long.

MR. AND MRS. GRAY

Mr. Gray, age 30
Mrs. Gray, age 28

Children: Robert, age 5

Married 6 years

Some years back I began to work with Mr. and Mrs. Gray on a short-term basis. Mr. Gray was a young surgeon, highly intelligent, ambitious, and hard-working, with rigid ethical principles. It was he who originated the referral.

In the first interview he came across as well organized, exacting of himself as well as of others. His main concern was his wife's excessive absence from the home, particularly in the past year. He complained of her growing preoccupation with gambling and objected to her involvement with "the fast set." She bet on the horses, had lost a good deal of money, and recently took off for a weekend at Las Vegas. He complained about her behavior rather than about the money involved. He felt that their five-year-old son was being neglected, as well as the marriage.

Worker notes Mrs. Gray's lack of concern and weak motivation.

With this much difference in their outlooks, separate individual interviews should have been considered.

Mrs. Gray seemed pretty cool in her response to all this. She was a strikingly attractive redhead, slim and well groomed. She denied that their boy was being neglected. She said her husband worried too much about the youngster. She assured me she had excellent sitters, which her husband could well afford.

She indicated that her outside interests had increased only because he buried himself in his work. She was willing to go along with counseling, but couldn't quite see why it was all that necessary. In response to my question as to her motivation, she assured me she had no thought of breaking up the marriage; he, for his part, wanted only that things improve. However, both agreed to consider giving more time to each other—and to Robert. Two more assessment sessions were agreed on.

In the subsequent sessions, she agreed that he was giving more time to his family, and he felt encouraged that she was making an effort to be home more. It seemed that a better balance could be achieved. It was in the third session that I again raised questions about their sexual relationship. Earlier, each had indicated that this was not a concern.

It now came out that there was little sex between them. In exploring this further, Mrs. Gray blurted out that his constant criticism of her behavior had gradually turned her off. I found there was no open communication between them in this area of the marriage. Mr. Gray was particularly uncomfortable in this discussion, while Mrs. Gray seemed bland and casual. Both agreed it was desirable to work on this aspect of their marriage, and a further three sessions were arranged.

An acute crisis results.

Two days later, I had a frantic phone call from Mr. Gray. His wife had left town in the company of another man. He stammered so much that he could hardly bring out the words. I saw him that evening. He was so shattered by this abandonment and by her harsh demand for a divorce and custody of the child, that he could barely function.

To make a long story short, it turned out that I continued to work with him for a period of more than a year and a half. His stammer continued, and he developed an eye-blinking tic. It was as though the carpet had been pulled from under his feet. He was a proud, shy man, respected in his profession and in his community, and he expressed an intense fear of psychiatry.

He has by now formed a trusting relationship with

While I knew he needed psychiatric therapy, at this point he seemed too fragile, too vulnerable, for me to suggest a referral.

me; he needs help and direction urgently, and I have the responsibility to carry on with him at this point.

Worker's flexibility in "giving" was important during this period.

In such an unsettled situation, the early use of structure related to daily functioning is an important therapeutic principle, not always appreciated.

I felt that a further abandonment—by me—could be disastrous.

During the subsequent weeks of this crisis period, I saw him several times a week, giving help of a supportive nature.

I thought it equally important to establish a definite structure in his home life. Arrangements for a live-in housekeeper were worked out. I interviewed several and we agreed on a middle-aged widow, a good cook, who seemed gentle and understanding. We decided on a fixed dinner hour which he thought he could largely hold to. (Even "workouts" at the "Y" were allowed for.)

The matter of how best to meet his son's emotional needs at this time was raised. Mr. Gray said he could count on his mother, a devoted grandmother, to make frequent daytime visits. The father's importance as a nurturing figure was stressed, and a regular half-hour for Billy at bedtime was readily arranged.

As a "gentleman," he had thought that he should give his wife grounds for divorce, the thing that was done in his circle at the time. (This was prior to the reform of the divorce laws—a period during which adultery was the only ground for divorce.)

I encouraged a different stand and enabled him to see that he need not be "the guilty party." In fact, his wife had already given him grounds for divorce, and it was she who had wanted to break the marriage. If she filed for the divorce, she could possibly remove the child to another city. To lose contact with his little boy would be devastating to him and probably to the child as well.

It turned out, in the ensuing divorce proceedings, that he was actually granted custody of the boy, as Mrs. Gray did not return to defend the action.

It was a good year and a half before Mr. Gray could accept a referral to psychiatry.* His tic and stammer had long since

---

*Counselors infrequently make a referral for psychoanalytic treatment. This is an expensive and lengthy process. When the client has the financial means as well as the capacity and motivation for further development, however, this should be considered.

Ego-building procedures and the right to personal pleasure were emphasized.

gone; he had gained a beginning confidence in dating other women and, with my help, had shed some of his inhibited attitudes and rigidities. The child was doing well and, with help, Mr. Gray had planned so that order was established in his home. His weakened defenses had been strengthened and his fear of psychiatry worked through. I was then able to refer him to a psychoanalyst whose personality I felt would fit his particular needs.

After three years of analysis which, he has since told me, benefited him greatly, he married an attractive and mature young woman. They now have another child and all four enjoy a good family life.

CLOSING COMMENTS

My failure in this case to effect a short-term service was due to an inadequate assessment. Mrs. Gray was able to cover up an extramarital affair as well as her decision to leave the marriage. I had assessed the marriage as having potential when in fact it was already broken.

From the case of the Grays I learned that the short-term therapist must at times be adaptable enough to work with one partner on a long-term basis. This became necessary when it was apparent that the sudden desertion of his wife left Mr. Gray almost immobilized. Time was needed to help him through the divorce procedure and the difficult adjustment period which followed.

CONSIDERATION OF SOME DIVORCE ISSUES

There are major issues arising out of divorce which the short-term marriage counselor needs to be aware of and able to discuss in the day-to-day work with couples. Since divorce laws vary from state to state in the United States and enforcement of judgments varies from province to province in Canada, a knowledge of the client's legal position is necessary. For example, if one partner leaves the domicile, this may amount to legal desertion. It is helpful for the worker to be acquainted with suitable lawyers to whom clients can be referred.

Financially, two separate households will mean dividing the available income. A lower standard of living is to be expected. Generally women retain custody of the children, and the majority will therefore have to work outside the home to support the family. As is well known, judges are reluctant to put too much burden on the man, the main earner, as he may lose the incentive to improve his financial position or fail to continue paying the agreed-upon support. Welfare workers are well aware that of women granted alimony or child support, only a very small proportion continue to receive it regularly. The financial difficulties of the career woman with children should also be noted—the problem of working overtime or attending special meetings, the expense and difficulty involved in obtaining adequate babysitters, and so on (Hunt & Hunt, 1977).

Child-rearing responsibility rests primarily with the custodial parent. Discipline becomes a problem for the single parent, whether a man or a woman. Often, more demands are made by the children, who can no longer play off one parent against the other. Physical, emotional, educational, and other concerns create extra pressure on the single parent. There is growing recognition that fathers can be both nurturing and competent single parents (Schlesinger & Todres, 1976) though only a minority of those who sue are as yet granted custody of their children. The task of child rearing is equally difficult for the man alone, and social sympathy is still typically reserved for the woman.

The emotional impact of marriage breakdown is hard on all—the man, the woman, and the child. The initial response, particularly in the first year, is often one of shock and fear (Hunt & Hunt, 1977).

In their study of divorced people, the Hunts found that despite the hundreds of books and articles on divorce, the divorced persons themselves are unprepared for the impact of the changed role and status, from married to divorced. Loneliness, anger, depressed feelings, pervasive guilt toward their children, as well as feelings of resentment against the children for interfering with their freedom and happiness are usual responses.

How do the divorced man and woman deal with lowered self-image and loneliness? Social life and the dating game often create problems for both the divorced man and the divorced woman. Friends and relatives are frequently unclear whether to continue their relationship with one or the other or both. For the man the pressure to prove his manhood, his superior sexuality, can create further problems. For women, it is often assumed that they are in urgent need of sex, that they can hardly wait to get into bed with their male date. The divorced woman is less likely than her male counterpart to be welcome at a dinner party.

A range of community programs is offered—social agencies, religious institutions, and such organizations as Parents Without Partners provide for group support—but the often stressful and disappointing search for a companion, whether a date or a mate, goes on. Wallerstein and Kelly (1979) refer to the cooperation between the courts and the mental health professions. A network of conciliation courts in the United States and Canada has become increasingly involved in working with divorcing and divorced persons and their families.

The development of no-fault divorce is a step in the right direction. Irving has pointed out, however, that this does not eliminate the traditional adversary position for which lawyers are trained. The need for the neutral mediation counselor, particularly in relation to custody issues and their emotional and social aspects, is gaining recognition (Irving, 1980).

The children suffer. Far too often, they feel pulled apart emotionally. As already noted, they often feel responsible for the break-up of the family; they may feel anger at one or both parents. In discussing the impact of divorce on children, Hunt and Hunt (1977) estimate that four of every ten children brought up in the 1970s will live in a formerly married, single-parent home, at least during part of their childhood. We are dealing with a massive social problem. At the time when the children need greater emotional support and attention, the parent is often too drained and overworked to meet their needs. The children are often used as pawns to hurt the former spouse.

Another risk for the children is that of role reversal, that the custodial parent may turn to the child as a resource for comfort, as a sounding board, a sort of parent—or partner—substitute. Of course, each child reacts differently (Wallace & Kelly, 1977). In children of kindergarten age fear of being abandoned may dominate. They look anxiously for a new daddy or a new mommy. Older children are torn by conflicting loyalties. Again, issues and problems concerning visiting rights arise. Unless parents cooperate, this becomes a tug of war. Fathers tend to visit younger children regularly. They tend to visit older children less frequently, especially those who are resentful (Wallerstein & Kelly, 1979).

There are further complicating factors. Aunts, uncles, grandparents on both sides, nephews, and nieces all may become involved. If any of these show partiality, this will also tend to disturb the child, as well as the parents.

Most divorced persons remarry. It has been estimated that the majority of remarriages take place during the first year after divorce. More men remarry than women. Of women over age forty, only a small proportion remarry (Wattenberg & Reinhardt, 1979).

What happens in remarriage? It seems that a second marriage has just about the same chance of survival as a first marriage has—36 percent of those couples married for the first time in 1975 will divorce, as will 38 percent of the remarriages (Glick, 1976). A second time round does not therefore ensure a stable marriage.

The formerly married couples who come for counseling have been through a great deal, and are usually highly motivated to improve the situation and to avoid a second failure in marriage. They may respond to short-term counseling. As well, I have found there is little resistance to referral to a family agency, should this approach be indicated.

The case of Mr. and Mrs. Green highlights the problems of living with a teen-ager who has been brought into the new marriage by one of the partners.

MR. AND MRS. GREEN

Mr. Green, age 39   Children   Alan, age 16
Mrs. Green, age 39

Married 1 year (a remarriage)

Implications of the referral. The sixteen-year-old probably felt displaced by his mother's new partner. Possibly he was told at age 7: "Now you're my little man."

Mrs. Green, a divorced woman, brought her fifteen-year-old son into a remarriage. She and her son had been on their own for over seven years. Her new husband had had no children in his previous marriage. After many years of being on her own and supporting her son, she had welcomed Mr. Green as an easy-going, cheerful companion, and after six months they had married.

After a year of marriage the Greens came to the center, expressing anxiety that the marriage was not working out. Mrs. Green in particular was unwilling to face the thought of a second failure at marriage. She was a refined, cultivated woman of university education and good taste. Mr. Green was a bluff, hearty man, somewhat blunt in manner, and very successful in his used car business.

The marital axis: she is reserved, he is outgoing.

Note the interaction: He is "sloppy," she is "meticulous."

In the first session each brought out the areas of difference and conflict. Mrs. Green felt that he embarrassed her socially by his lack of polish, although a number of her friends did accept him. She complained of his sloppiness, and he complained of her overly meticulous housekeeping. She complained that he was abrupt and irritable with her and her son. Materially, she agreed he was generous, always ready to go out for meals with her and to entertain at home, provided that she didn't make a fuss over everything. Both agreed that sex was satisfactory, and he offered that they got along with both sets of in-laws, although rarely together. It seemed that on the whole their relationship had more assets than liabilities—the complaints were not really major.

Again and again, however, the reaction of the son to Mr. Green came out as a focus of family and marital upset. Mrs. Green said she felt as though she was being sawed in half by the two of them. Of course she loved her son. He was a fine student. She approved of his friends. Here Mr. Green interrupted excitedly to say that the boy was rude and argumentative. She admitted that he was difficult, but on the other hand, Mr. Green demanded respect, was harsh with him, shouted at him, and would frequently order him away from the table. Mr. Green said this was because the boy was usually commenting negatively on his—Mr. Green's—table manners. In other words, the boy didn't know his place or how to mind his own business.

After a couple of sessions with the Greens, I realized that 16-year-old Alan would certainly undermine and sabotage any benefits that could result from counseling. Mrs. Green was able to see that in nearly eight years alone with the boy after her divorce, they had become very close and interdependent. Mr. Green said the boy's father had moved out of town over five years ago and had hardly showed any interest in him. Mrs. Green admitted that Alan tended to glorify his missing parent. Mr. Green felt downgraded. Although he had tried hard, he was never accepted as a substitute father.

Despite my efforts to help Mrs. Green put some controls on her son's behavior and to encourage Mr. Green to ignore the boy's goading, the situation did not change. She still felt guilty for depriving her son of his father, and I tried to reassure her on this. I pointed out to Mr. Green that by reacting so strongly, he was giving Alan the privilege of upsetting him, an adult.

Since we were getting nowhere in these talks, I suggested it might be helpful for me to see young Alan on his own. I had three sessions with him. Alan was a good-looking, well-grown boy for his age. In the first session he blasted and swore at his stepfather, saying that he "hates his guts," that his mother had made a terrible mistake in tying up with such an ill-bred, loud-mouthed man, and that he wished she would get out of this miserable marriage. He was sure she was unhappy and just hiding it because she was ashamed to admit her mistake. I permitted, even encouraged him to pour out all his hostility.

I empathize by accepting his angry *feelings*. This is not condoning his objectionable *behavior*.

I emphasized how his feeling of loyalty toward his own father must add to these angry feelings. We talked about his father and his recollections of him. He remembers him as being lots of fun and very kind. He has not seen him for many years but does hear from him on his birthday and at Christmas. I verbalized for him that it would be natural for him to have some hurt and angry feelings, too, along with his love for his father. He listened attentively. I told him, here he was at an age when most young men are pulling away from their fathers, and he was stuck with a second one, and who needs that?

The reality of the absent parent is raised. Alan's ambivalence—his love and anger—are accepted as natural.

This interpretation fits more easily in a one-to-one interview.

At the end of the session, he had calmed down, and I said I would like to meet with him again to discuss his own plans for the future, his interests and vocational ideas.

In the next session we discussed his ambition to be an engineer, and that in another two years he would be able to go to college. He hated the idea that his loathed stepfather would have to foot the bill; again I accepted his feelings. I pointed out that with all this resentment and disgust for his stepfather, it must be hard to feel financially obligated. I continued, though, that he had no obligation to love Mr. Green or even to like him.

I relate to the emerging adult. I give him a further opportunity to talk and express his hostile feelings, something he cannot do to his mother without upsetting her.

"Oh," he said, "I'll pay him back every damn cent when I get on my feet."

I asked him what would happen to his mother when he went away to college. Perhaps he should stay home and take care of her? In fact, if the marriage broke up, would he not feel obligated to take care of her? I wondered whether this was a role he was prepared to carry for the rest of his life. Of course this shook him up quite a bit.

Now feeling understood and empathized with, he is ready to be faced with some pointed alternatives.

By the third session he had warmed up enough for me to be able to say to him, "Look, young man, you've got a good future in front of you. Your mother is a big girl now, you've been a great son to her, but she has to work out her own destiny. I don't think you want the responsibility for breaking up this

A cognitive approach, appealing to his intelligence.

For behavioral change, the technique of role playing is used. It is an effective way to prepare for and rehearse difficult situations clients will have to cope with more suitably. Also, when the client is placed in the shoes of the other person, he gains an understanding of how it feels to be that other person.

marriage. If it is to break up, let her take the responsibility for doing that.''

I pointed out to him that he didn't need to care for or admire his stepfather, but I did think he was intelligent enough to consider a more neutral stand, just being civil and polite. I said this would be a challenge in view of his feelings, to which he was still entitled. I did think, however, he had the stuff to cope with this. He agreed to have a go at it.

In this last session, I now suggested that we role-play a few of the awkward situations he will have to deal with. He suggested two—an argument over T.V. with Mr. Green, the "know it all," and a scene at the dinner table, where Mr. Green's noisy table manners disgusted him.

At first, I took on the part of Mr. Green, and Alan acted himself, watching T.V. I acted as the expert on football, having seen top players over the years. I said he could learn a lot from me. This brought on a good argument. Then we reversed roles; he became Mr. Green and I became Alan, acting rude and provocative. This stumped him and he got the message. We switched roles again so he could practice what it was like to be civil and polite to someone you dislike so much.

We then role-played a dinner table scene, putting soup on the menu as the first course, ending with Alan being ordered to leave the room. When Alan was put into the role of Mr. Green, I really laid on the snide remarks and innuendoes about people with lack of breeding and bad manners, in a superior tone of voice. Alan became uncomfortable and agreed, "Maybe I did overdo it a bit."

As the session was ending, I told him it wasn't easy for young people to find their way in becoming adult in today's world. With his career choice settled, I thought he was a step ahead, and that in time he would find a nice girl and make his own kind of good marriage. We shook hands, and I wished him luck.

In retrospect, I think the pay-off came when Alan realized that he might have to make a great sacrifice to take care of his mother if she divorced Mr. Green and turned to him in her loneliness, as she had done until her remarriage. He took our discussion seriously, understanding that the more mature role for him in the next few years would be to move away from those close ties he had to his mother. He could then look forward to a more adult-to-adult type of relationship with her.

Meanwhile, in my sessions with the parents, I suggested that Mr. Green had taken on the impossible task of becoming a substitute father much too quickly. He did not have the responsibility to be the heavy-handed father. The teen-age boy, as an adolescent, was learning to cope with the normal struggle between dependence and independence. I told them that Alan had good potential, that many of his unpleasant and irritating ways were part of the normal developmental process. This helped Mr. Green to see that even if he were the real father, he would still come in for some pretty tough times. With Mrs. Green becoming less protective, Mr. Green became less authoritarian.

Mrs. Green accepted the ongoing task of separating and releasing her son from the tight bond which had developed out of her years of being alone. She became less critical of her husband, who began to extend himself to please her. He became more relaxed with Alan, commenting that the boy was now easier to get on with. I commended them for their good efforts here.

In the follow-up call two months later, Mrs. Green said the home situation was much better. Alan was busy enough and happy, she thought, with friends, sports, and school.

Stepparents are prone to overwork at parenting. Especially with older children, it is wise to move in slowly, as a friend.

Use of generalization to support Mr. Green; the main factor is the boy's stage of development.

Behavioral change occurs with a modification of the negative interaction.

CLOSING COMMENTS

This conflict in a second marriage worked out well after nine sessions, six with the parents conjointly and three with the teen-ager on his own. Some of the same elements in the coalition between the formerly married Mrs. Charlson and her daughter (Chapter 8) were present with Mrs. Green and her son, although the Charlsons were not able to work it out.

It is more effective to work with teen-agers on their own in cases where the marital conflict cannot otherwise be sorted out.

Because of the complexities inherent in second marriages, premarriage counseling for such couples, the widowed as well as the divorced, is desirable. Of course there is always the chance that the new marriage may not take place as a consequence of premarital discussions. Such an outcome is far preferable to a second failure with all the pain and hurt involved.

There is growing recognition that services for such couples should be readily available (Messinger, Walker, & Freeman, 1978). Preparation for re-marriage after divorce is comprehensively discussed by Walker & Messinger (1979).

The short-term marriage counselor should bear in mind that the couples they see have, despite their misery, reached out for help at a critical juncture in their lives. For the most part they have taken a first and difficult step toward seeking the possibility that a lost and once-valued relationship might somehow be revived.

Also, it is worth repeating that one remarriage in three will break down. I recall a woman whose second marriage was far more complicated than the Greens'. There were hassles with her, his, and their children and in-laws as well as other problems. She told me, "If I had known the misery I would go through with the divorce and the pressures of my second marriage, I would have tried harder to keep my first marriage going." A referral for family unit treatment was effected and after two years this is still under way. That is, the "blended" family is particularly vulnerable to marital and parental upset.

Finally, it behooves the marriage counselor, short-term or otherwise, to line up initially on the side of marriage and to view divorce as an alternative only when a barren or destructive relationship has taken hold.

8

Contraindications to Short-Term Marriage Counseling

As has already been stated, not all marriages can benefit from short-term help. This is still an unsettled area, both in the literature and in the field of practice. Until research can validate definitive contraindications, it is wise to keep a flexible approach. It may sometimes be necessary to add a fourth session to the initial phase of treatment. In the event of any doubt, the beginning counselor should seek supervision or consultation, with referral as a possible alternative. From my experience and that of colleagues, however, I would suggest that in situations such as the following, short-term marital counseling is contraindicated:

Overt psychosis in one of the partners.

Chronic drug addiction or alcoholism.

When one partner lacks impulse control, as in a longstanding pattern of physical violence, often coupled with a strong provocative pattern in the mate.

When one partner has a deep-seated and persistent intrapsychic conflict—for example, the man who talks himself out of one job after another, and without the wife's collusion.

When there is deadlock in the conjoint interviews after the initial phase —that is, when there is a mutually destructive pattern, but no motivation to change or to break the marriage is indicated or apparent.

When the individuals are unable to share a worker and are too self-pre-occupied to hear each other—despite the misery, they cling to each other destructively.

When there are problems of persistent sexual dysfunction, such as primary impotence, in which case a more specialized service may be indicated.

Finally, cases of extreme poverty do not lend themselves to the approaches I have been describing—for example, where eviction is pending the couple are obviously unable to respond to marriage counseling as such. At this point the emphasis must be on meeting their primary needs, although such couples may and should be worked with later.

Nearly all couples can benefit from a few sessions with an understanding and responsive counselor, even if they do not continue past the initial phase. In itself a skilled and sensitive referral may have therapeutic as well as practical value. This is an important service which the short-term marriage counselor performs from time to time.

The following steps are involved in an effective referral process:

1. An intimate knowledge of the community resources available and the services they offer.
2. Personalizing the referral, that is, knowing or getting to know specific individuals; drawing on colleagues who can recommend suitable names for the particular need.
3. Dealing with the client's fears and misgivings about the referral, particularly a psychiatric referral. It needs to be emphasized that psychiatry is usually voluntary, and that to accept it or seek it out is a sign of strength, not of weakness.
4. Sharing information with the referral person (with the client's consent), and being assured that in fact the client will be accepted for service. Practitioners are well aware of the risk clients face in being shunted from pillar to post by a thoughtless or casual referral.
5. Preparing the client to accept the referral, mentioning a specific name to be contacted,* explaining that this person is someone the counselor knows or whom a colleague has recommended and who will be available; assuring the client that this is an optional service which he or she is free to take or to leave and, if necessary, to seek out another therapist or resource. The couple are, however, encouraged to carry on for at least two or three sessions before making any further change.
6. Following through to be certain that the referral was implemented.

*It is advisable to supply two names, in the event that one is not available.

The case of Mr. and Mrs. Wood is an illustration when short-term marriage counseling is contraindicated. Their narcissistic needs precluded them from being able to listen to each other. Their capacity to share the counselor was minimal at best. Although the assessment was made in the first interview, a second interview was offered. This practice enables beginning practitioners to confirm the initial assessment or to seek consultation for an alternative plan.

MR. AND MRS. WOOD

Mr. Wood, age 48
Mrs. Wood, age 47

Married 19 years

Children: Son, age 18
Daughter, age 15

Referral, December 19

Implications of the referral. Is the lawyer more motivated than the client?

Mrs. Wood telephoned for the appointment at the suggestion of her lawyer. The lawyer thinks she is being taken advantage of by her husband, that she is acting like a "patsy." Had she been to the lawyer seeking a divorce or separation? No, she said, she had only been to see him about making a will. When I asked how she saw the problem, her response was vague, but she did say that her husband was now willing to come.

As she is vague, I make our assessment policy clear.

I said we usually arrange for an assessment of one to three interviews and then decide with the couple whether our service is suitable. Mrs. Wood said they were both prepared and ready to come to see me. I made an appointment for the following day.

First Interview, December 20

The couple arrived together, a little late as a result of a storm. Mrs. Wood strode in, shook me heartily by the hand, and introduced herself and her husband. She is a tall, solidly built woman. Her blond hair hung straight nearly to her shoulders. She looked somewhat odd, wearing a long, flowing, multicolored cape and high, black knee-boots, laced in white. She was carrying an enormous hand-knitted bag. He looked more sedate and conservative. They sat down together on the sofa.

Unusual appearance is a significant personality cue. Though nonverbal, the language of dress sends a message.

I asked what had brought them to a marriage counselor. She was staring at me, rubbing her hands tensely. He spoke: "It's a problem of communication. She doesn't try to understand my point of view." I asked Mrs. Wood if she knew what he meant.

Note that self-preoccupation blocks communication

Worker turns to factual information in an effort to refocus the interview.

The son's leaving home would create stress for Mrs. W.

Mrs. W's somewhat confused response demonstrates her poor judgment in expecting her husband to respond positively when she downgrades him.

The marital equilibrium was upset by his move out of the patient role, and out of the dependence on his wife.

She turned on him sharply. "I've been very open and honest with *you*. It's *you* that keeps things in; you don't share the good, and you don't share the bad with me. There's just nothing, nothing." He shrugged and muttered. I was having a hard time getting them to focus on anything in particular, so I asked them for brief factual material. They had come to Canada from Belgium seventeen years earlier. They have a daughter aged fifteen who, both agreed, is a nice, sensible girl and is doing well at school. Their son, eighteen, was fired from his job a few months ago and is now working in the States. She misses him very much. Her husband indicated that she is very much attached to the boy and he to the girl. Both agreed they are pretty good youngsters. The boy is earning good money and writes regularly.

In another attempt to focus on problem identification, I asked if I could hear what good or bad things she was referring to earlier on. "Well, for the good," she said, "his mother sent us a letter. Actually, the letter was addressed to me, and in it was $900. I was to give $50 to each of the children and to my husband, and the rest, his mother said, I should keep for myself for taking such good care of my invalid husband." In a bitter and angry voice, she said to him, "You didn't say a word about my joy, or my pleasure at being appreciated, and at getting this gift." He interjected that his mother was a very eccentric woman and she said, "Yes, she is eccentric." I asked how he felt at being called "an invalid." He said it didn't make him feel good at all. I asked if she could understand that, and she said, "That's childish—he should know better. He should think of *me*. I thought only of him for fourteen years."

It emerged that he had suffered with stomach ulcers for fifteen years and had been operated on for this ailment about a year ago. He now feels like a new man and has no pain at all, he said. She turned on him again. "You're a changed personality." He hinted that maybe she needed to have him helpless and dependent. She snapped back, "That's ridiculous. So I'm a masochist, am I? I have to be ordered about and stepped on." She turned to me and added that his condition was "psychosomatic" and that he had been to a psychiatrist.

I commented that they were using a lot of psychiatric vocabulary. She said she had been called in a few times by the psychiatrist too. Yes, a few years ago, she did have some psychiatric treatment, but it did her no good at all. Over the years, there were a number of doctors involved for her husband, and they all told her the same thing as the psychiatrist—keep him calm, don't excite him, take care of him, he has to be very careful not to get upset because of his ulcers. I turned to Mr. Wood and he said, "She's a very good cook and she did take good care of me, that's true. But she tried too hard. She tends to make unusual and spicy recipes."

Note the contradictory and conflicted message. It is a masked criticism from Mr. W. He is really saying that her meals are bad for his ulcers.

I asked her if she feels to blame for his condition, and she said, "Yes, I've always felt to blame."

To help Mrs. W. out, I clarify that she is not the cause of his ulcers.

I asked him to tell me when and how his ulcers developed and it turned out that the problem began when they came from Belgium. There was the stress of getting started; he had a hard time and had made a precarious living, it appears, as a draftsman, although he was vague about this. I had the impression that his widowed mother, who owns property, periodically produced a windfall but that this source of income was irregular.

I pointed out that with all these pressures, it must have been difficult not only for him but for his wife too, and in addition, it must have been hard for her to shoulder the burden of blame, as there were many contributing factors to his condition. I repeated that it was an oversimplification to blame his wife, and I thought it was unfair if the doctors had done this. He nodded, but not too strongly.

Mrs. W. now shows further lack of control; she is unable to stay with the topic, moves from one thing to another. This differs from the "topic switch," which serves consciously or unconsciously to derail interaction.

She said she's been choked up over all these years. She went on and on, somewhat like a yo-yo, off on tangents, mainly to show her virtuous, long suffering and his cruel withdrawal into silence and neglect of her. During all this, he kept calm and detached. He said, "Look, I just feel helpless. It's hard to keep her to a logical conclusion, with a logical discussion. Our friends don't like to come to the house any more, because of her." Here, she interrupted, screaming at him, saying, "That's ridiculous. Last week, we had so-and-so and so-and-so in. What on earth are you talking about?"

Again the masked criticism. This type of contradictory message furthers client confusion, and it sparks off Mrs. W.'s mercurial moods.

He then let this go, and said, "She's a good mother, and she works hard, but the children too feel embarrassed in bringing friends in, because of her."

Again she ranted, "How come I see all those long-haired boys and girls with blankets if they don't come to the house? I get on fine with the kids." He said, "Yes, she's good at raising kids, keeps them in line. I think perhaps they're afraid of her." Agitated, she said, "I'm a castrating woman too, like the psychiatrist said!"

She went back to the letter, from his mother. She again raised his cold and begrudging response, though earlier she had agreed it didn't make him feel good to be called "the invalid." I asked him whether he had been reacting to that. As a matter of fact, his daughter had brought him the letter to read, but Mrs. Wood was in the kitchen at the time. He didn't even have time to finish it. Besides, he was upset about something else "which we needn't go into here." I questioned why not, and then she brought out, in a muddled way, the episode of their holiday last summer.

A "holiday" when couples are in conflict usually creates further disturbance.

This was a two-week holiday, their first in years. Apparently he thought it would be a good idea to invite the couple next door, with whom they were quite friendly. She said that the woman was her one and only friend for many years. He thought if this couple came along, it would help them have a nicer holiday, as they themselves had so little to communicate to each other on their own. But, she said, it was a terrible "betrayal" because before long he and the other woman were madly in love, and this betrayal was from a friend, who was walking around starry-eyed like a stupid teen-ager, looking at him dotingly.

She's spilling out too much. Her lack of control and judgment demonstrates weak ego functioning.

Mr. Wood came in here with, "You had an affair with her husband some years ago." This came out very casually and quietly. What irritated and upset her even more than his affair was that, as she said, "You plotted behind my back. I knew nothing of it, and you two sent the husband into the cabin to try to get him to make love to me so that you two could be together. . . . He kept pushing me against the kitchen wall, and he kept trying to get me into the bedroom and into bed. But," she went on, "I know about him, and I've been in bed with him, and he's not that good, anyway. I've had enough of him. He's not even as good in bed as my husband. Besides," she said to him, "that was completely different. It took place five years ago, and you said you didn't mind as long as it didn't interfere with us." She went on, "I also told you about the few times I slept with the doctor, and shared everything with you." Again, she said she was more perturbed about her friend's betrayal than her husband's behavior. She was wound up, telling him he must be blind. What could he see in that plain-looking woman, fifty-three years old? He was "probably looking for the mother he never had." He indicated quietly that the affair was over, and he was relieved to have it over. She didn't seem to want to press this particularly, so I left it. However, she tossed out, in the meanwhile he would probably have liked to arrange a partner switch of all four under one roof.

I try to stem the tide and refocus on something positive, but—

I thought, to cool the situation a little, I would try to bring out something positive. What had they seen in each other originally, when they married? He said, "I think I must have loved her; she was a good-looking girl." They had married late—she was 28 and he 29. And what about Mrs. Wood? She said, "I don't know. I don't think I loved him. I wasn't sure. We only knew each other for four months when we married, then the visa to Canada came through. I was very worried. I was fearful about going to a strange country with him." He said he had never known about that. His manner and affect were consistently flat during the interview.

He seems apathetic and resigned to his situation.

Another effort fails.

I asked if there was anything good she could think about in relation to him. She had said that he was good in bed. Was there anything else? She kept saying, "I don't know, I don't know."

I asked what they expected from me, what they thought I could do for them in this situation. She said to me, pleadingly, "You don't threaten him; maybe he will listen to you." He said calmly that he thought *she* should have someone to talk to on a regular basis. I asked him directly, does he want in or out of the marriage? He hedged here, and she nudged, and finally he admitted he wanted to be out of it.

Each wants me to change the partner!

She is locked into the marriage by her pathological need for him. He similarly makes needling but hollow threats to leave her. In their interaction they are drawn to each other like moths to a flame.

At this, Mrs. Wood burst hysterically into loud sobbing, and at the same time blurted, between sobs, "He'll be lonely, he'll get sick, he won't admit it; he'll be too proud to come back to me." He said, "See, I'm helpless—what can I do?"

Worker puts her own feelings to use and confronts him with *his* feelings of

Since I was feeling rather helpless myself by this time, but didn't want the session to end in this manner, I decided to challenge him by asking him bluntly, "What do you mean, help-

helplessness—a valiant attempt to keep control of the interview!

The use of direction, hoping with the partner's help to establish some order.

Question as to general health is essential in such cases. Disturbance in sleeping and eating patterns is significant.

less? Just look at her, all upset and distraught. What do you feel when you see this?'' He said, ''I'm sorry for her, but she gets all wound up, and she doesn't stop.'' ''Well,'' I said firmly, ''if you feel sorry for her, tell her—it could comfort her. Try it.'' He did so, and she began to quiet down. ''You see,'' I said, ''you can help.''

I asked about their physical health. Mr. Wood's is better. How about Mrs. Wood's? She sleeps okay and eats okay. I wondered if she had any medication to help her under pressure? The family doctor has discontinued this because she took an overdose a few years ago. I asked if she felt she had been helped by the psychiatrist. She said she had been hospitalized for a few weeks after the overdose and then had outpatient treatment for about two years, ''but it was worthless, and I would never bother with that again.''

I said I did not consider, from our session today, that this marriage counseling agency was a suitable resource to help them over this troubled period. I thought that individual help was indicated. I had in mind a family agency where this could probably be arranged. I would like the three of us to meet together about this next week, if they were willing. Mrs. Wood said she would like to come back, and he nodded.

Worker's Assessment and Plan at this Point

Joint interviews will not be effective; they are unable to share a counselor, as individual needs are paramount. At the same time, the rigid interlocking pattern precludes separation. Although he said he wants ''out,'' this was probably only to needle her. A referral is indicated.

Worker offers a little support to Mr. W. along with the mild confrontation about his silence, defined as "not too helpful" rather than as hostile.

Technique of generalization is used to help Mrs. W. leave the interview less distressed.

I commented again that just saying he was sorry had really been helpful to her. I also said that his quiet and silence had not been too helpful, and that this so often tends to upset the other person even more. I continued that this is true not only of Mrs. Wood but of almost everyone who finds themselves upset and in an argument. Mrs. Wood seemed to appreciate this kind of support and nodded. She had really calmed down by now, although I imagined she still felt pretty tense inside. I decided to explore referral to a family agency where psychiatric consultation would also be available.

Second Interview, December 27

Both came on time. They were going to his brother's for dinner. She looked more attractive; her hair had been curled and set. He volunteered, "I didn't have to do anything, as she was quieter." She pointed out that he'd been away all week, and they hadn't had much time to talk, anyhow.

Important to note an area of health. She is able to carry a teaching role.

She expressed concern about her job. She teaches English to immigrants several evenings a week, and loves it. She thinks the school may be closed, as a strike is imminent. I expressed interest in this activity, and said I felt that since she was bilingual and competent in this area, it would be useful for her to find a similar job in which she could be involved in interesting and constructive work.

Recognition of her competence is necessary. She has some skills to build on, a productive treatment approach, if she were to accept a referral for individual help.

During the session, Mr. Wood was again passive and bland. I asked if they had talked together at all about the last session. She said, "We never talk." He said they rarely do. She now began to get wound up again, but I decided not to allow a recurrence of the first interview and tried to get to the issue of the referral.

Mr. Wood said she needed someone "to sound off to." I told him I thought that he had some difficulties of his own still to work out and could benefit from an understanding outside person.

I told them I had talked to a worker at the family agency. I had not given their names or their situation, but understood that she would be available should they mention my name and want to be seen. I said I felt an ongoing, individual resource would be useful for Mrs. Wood and for Mr. Wood too, until their situation became clearer. She said she didn't think she'd like this idea. I said she should think it over and call me in a week. If I didn't hear from her, then I would phone her. "I feel you are entitled to get some further help," I said. I recommended to Mr. Wood and to his wife that the family doctor should be consulted again in the interim, to reconsider providing some medication for her. He hinted she took alcohol instead of drugs. She argued here that she never took enough to get drunk. Here I just said that the doctor should know what

It is important, where one spouse seems more disturbed than the other, to include both in making a referral for further service. This prevents one labeling the other as "sick."

she's going through, as he has known her for so many years since she came to this country, and I felt he should be consulted.

I also gave her the name and the telephone number of the social worker to whom I had talked about them. I said this social worker was known to me, was kind and able, and would be a useful resource for individual help as well as for marital counseling. At this point, I said I felt individual help was indicated.

Telephone call from me to Mrs. Wood

This was a follow-up telephone call. I wanted to show Mrs. Wood that I had not forgotten. She said she had been out and had just come back from one of the church groups she is interested in. She is thinking of reviving her interests in the humanist movement and has come back to the Unitarian Church. I gave her credit for this initiative, particularly since her teaching work is somewhat in jeopardy at this point. She went on to say that she is still reluctant to see any social worker or psychiatrist. She thinks she can cope on her own. She is very discouraged about her husband, and the session with me just confirmed that he is not going to do anything about changing himself and his behavior.

> Note an area of strength—on her own she seeks and has found an ameliorating outside activity.

I again talked with her about seeing her doctor. She said that her annual check-up was coming up next month, and she would ask him about some medication. She willingly gave me his name and permission to talk to him. I did so. He has known them for years and has a good understanding of their problems.

CLOSING COMMENTS

The assessment of Mr. and Mrs. Wood and of their relationship is not fully explored. Probing techniques might stir things up and further weaken their defenses. Sufficient material, however, comes out to indicate deep-seated personality problems in each of them and a highly rigid and longstanding pattern of negative interaction in the marriage; crisis prone, they will probably need periodic help.

Working with borderline, ego-impaired, inadequate personalities such as Mr. and Mrs. Wood can be frustrating, particularly when help is rejected. This case demonstrates, however, that it is constructive to encourage the type of concrete activity that Mrs. Wood was herself able to seek out and make use of. This helps compensate for lack of a kinship or friendship support system.

If a volunteer organization is available in the community, this can be a helpful resource to get clients involved in giving a practical service to others, which is ego building. From my experience, this has more potential for helping someone like Mrs. Wood than persisting with the psychiatric referral, which is futile at this point.

In cases where a client shows signs of being overtly psychotic or is seriously depressed, psychiatric referral is essential. Nonmedically trained workers must remember that any threat of suicide, or damage to self or others, must be taken seriously.

Contacting and alerting the client's medical doctor has proved to be an important resource when the cient is unwilling to accept a referral from the worker. The patient finds this less threatening, as he knows the doctor and has some confidence in him. The doctor may also know and be able to involve a responsible family member. Thus the medical doctor is often the most effective person to make a psychiatric referral when this is imperative.

INTRODUCTORY NOTE

The case of Mr. and Mrs. Charlson also turned out to be unsuitable for short-term marriage counseling, although this was not perceived during the assessment period. It may be helpful for the reader to examine the early sessions to determine where and why the worker missed the significance of the relevant messages.

MR. AND MRS. CHARLSON

Mrs. Charlson, age 38
Mr. Charlson, age 39

Married 5 years, a remarriage

Children: Elise, age 17
Lil, age 3½ years
Bill, age 14 months

Referral

As Mrs. C. has initiated a legal contact, her motivation for counseling will be in doubt.

Mrs. Charlson telephoned. She was referred by her lawyer, who thought there was a possibility of bringing the couple together before she proceeded with her request for separation. She mentioned that she had been married previously. She had been divorced from her first husband three years after they were married and had one child from that marriage.

First Interview, January 18

The couple arrived together and sat together on the sofa in the office. Mrs. Charlson looked younger than her stated age of thirty-eight. She is an attractive brunette, nicely groomed, with a warm and friendly smile. Mr. Charlson, blond, balding, and rather bulky, had a heavy chest and large stomach. He leaned back passively, his face somewhat expressionless.

I explained that the agency provides for short-term marriage counseling and that our usual practice is to assess with the couple after one to three sessions whether further sessions will be helpful. If not, another plan will be discussed with them.

Explaining the limited service early on, is particularly important when a lawyer has been involved.

Mr. Charlson looked so self-conscious and disengaged that I decided to ask for a little factual information before beginning on the matter of the visit to the lawyer.

This may ease him into the session.

Both are full-time teachers. Mrs. Charlson teaches design and art at a private girls' school. Mr. Charlson teaches mathematics and physics in a high school. A middle-aged neighbor, widowed, comes in daily as a babysitter. Mrs. Charlson's daughter from her previous marriage is seventeen and there are two children from this marriage, a boy of fourteen months and a girl three and a half years old.

Mrs. Charlson's parents are living in the country. She was the oldest of six children and carried a good deal of responsibility for the care of the younger ones, as her mother has never been strong.

Mr. Charlson's father died when he was three years old, and his mother died when he was six. He was brought up by a foster couple. The foster father died suddenly three years ago; the foster mother died when he was ten. Mrs. Charlson said both she and her husband adored the foster father. He was a wonderful parent to Mr. Charlson and worked hard to provide him with a university education.

I commented that this must have been a great loss to Mr. Charlson after all the other losses he had sustained, but he showed no reaction. I remarked that it was difficult for him to show his sorrow. Mrs. Charlson explained that he never shows any sorrow, that he never shows any sad feelings. In fact, she added, he's a "Stoic," but I said, "It's hard even for a Stoic not to feel such a loss."

Now Mr. Charlson quickly snapped back at me, "That's not what changed me in the marriage." I pointed out that he had jumped to a conclusion here. I had not thought this was the cause of their marital problems.

Technique of suggesting that what he does to worker is what he probably does to his wife. This is confirmed, and gets the interview under way.

I turned to Mrs. Charlson. "Does he tend to jump to conclusions like this with you?" "Yes," she began, "he generally assumes that something has gone wrong; he is very critical of me, and jumps to conclusions about the behavior of my seventeen-year-old daughter. In fact," she continued, "he threw my daughter out of the house a few days ago." She said, "Everything is wrong between us; there is nothing in this marriage any more."

Precipitating factor—conflict with the stepdaughter.

I asked for some details of this incident which threatened to break up the marriage. Mr. Charlson was sitting very quietly, waiting for Mrs. Charlson to talk. She said, with some heat, "My daughter wouldn't pick up a glass that he broke, so he told her to leave the home." "Actually," he said, "this was not the fact." He had told the girl to clear up after supper, and when she refused, he got angry and threw the glass on the floor. He said he'd had a couple of drinks and really had no intention of sending her packing. (It seems she had moved in with the babysitter.)

Mrs. Charlson said, "You knew what you were doing. First, you threw the glass on the floor, and then told her to clear up. When she refused, you threw her out." I pointed out that their two stories left me unclear as to whether he had intended the girl to leave, and whether or not he had actually been drunk. Mrs. Charlson said, "Drinking wasn't the point. My real complaint is that he has no use for my daughter, who is a really fine girl."

This private language indicates a coalition to keep husband out.

Mr. Charlson responded, "You keep on protecting the girl, and you gang up on me, even talking to her in French, which you know I don't understand." (Mrs. Charlson is French-Canadian, Mr. Charlson is English-Canadian.) He insisted that he treats the girl well, that he moved into their present home so that she would be near to what he considered a good high school. In fact, he wants the girl to have a college education and wants the best for her. "She can come home tomorrow."

I raised the question of drinking—was this a serious problem in the marriage? Mr. Charlson said, "I used to drink with the boys before I got married." She indicated that he still likes to take a drink but that her problem was that he ignores her and rejects her daughter. Ordering her out was "the last straw."

Mr. Charlson said, "I feel unwanted in the family. I feel I pay the bills, pick up the garbage, and that's it!"

The role of stepfather has not been worked through.

Since there was so little between them, and both felt unwanted, I asked why Mrs. Charlson had not pursued the separation. She replied somewhat lamely, "I still love him." I asked if he knew that. "No," he said, "I did not." Does he want to retain the marriage? He said he does. I asked if he knew it would be necessary for his wife to feel more cared for. Mrs. Charlson interrupted, "He gets behind his paper in another room and ignores me."

The central problem revolves around the daughter.

It seemed unprofitable at this early point to pursue this negative interaction, so I refocused on their relationship to the daughter, Elise. Mrs. Charlson had been alone with the girl for 10 years before she remarried. I asked if she felt guilty because she had deprived Elise of a father. "Yes," she replied, "I do." I said this would create a tight bond between them, and that bringing up a child alone, working for her all these years, could set the stage for the kind of alliance where Mr. Charlson feels out of it. I asked, "How about this?" He said, "The girl has always been between us."

Is the teen-age girl the scapegoat?

I again questioned the matter of his drinking. He insisted he has never lost a day's work in his life on this account. "I know how much I can handle, and I can't take too much, because I do get upset and bad-tempered." She put in, "It's not just the drinking, it's the way you treat me and Elise." I said it seems as though Elise is being used as a sort of football here, and asked, "Who's the one getting hurt when you two are too angry to talk to each other? You fight with Elise and tell her to get out when you're really mad at your wife, and it seems, Mrs. Charlson, that you're usually ready to get back at him by speaking in French to Elise." "Yes," said Mrs. Charlson, "it is Elise who gets hurt."

The circular destructive interaction is pointed out.

I pointed out that it's a burden for the girl to feel that she's between the two of them. "Well," Mrs. Charlson indicated, "Elise has said that when she's eighteen she will leave if we are still fighting like this." She went on, "I don't want my daughter to go." I said that today many young girls live away from home, that it's a part of growing up, as long as they don't leave because of anger, hate, or resentment. I added, "Elise has to make her own life." Mr. Charlson felt pretty good at this.

Toward the end of the interview, I summarized by saying, "You seem like two unhappy people who somehow want to keep the marriage together." I asked if the marriage was good enough for both to be willing to work at it. This would be essential for any improvement to come about, and if we were to continue to work together.

Mr. Charlson said, appeasingly, "I was hoping to get a trailer, and we could have a family holiday together, and I want Elise to come too." I suggested that although this was a good idea, we should stay with tomorrow, and next week, and with the problems they are facing now.

As their problems seemed to revolve around Elise, I asked Mrs. Charlson to consider the impact of her talking French to her daughter, and as a start, to discontinue this practice during the coming week. Mr. Charlson agreed to tell Elise that he wants her to stay, and that he and his wife are going to try to work out a better marriage.

Interpreting their role as clients.

Mr. C. wants the marriage, and shows signs of giving way.

Significant tasks are set.

Second Interview, January 25

Mr. and Mrs. Charlson were both prompt. He said, and she agreed, that they had a better week. I asked in what way? He was quiet, and she said, "He was kinder, and treated me more like a person." No, she did not tell him this; she thought he knew. He said, "She didn't bark at me." What had he done for her? She answered, "He didn't run to his paper right after dinner, the way he's been doing." Yes, Elise is back home, and Mrs. Charlson said she didn't talk to her in French at the table.

We were soon into the subject of Elise again. He said that their babysitter has a daughter who is a "no-good teen-ager."

Mrs. Charlson said, "When he talks like this about teen-agers, I resent it. He seems to think that all teen-agers are no good, and that the best thing for this woman to do would be to kick her daughter out, just like Elise." He said he didn't have Elise at all in mind when he said that.

It is useful to get specifics when generalized improvements are offered. These certainly sound minimal!

The repetitive problem of Elise. Note the mother's overidentification with Elise (Mrs. C., by overidentifying, feels like *her daughter, not just* with *her. It is as if she were in Elise's shoes and couldn't get out). His resentment of Elise is com-*

pounded by his feelings about "rotten teen-agers." His own teen-age problems may be stirred up, and he is overreacting.

Mrs. C. is nowhere near ready to face releasing her daughter. My raising this was precipitous. It would have been better to question whether they are not both overreacting to Elise.

When I asked Mrs. Charlson if she had thought about our talk last week, about Elise being able to leave home, to go to college, for example, not in anger or with guilt, and that this in fact might be good for her, Mrs. Charlson was reluctant to get into this, and went back to his reaction, when he comes home from his school and talks about those "rotten teen-agers."

She again thinks he is talking about Elise, and said, "When you generalize, what else can I think?" He replied, "I'm just mad and letting off steam. I don't mean Elise." He added, "I know these generalizations aren't valid."

I asked Mrs. Charlson what she expected or wanted from her husband. She replied, "I want him to talk more gently to me. I hate it when he shouts at me." She then brought out that on the very day of his foster father's funeral, "He came home, got rough, and gave me a black eye." He was quiet for a while, and then said, "Yes, when you went at me twice, and you were so mad about something." He added, "If I did that, it was because I was upset. How often have I put a hand on you? Once in five years? You know I wasn't myself."

I was reluctant to get into this highly charged three-year-old battle. There is enough irrational warring going on right now.

She responded, "It's not the physical attack. It's the inner humiliation that doesn't heal." Again she moved on to the subject of Elise. She said to him, "She's yours by marriage, but she's mine by blood." I pointed out that what she was saying is provocative; in effect, she is telling her husband, "Elise and I have a coalition going; we have a barrier to keep you out."

Note that Mrs. C. clings tightly to the relationship with her daughter.

Now she began to cry freely, and said, "I suppose so, because I feel he turns away from me, as well as from Elise." While she was weeping, I asked if he could help her with this, and he said, "Well, I'm a Stoic; I can't change. That's the way I am."

Note these extremes in feeling responses. One partner craves affection, and the mate is emotionally detached.

"Mr. Charlson," I said, "as a teacher, you know very well that behavior can be learned." He topped this off by saying, "Well, that's why I teach math and not the humanities." Here she came in with, "You're a good teacher, and the students do like you."

When I challenge him, she protects him. I point out

that support alone will not bring change. Protecting the mate serves to keep the system intact.

I said, "I'm glad you can see some good things about your husband, but right now I'm hoping for some change, which is the reason you're here." Mr. Charlson commented that he tends to do things rather than to verbalize. I suggested that he could then do more to let his wife feel cared for, as she is the one who wanted "out" of the marriage. He said, "Oh, I'll try, but she's so wrapped up with the children." She snapped back, "That's because I don't have a husband. I thought I did at first, but the good times soon dried up."

If they had had such good times at the beginning of their marriage, I asked, what had caused things to get so much out of hand? Neither could say—only that things had deteriorated. I asked again, since there is no affection, is there any sex between them. Silence. A long pause. I asked, "Is that a taboo subject?" He said, "There's none." "Since when?" I asked. More silence. I said, "You do have two children." Mrs. Charlson: "There's been nothing for the past fourteen months, ever since the little boy was born."

At this point it came out that after the last baby was born she had wanted to have her tubes tied, but he wouldn't give his consent. She had said, "Look, I'm thirty-eight—I don't want any more children." She continued, "Before this, sex had been wonderful." He agreed. "What a loss for you both," I said.

His wish for more children is unrealistic. Does he need to bolster his security as a male?

About his wish to have more children, he said, "When we were married, we made an agreement that we would have three or four children." He indicated that the last baby, a boy, had been unwanted by Mrs. Charlson, so I said, "You feel that both you and your little boy are not welcome? Then why do you want more children?" His eyes filled up.

Denial of his feelings.

I commented that he looked sad. He touched the corner of his eye, and lit a cigarette. He shook his head—"No." He smoked constantly during the interview.

She argued that there were enough children and she didn't see the need to have more. He said that although he had never referred to their agreement, he had resented her refusal to have more children. This, in fact, was what had turned him off sex.

She said, self-righteously, that she could have had the operation without his consent, but she knew that wouldn't be a good way to do things. He said that now he doesn't feel resentful any more. I asked whether she knew he had changed his mind about this. No, she didn't. I asked him, "What made you change your feelings about this?"

"Oh," he replied, "I've learned to live with it. There's no alternative." I said that he sounded more resigned than convinced. He just shrugged.

I said that today I was concerned because there was so much emphasis on everything wrong between them and so little on what could be done to improve their daily living. I said that at the beginning of the session it sounded as though there were an improvement, but I wondered if they were able to maintain this. I thought they would have to work together on how to keep Elise more in the background and try to revive some of the good things they had earlier in the marriage. Unless they could begin to work along these lines, I really questioned whether short-term service was going to be the answer to their difficulties.

I hoped to put some limits around their somewhat vague and extensive complaints. As well, I do question whether short-term counseling is appropriate for this couple. I am aware that Elise should perhaps be involved, but how and when is not clear to me at this point.

Third Interview, February 1

Mr. and Mrs. Charlson came early. They indicated again that they had a better week. She comes into the living room, where he sits, and they have coffee together. Before, she used to go into the kitchen; previously, they didn't sit in the same room. I asked, "And what has Mr. Charlson done that seems better?" She continued, "He puts his arm around me at night." She continued, "He said that last week here he had felt as if he had been through the wringer, he had felt so drained." Here he added that it was worthwhile, as now she understands his hurt, because she hadn't wanted the baby boy and wanted to have her tubes tied even before she was pregnant.

Here we are, back again with Elise.

Then he went on to voice his resentment that Elise had brought a girlfriend home who stayed for three days. He said, "We should be a family on our own." Quite an argument followed here, she insisting that the girl had stayed mostly in the daughter's room and joined them only for meals. Again he complained that she takes too much interest in Elise, that Elise doesn't do enough in the house. She argued that her daughter does the dishes all the time, that she puts the two little ones to bed, and that she has never refused to do anything asked of her. He insisted that the girl is not really asked to do things.

Mrs. Charlson said, "I wonder what I do for her that you think is too much. Tell me." He was vague but admitted he wants to be able to tell Elise to do this or that but he is afraid. Mrs. Charlson said, "But you do that all the time."

He insisted that he wants the authority. Mr. Charlson said he would be willing to work with Elise after dinner if she were more respectful. More arguments followed, which I interrupted by saying that they would still have to get together on what is to be expected from Elise. Mrs. Charlson complained that Elise did things for them but gets no notice. She cooks dinner three times a week, now that her schedule brings her home earlier. "You didn't even comment—you just shove your face into the stew." "No," he said, "I told her it was good." "You didn't tell Elise," she interjected, "you told me, and even when you told her to leave, she said she was sorry for you."

I suggested that if he could be more positive directly, Elise might be surprised and encouraged. I went on to say that he feels out of it but that he certainly manages to keep himself out of it too. He agreed to give Elise some recognition when it was deserved.

I raised the question of what they do for recreation. Do they ever get out on their own? He indicated they were pretty busy and tired after a day's work. They used to get out and see friends more when they were first married, and I suggested they try to find time to get back to this.

I suggested that we limit ourselves to another two sessions, and then decide if this is the type of help that they need, or whether another plan should be considered.

Fourth Interview, February 8
They again sat together. I commented that Mr. Charlson looked glum and solemn. "Yes," he said, "I'm tired. I've had a hard week." She said, "He's been barking at me again." It seems she was driving the little girl to the pediatrician because the child was ill. She went down a back street, lost her way, and he got angry and swore at her. She was going to give him the old silent treatment, and then decided she would give way. For thanks, on the way to work the next morning, he muttered and barked again. "Oh," she went on, "he's so uncommunicative. I'm so fed up. I don't know what to do." He was annoyed and

---

Margin notes:

No doubt Elise has learned subtle ways of downgrading him and clinging to her prior right to mother.

Direct guidance is offered.

If they get more involved outside the home, there may be less tension inside the home, where even small improvements are not maintained.

The same battle is on again.

said, "She was nagging again this morning, and at eight o'clock, I just can't take it!" It seems she had asked him the same thing four times, and in response he had said, "—dammit, there she goes again." She said, "This made me feel it's completely hopeless."

I could have redefined her negative "nagging" as positive, i.e., wanting his opinion and attention.

I said, "With a little child ill, and both of you tired, it's only natural to get irritable, and it's really not fatal." "Maybe that's so," Mrs. Charlson went on, "but he forgets I have to do everything—work, run the house, and take care of everything." To him she said, "I don't even get a kind word from you."

I try, without success, to put a realistic perspective on these incidents.

I said, "It sure sounds as if we're back to square one, and getting nowhere fast. I'll soon feel helpless too."

A useful technique when the worker's feelings are getting in the way. By now, I'm feeling frustrated and decide to put my feelings to use, *before* I get really fed up.

This prompted him to say, "But the rest of the week went okay." I asked him in what way it had been okay. She complained there still isn't any sex. He replied, quite gently, "You're so afraid of getting pregnant." I asked about birth control. He has used a condom; that's how they had the "accident." She went on about how rejected she feels. He said, "I do too." She said, "But I thought you just lost interest."

It brings a response from Mr. C! It seems he wants to keep the marriage, but does not want to change.

I asked if they had discussed this before, as sex had been so good in the past. "No," nor did they talk during lovemaking. He just knew what to do that pleased her. I suggested they talk now about alternative means of birth control. She told him she had thought of getting refitted for a diaphragm. She had used this before the birth of the first child. He encouraged her, saying he would be glad if she did. She agreed to go to her gynecologist and get this settled soon.

At last, I got some problem solving under way.

I suggested that much of their mutual irritation might be linked to lack of sex, as well as to their negative pattern of arguing broadly rather than discussing and settling a specific difference, as they had done so well just now.

They are given encouragement for a more positive way of working.

I pointed out that Mrs. Charlson has been consistently positive about sex and how well he satisfies her in this. I asked how this made him feel. He didn't answer, just looked at me uncomfortably. "Oh, heck," I said, "how about giving her some positive feedback? You must know it's not that risky."

The going looks better, so I move in more daringly.

Now she was watching him with a smile. I suggested that he take a look at her right now. Does he like the way she looks? He smiled, a little more alert and responsive. "Not too bad," he said. "Well," I said frivolously, "so it's really not that bad?" He repeated, "Not bad at all." He laughed. She laughed here too. I said, "You know, Mr. Charlson, it's like learning a new language, but a friendly comment means so much to your wife, I think it's worth your while to get into the act."

"In any case," I continued, "I think you came through pretty well just now, the way you looked at her." "Oh," he said, "I could even say she looks great." I added, "The way you're beginning now to share a little of the positive, who knows what will happen?

"Now," I went on, "Mrs. Charlson, if you can reinforce these small changes, you'll soon have him swinging from the branches." They both laughed, and left in a relaxed mood.

The use of a light touch, as a technique to ease tension and the weight of it all. It helps the counselor as well as the client.

Fifth Interview, February 15

Today she looked really attractive. She said, "I feel much better. I can't stay mad anyhow. I got a lot off my chest." He said, "I'm pleased the days of silence are over." She reported that he included Elise when he took Lil skating on Saturday. He thinks Elise is now willing to do more and also washes up after dinner, when Mr. Charlson makes the suggestion. She had told Elise that things are going better between them, and her daughter said she feels things are better too.

At last, some positive changes appear to be taking place.

Little Lil, three and a half years old, had commented, "You and Daddy don't fight any more." Mrs. Charlson felt terrible to think that the child had noticed so much, and had said, "No, we don't." I said all parents get angry with each other at times, and it helps to be able to say to the child, "We get angry, but we still love each other."

She announced, "I'm having the tubal ligation." He said he'd agree. "But," she added, "you said you'd agree, but only with a gun to your head." He said, "I don't think I can say I don't want more children; that's asking too much, but if you don't want them, that's it."

The negative interaction is well entrenched.

She got upset and began to weep. "That's not very flattering. I feel I'm just a sort of baby machine. What about *me*?" I pointed out that his wife had been to a lawyer; she wants a place in the sun and to be loved for herself too. He agreed. "That's why I'm here." "He's so stubborn." She continued, "His brother has nine children. Maybe he wants the same." He denied this. "Look, I'll even tell her to have that operation if she feels I still resent it."

For her to have the operation could have serious emotional consequences for someone like Mr. C.

I thought, in view of the differences they still have on this issue, that it should be deferred, and an immediate decision not made, as it was more important for them to get back to sex with adequate birth control.

He said, "I know it's no good to have kids if it's just going to break us up, and I agree to go along with you." This calmed her. I said, at the end of the interview, that in the sixth session we would discuss a summary of what had or had not been accomplished here, and what goals should be set if another three sessions were to be arranged.

Now it comes out! Alcoholism, with violence!

About four days later there was a telephone call from Mrs. Charlson. Her husband had been on a drunken binge. She can't go on. He had beaten her up badly, and she can't protect him any more. She had gone back to her lawyer, to continue with the separation.

Note their collusion in coming with an agenda that omitted the key problem.

She said she had originally promised her husband that if he came to counseling she would not push his alcoholism as a problem. She had agreed there were so many other things that were wrong between them. He had persuaded her that if things were better, the drinking would not be an issue, and she went along with this.

I asked how long the drinking had been going on and what his pattern of drinking was. She said, "It's always been there. About every two months or so, it's pretty bad. By then, it accumulates. He comes in late at night, gets rough, and knocks me around."

It is important for the spouse to be strengthened in her (or his) effort to disrupt their destructive interaction.

I told her it was important for him to take the consequences of his behavior, and that her decision to separate was wise. The best thing she can do for him is to make him realize she will not continue in this way.

Technique of using a rigid

Protecting him from the consequences of his behavior was not in his best interest or that of the family. Separating could be

behavior pattern—in Mrs. C's case, her strong need to protect, by redefining and redirecting it.

a way to propel him into getting some help, while he is still a comparatively young man and before irreversible physical problems arise. In fact, I told her, this would be *true* protection.

I said I wanted to meet with them to discuss the present situation and future plans for help.

Sixth Interview, February 21

This was arranged in response to a telephone call from Mr. Charlson asking for an appointment. Today Mrs. Charlson wore dark glasses, sat still, and looked solemn. She did not want to open the session. I asked why he had called. He just looked at his nails, which were bitten down, and waited quietly. Characteristically, she spoke. "He has a summons in his pocket to appear in court in two weeks." "What happened?"

He admitted he had come home in a drunken rage and had put out a cigarette on the back of her hand. He had thrown a few ashtrays around. He said, "I wouldn't drink if she treated me better."

I said, "But this must have begun before your marriage five years ago." Here she said that his foster father had told her he thought marriage would help him. Mr. Charlson continued to defend himself, saying, "She doesn't respect me, she gets mad. I feel helpless." Now Mrs. Charlson was up in arms. "Don't give me that. You lean on me like a child and still demand respect."

The alcoholic's conflict between a deep need for dependency and the strong fear of it.

Again, desperately, he pleaded, "She's embarrassed me by not paying the bills. I told her to budget." I asked why Mrs. Charlson should do this, since they were both working. But he just turned to another complaint. "She won't even let me go fishing, which would be a harmless outlet." She broke in, "You know you'll only go with a crowd that gets drunk. You'll kill yourself, or fall in the river."

He continues to project the blame on her.

More protectiveness from the mate. She has a "rescue mission." This pattern is often characteristic of the alcoholic and his wife.

Denial is strong, also typical of the alcoholic.

He kept insisting he had no drinking problem. I said, "I know it's hard for you to see this, but I must point out that your wife wants a separation because it's a problem for her and the children. Your family life is affected even though you say it doesn't affect your health or your work.''

Here Mrs. Charlson began crying and said, "If I get a separation, he keeps telling me he'll drink himself to death.'' I said, "That's his problem. He has to find a better way to solve his tensions than getting into this kind of destructive behavior. It could also get him into trouble with the law.''

Finally he admitted he may have a drinking problem but he really thought that getting counseling first would solve the problem. Again he went back to fishing as an outlet. "Why this?'' I asked. He said, "She objects even if I only go two or three times a year.'' He was ready now to promise anything. "I'll stop drinking for a whole year.'' I asked, "What will happen when the year is over?'' She said, "I don't believe you— you've promised before. You've beaten me many times, and badly. Elise, too, has had it from you, and even your best friend says you're an alcoholic.'' I turned to him, "Mr. Charlson, you can't see the risk for you. No one can force you to get help with your drinking, but your wife has the right to say, 'I won't live with this fear any longer.' ''

She reminded him, "How often have I told you—don't come home when you're drunk, don't drive, go to a motel.'' Again he argued feebly that fishing was a good outlet, that all of his friends don't drink; only some do. Mrs. Charlson said, "They *all* drink. It's just a booze party or you wouldn't go. In fact, you could go every weekend if you didn't drink.''

I stopped her here and asked, "Why should he go every weekend? Don't you and the children have some right to his time too?'' She answered, "I'd put up with a lot, if he'd only stop drinking.'' I said to her, "That's one of your problems. Perhaps you put up with too much.''

About his drinking himself to death, I told her she needn't feel responsible as, if she stayed on, he still might drink himself to death. In any case, it sounds as though this pattern would go on and could destroy them all. I said I thought she had made a courageous and necessary decision about separation, not only for herself and her chilren, but actually for her husband too. This could turn out to be a constructive plan for all of them.

Mr. Charlson looked pretty downcast. I pointed out to him that divorce was not the issue at this point, and he had the op-

Again, her ambivalence is evident, with her need to protect and watch over him.

Worker has to be consistent in holding to the realistic risks, and to strengthen Mrs. C's resolve to separate.

Again, she is overgiving. I interpret this as negating the rights of the rest of the family.

Some hope is offered.

tion of going to A.A. as a resource for treatment. I said he was an able man, with many years of living ahead, and that his health was not yet affected. I suggested, however, that a medical check-up would be important to confirm this.

Raising the realistic medical risk.

I said Mrs. Charlson would need ongoing help in the difficult period ahead, and I would like to arrange a referral to the family agency, and with her agreement to share their situation. She nodded her willingness. I told them that with alcoholism in the family, the agency sometimes undertakes to treat all the members of the family as a group, along with A.A. when it seems timely and appropriate. This will depend, however, on how the agency perceives the situation.

A few weeks later, Mrs. Charlson phoned me. A six-month legal separation had been arranged, and she is now in touch with the family agency. She still hopes he will be helped and the family will get together again. I encouraged her and stressed that she was certainly doing her very best to help them all.

CLOSING COMMENTS

In reviewing the case of Mr. and Mrs. Charlson, it is obvious that there were contraindications to short-term marital counseling from the outset, which were missed by the counselor. However, the outcome of the service proved beneficial for the family.

The couple had colluded in denying the all too common problem of alcoholism. Obvious signals of this, however, were present in the first interview and in the second as well. I allowed the couple to divert me to relationship issues until five sessions later when the key problem exploded and referral to other resources was found necessary.

Although there had been some indication of improvement in their negative interaction, and some pressure removed from the teen-age daughter, the case clearly shows that a focus on relationship treatment was inadequate in and of itself. A serious alcoholic problem can never be a secondary concern. This is confirmed in an article by Davis (1980), who concludes: "Without a committment from all concerned to work toward eliminating the problem drinking as a first priority, an error is being made." In other words, when alcoholism and/or violence is present in a marriage, it is essential to strengthen the "victim" to act differently and to promote a firm stand in the use of meaningful consequences so as to create a crisis. This appears to be necessary in order to motivate the spouse to face rather than to deny the problem and to take active steps for treatment.

To repeat, treatment for the alcoholic should be the primary concern, regardless of whether the "victim" provokes, seeks punishment, or protects the mate. The familial interactional difficulties can then be worked with.

The worker recommends Alcoholics Anonymous. This resource has been acknowledged by many psychiatrists as generally more effective than psychotherapy. A variety of other approaches have had their successes and failures. The structured program of the A.A. meetings, however, and the use of group controls and group support, along with the "buddy system," serve to strengthen the weakened ego of the alcoholic and are less threatening than individual help. Al-Anon can be similarly effective for the wife.

There is currently some controversy regarding the effectiveness of A.A. as opposed to family therapy. Davis's article suggests that both approaches can be mutually reinforcing in the treatment of alcoholics.

This case also raises the disturbing problem of wife abuse (Flynn, 1977) and violence in the family (Ball, 1977), which are more openly acknowledged today as serious social concerns.

9

Preparation for Marriage

Many years ago at a public lecture on sex education, a woman asked the speaker: "My child is six. When should I begin his sex education?" "Madam," said the speaker, "rush home quickly—you shouldn't be here in the first place. Sex education begins in the nursery."

It is well known that children learn very early how a husband treats his wife, and how the wife treats her husband. They sense when respect and affection are present in or absent from the home. We can't go back to the nursery, but fortunately people can learn at any age, although as we get older the unlearning process becomes more difficult.

Engaged couples rarely seek premarriage counseling. Why should they? Behind the rose-colored glasses, they rarely see the need to learn anything about sex or marriage. Nevertheless, the caseload of the short-term marriage counselor will generally include a small proportion of engaged couples seeking help.

The few who come usually have severe, even acute, problems. Strange as it may seem, small and seemingly unimportant matters can trigger a highly explosive situation. Whom to invite to the wedding? What to serve? What will be the color scheme—his mother looks better in yellow, and her mother favors pink. All this with the wedding date set for less than a month away.

Why are the young couple caught in this hassle? Perhaps the young man is to be subsidized by his father; maybe he is working for him and he puts pressure on his fiancée to give way.

Or the woman may be tied to her family, who may feel socially superior and want to assert their position, and therefore pressure her betrothed to give way. In any case, they are far from ready to take on the tasks of the beginning phase of marriage. They need to grow up first. Sometimes counseling can be effective in helping them to cope with such family situations, by presenting them with alternatives. Where are their priorities? Is it his side, her side, or their side?

A small issue can become a major one. Parental conflict or domination persists long after the wedding ceremony has been performed. How will they deal with that?

I recall one engaged couple who came to me two weeks before their scheduled wedding date. The minister had referred them because of intense quarrelling between them. She appeared in the office wearing dark glasses which she removed, revealing a black eye. He admitted he had struck her; he was sorry but she had provoked him and had hit him first. She denied hitting him, but did say she had upset him.

To summarize briefly, they had known each other for nine months, and this was not the first violent incident. I told them both that he needed intensive therapeutic help, that he was not ready to undertake marriage without creating misery both for himself and for her. I advised them to defer the marriage. She resisted this, asking how long it would take. I explained that lack of impulse control with violent outbursts will not yield to short-term therapy. I told her firmly, "What you see is what you'll get." I added that if she persisted in entering into such a hazardous marriage, she too should undertake individual therapy.

She insisted, however, that once he got away from his "terrible" family and his miserable home atmosphere, they would get along and be happy together. He too thought things would quiet down when they were on their own. She was determined to be married before her thirtieth birthday. A friend had made a shower for her, and the wedding date was set.

It was frustrating to realize that I could do nothing for them. I did urge her, however, to take responsibility for birth control and she accepted an appointment with a gynecologist.

Two months later, she telephoned and urgently requested that I see them again. This time, she had her arm in a cast. He tried to say that she had fallen on the ice when they were skating, but she was now too frightened to protect him further. She said he had broken her arm in a fight. She wanted advice from me about a divorce. He said he would not contest it, and I gave them the names of two lawyers.

A PROGRAM FOR PREVENTION

Apart from such cases coming for a clinical service, the center recognized the necessity of promoting "prevention" and reducing the risk of marital breakdown by reaching out to engaged couples in the community. Accordingly, a number of programs were set up. Three levels were involved.

One was an educational interpretive program. These were the so-called one-night stands. The center provided speakers for a wide range of community groups, such as religious institutions, service clubs, high schools, university campus groups, and so on. These meetings served to offer an interpretation of the type of service available at the Marriage Counselling Centre of Montreal, at the family service agencies, at clinics, and at other resources. Since many people still tend to think that the marriage counselor will tell them who is right, who is wrong, and exactly what to do, these single meetings offered a useful explanation of the counselor's role as impartially enabling couples to help themselves.

A second level of prevention involved working at the Centre with small groups of premarrieds in a course of ten weekly sessions with one leader. The idea was that working with a group of five or six young couples who do not normally seek marriage counseling would provide them with some useful preparation for marriage. For the practitioner and teacher it would provide a perspective not available when one is confined to an office giving a service to seriously troubled couples.

A third level consisted of courses of ten weekly sessions offered to non-social-work professionals involved in pre- and post-marriage counseling. These were ministers, medical doctors, and lawyers. The work with these professionals will be described in Chapter 10.

RECRUITING GROUP PARTICIPANTS

The Marriage Counselling Centre of Montreal offered its first premarriage counseling course in the spring of 1956. We decided it would be best to introduce the new program at a community meeting to be held in a health and socializing center, such as the local YM/YWHA. The object would be to present the course as progressive and preventive rather than as problem-oriented. The meeting was advertised under the caption: "Are You Ready for Marriage?" A psychiatrist, a gynecologist, and a marriage counselor (myself) were the panelists. The doors were figuratively bulging, with young people standing in the hallways. It was a real overflow turnout.

Many remained standing throughout the two-hour session. This confirmed to us that the meeting was a great success. As the couples left, forms were made available describing the ten two-hour sessions with starting dates and times. A nominal registration fee was mentioned. Interested couples were asked to return the forms by a certain date. All available blank forms were taken away.

We were of course delighted by the enthusiasm this opening meeting had engendered. I recall my concern and anxiety for days afterwards: how would we handle the large number of anticipated requests? If each group were limited to six couples, how on earth would we be able to provide the trained leaders who would be needed? With the small professional staff available, we could never handle the crowd we saw coming.

I needn't have worried. When the date arrived for the forms to be handed in, imagine my astonishment to find that only one couple had signed up for the program. What had happened? We could only surmise that the young people coming to the Y would be familiar with many of the members who had come to the opening meeting, indeed would have close friends among them, all of whom had attended. It could be embarrassing to meet friends at registration and wonder why they were taking the course—they must be having trouble!

In any case, we then decided to send notices to different religious institutions, colleges, service groups, and similar organizations, announcing the course, with the limit of six engaged couples, pointing out that relatives or friends would be placed in different groups which would meet on different evenings. This, too, did not draw more than a sprinkling of couples. We later added spot advertising on the local radio, which turned out to be quite useful. We did manage by various means to get together two such groups twice a year, but even this modest achievement was not easy to maintain.

Some years later, Dr. David Mace, a distinguished leader in marriage and premarriage counseling both in England and in the United States, attended our annual meeting in Montreal as the main speaker. I discussed this problem with him, and he told me that his experience in England had been similar. It was extremely difficult to catch the group of premarrieds for this kind of intimate, ongoing experience. A single meeting or lecture will attract them, as it is nonthreatening and does not touch them in a personal, meaningful way.

THE SCREENING PROCESS

Screening is an essential aspect of this type of group counseling. Registration begins a week or two before the first session. Each of the partners is asked to complete a premarriage inventory form. This asks for information about marriage plans, how long they have known each other, previous marriage or engagement, current relationship to parents, in-laws, siblings, education, religion, employment, friends and hobbies.

Each of the partners is then seen in a brief interview. The group leader utilizes this information in making a tentative assessment of the individuals.

A conjoint interview with the couple follows. This has several purposes. The aims of the course and the couple's expectations of it are discussed. The role of the leader and the role of the participants are explained. This interview is also brief, taking approximately a half-hour of time. However, it provides the leader with a glimpse at the couple's pattern of communication and interaction—who leads, who follows, and to what extent. They are told that the individual concerns and issues that couples raise will also be related to the group as a whole. In other words, the group, rather than the individual, is the client. This they find reassuring.

A further purpose of this conjoint interview is to distinguish those couples who can use the group advantageously from those who, because of a severe problem or crisis situation, require a separate counselling service. It is explained to such couples that the group will not meet their individual needs adequately. These couples are also told they may be able to benefit from the group experience at a later date.

Group Composition

But more than individual and couple assessment is needed to ensure effective group functioning. Two criteria in forming the groups are of special significance. As indicated, friends or relatives are placed in different groups, to meet on different evenings. In addition, it is wise to avoid an extreme disparity in intellectual interests and ability which may tend to slow up or inhibit communication within the group. A truck driver with an elementary school education and a lecturer at a university may not be on the same wavelength.

Aside from these contraindications, contrast and balance are useful principles in group composition. Social, economic, religious, and occupational differences between couples are desirable. A mix of personalities is useful as well—for example, the shy and the opinionated, the peacemaker and the doubting Thomas. This provides an opportunity to understand and accept differences in others as well as in themselves.

Discussion Method

In the first session, the leader can use information derived from the screening interviews. For instance, often we find it is the women who coax the men into coming. As one reluctant young man put it in a screening interview, "I don't want anyone telling me how to run my marriage." Another said sheepishly, "I hope I won't be asked any embarrassing questions" (Freeman, 1965, p. 39; reprinted Munson, 1980, p. 318). These cues enable the worker "to start where the group is." For example, when they gather in the informal setting found most suitable, easy chairs and coffee available, and introductions are over, the leader may say, "I believe most of you men have something in common—you weren't exactly eager to come in the first place!" The worker restates the positive, health-oriented purpose of the group and the discussion leader's role as resource person to help them clarify the kind of marriage they themselves wish to develop.

The group tends to move into discussion of their expectations of marriage, when the topic is suggested by the leader to get the ball rolling. A range of idealistic responses comes through freely. These indicate initially that a good marriage is supposedly a ready-made affair. They begin by defining "love." Conventional intellectual ideas of constancy, loyalty, devotion, trust, and so on are offered by the participants, some with a romantic flavor. I recall a young woman saying that "love is the gift of oneself to the partner, who should always come first." This gives the leader an opportunity to challenge them on unrealistic expectations and to play devil's advocate in a light way. I may ask, for instance, "Will no one here question this high-minded perfection?" This will help to move the group to more practical discussion.

The group is encouraged to set up the agenda for subsequent sessions. Topics such as budgeting, buying on credit, friends, relatives, sex, birth control, religion, outings and holidays, and in-laws are raised. The subject of parenting, and if and when to have a child, is also brought up. Topics may and do run together in different sessions, although the leader tries to give direction and explore different aspects of a theme before moving too quickly on to another subject.

The group "gels" and becomes close-knit within three or four sessions. The leader encourages interaction and the raising of areas of agreement as well as differences in thinking and feeling between the members, and at times between a couple. No one couple's differences are exposed for too long, as others in the group with related concerns are drawn in by the leader. Issues of togetherness and of autonomy may become quite heated. This may become linked to who does the housework when both partners will be working. In one group a young man admitted his "addiction" to watching hockey on television. His fiancée complained she felt neglected and out in the cold. He resented her interference with "his right" to some enjoyment on his own, and he appealed to the group. She became angry and burst out: "And where do I come in?" Soon everyone became involved. He was advised not to go overboard on the hockey. She was encouraged to find an interest of her own. The right to individual interests was stressed, but not to the exclusion of common interests. Otherwise, as one member put it: "Why marry? Stay single!"

Role playing is used frequently. For example, on the subject of relationship to in-laws, one man declared that his fiancée's parents were fine but that he was struggling with his own bossy, widowed mother. He and his fiancée couldn't even look at bedroom furniture without his mother tagging along. The situation was role-played with several men in his group to help him deal with his mother differently. The following week he reported back to the group, which could hardly wait to hear what he had to say: "Radar must have been operating. My old lady really improved since we role-played her!" Some members told him that *he* had improved, that he had learned not to stick his neck out by apologizing to her for every move he made (Freeman, 1965; reprinted in Munson, 1980, p. 319).

At a later session, when budgeting and saving were being discussed, another man said his parents were going to put the couple up for the first year or so, so that they could save their money for the down payment on a small home of their own. The woman said she was very fond of his parents and didn't mind living with them if this was what he thought best.

They were soon challenged by others in the group as to how they could tolerate risking interference by in-laws. The young man insisted that his folks were easy-going, and the woman agreed. Then he added, "My mother would be only too glad to teach Eileen how to cook!"

"Wow," another woman burst out, "I'd sure hate that!" One of the men said, "Imagine making love with your parents outside the door!" Someone else asked, "Is this necessary financially?" When the details came out, it appeared that they had an adequate income between them, and that his prospects were good. Then, as another member put it, "You'd be better off away from your parents, even in one room, and you'd have a heck of a lot more fun.''

It developed that the woman came from an affluent family, and the man felt it incumbent on him to provide her with a home of their own as soon as possible. He had thought that living with his parents, with no rent to pay, would speed this up. It came out, however, that he had not made this clear to his fiancée, and she had gone along with his plan, though somewhat reluctantly.

"Actually," she told him now, "I think I'd prefer us to live in a small place on our own, even if we had to wait two or three years to buy a home."

The leader then commented on the frank and helpful nature of the discussion, but suggested that the couple should give such an important matter greater consideration on their own. The leader then pointed out that such joint decision making after reflective discussion was indicated for all of them.

This example shows that couples can at times learn more from each other than from the leader. It is interesting to see how communication improves, how a small behavioral change can bring about attitude change as the group progresses. (For more detailed description of these groups and the techniques found helpful, see Freeman, 1965.)

FOLLOW-UP AND CONCLUSIONS

Over the years an annual reunion was held by each group. Some of the member couples had moved away so it was not possible to keep track of all of them. We learned that a small number broke their engagements and did not marry. Group members said they thought this was for the best. In those cases they sensed trouble ahead. Some of the couples became close friends when the group was over, an interesting fringe benefit.

In summary, the short-term group experience was well received by the participants and was a rewarding experience for me as a marriage counselor. Of course there is no guarantee that marital bliss will ensue for the "graduates" (Bader et al., 1980). Still, the notion persists that these couples are on their way a little more prepared, more realistically ready to work at developing a wholesome family life.

Since the early 1960s there has been a mushrooming growth of preventive programs across the continent. Family life education, sex education, marriage enrichment, and numerous related programs are now widely offered in welfare agencies, in high schools, colleges, clubs, religious institutions, and elsewhere. As well, there is a trend for the growing number of "cohabiting" couples to seek counseling before marriage.

For those interested, a comprehensive review of developments and current problems in the expanding field of premarriage counseling is available in the literature (Schumm & Denton, 1979).

10

Sharing the Short-Term Approach with Allied Professionals

We now turn to the third level of "prevention," the extension of the center's services to key community professionals such as physicians, lawyers, and clergymen of all denominations.

It is well known to practitioners that premarrieds as well as couples in marital difficulty do not for the most part seek out a marriage counselor or psychiatrist in the first instance. Instead, it is easier and less threatening for them to request help from their clergyman or doctor, whom they already know. The lawyer, too, is sometimes called upon for advice about separation or divorce. Yet such counseling is not central to the function of these professionals, and their training may not have equipped them for it.

It therefore seemed to the staff of the Marriage Counselling Centre that sharing the time-limited approach with physicians, lawyers, and ministers could be both practical and constructive. With this in mind, we decided to initiate a course under the aegis of the continuing education department of McGill University, entitled "Short-term pre-marriage and marriage counselling." The expectation was that these professionals would be encouraged to give a brief counseling service on their own, or alternatively to make a knowledgeable referral to a suitable resource.

The course was limited to eighteen members, consisted of ten weekly sessions of two hours each and was well attended each year over a ten-year period. It consistently attracted mainly clergymen; few other professionals enrolled.

Why so few physicians and lawyers were involved is a matter of speculation. The medical practitioners who did attend suggested that for the most part their educations prepared them to treat illness, but did not include dealing with child-rearing difficulties, marital discord, or, in particular, sexual problems, with which they are faced continually in their practice. Some of the lawyers said that the adversary role to which they were trained implies a conflict of interest. When faced with legal grounds for divorce the tendency is to move ahead in that direction and marital reconciliation is just not in the cards.

It must be said, however, that those from the fields of medicine and law who did attend these courses were actively interested and participated fully in the sessions. These professionals bring an important specialized knowledge and perspective which social workers do not possess. Later, a number of them became effective sources of two-way referrals and of consultation, to and from the staff of the center. At times they also contributed as valued team members in ongoing treatment of particular couples.

In this connection the special therapeutic intervention which the general practitioner may provide, however briefly, has been studied and described with outstanding clarity and up-to-date relevance by Dr. Michael Balint, as far back as 1957. The trend toward family practice in medicine may bring about significant change in this area and may so widen the scope of physicians that greater emphasis on the promotion of health and on reducing the risk of marital breakdown will result. In recent years the growing involvement and contribution of the medical doctor, who is also trained as marriage and family counselor is reflected in the membership of the American Association of Marriage and Family Therapists.

Interest in closer cooperation between family and marital therapy and the legal profession is also gaining attention. This is discussed in a special issue of the *Journal of the Association for Marriage and Family Therapy*, July, 1980. It is pointed out in this issue that some of the law schools have begun to offer courses in interviewing and counseling, and a few programs are now offering law degrees combined with doctorates of Psychology or Masters of Social Work degrees (Steinberg, 1980).

Although not dealt with here, it should be noted that clinical psychologists continue to provide a significant segment of well-trained marriage and family therapists. Still, many psychologists who are not specifically trained in this area are called upon to give a marriage counseling service, and the need for additional know-how has been expressed. Educational counselors are also becoming increasingly active in this field.

COUNSELING IN THE RELIGIOUS MINISTRY

Ministers of religion have been with us since time immemorial, long before psychiatrists and marriage counselors came on the scene. Pastoral counseling has an age-old history of helping people in trouble, of dealing with crises such as illness or death, as well as marital conflict and children's behavior problems. Some theological centers have developed high-quality programs for training pastoral counselors and provide supervised field practice in mental hospitals and in other settings.

The consistent response of clergymen to courses offered by a professional marriage counselor, however, would indicate recognition by many of a need to strengthen their knowledge and skill in this area. The highlights of a typical course follow.

The First Three Sessions

At the opening of the first session on short-term marriage counseling, I vividly recall entering the room to find a group of dignified clerical gentlemen seated around the table. There were several Anglican ministers with collar reversed, a number of Orthodox Rabbis wearing skullcaps, and, between the Presbyterians and Unitarians, a Reform rabbi. My new role as "teacher" of religious leaders found me somewhat apprehensive.

After they introduced themselves, I commented that there was quite a mix in the room, but that they all had something in common. "Yes, indeed," came instantly from one grave-looking gentleman, "have Bible—will travel." We all laughed. I told them I knew I would be preaching to the converted, but hoped to "holler in different places." I said I would welcome their reactions to my plan for the course, which was subject to change if they wished.

Topics are provisionally lined up by group members and the leader. For married couples, the topics usually include child rearing, teen-age problems, infidelity, alcoholism, and financial and sexual difficulties. For premarrieds, difficulties such as parental disapproval and premarital pregnancy often arise. The use of community resources and the possible need for psychiatric referral are matters usually added by the leader.

We then discuss our respective responsibilities for the course. I indicate our "contract" should include what I would contribute as group leader and what their contributions should be as group members. I would take the responsibility to provide guidelines for the short-term approach to marriage and premarriage counseling and would welcome questions and differences of opinion from the members. I would like to use illustrative material, live examples from my own practice and from theirs, current or recent, from which we could together draw useful practice principles. I told them to expect the occasional use of role playing to liven things up, and they agreed to go along with this.

At the first session and into the second I share a theoretical framework for making a marital assessment on which the treatment plan is to be based (see Chapter 1). It is understood that members have a rich life experience with a varied knowledge of human behavior, which lends itself to the eclectic approach as used by the leader.

Notions of mate selection and the complementary balance which often draws people together are presented—for example, how the reserved type is drawn toward the outgoing one, each providing something the other is lacking. This creates the emotional "fit" which may work well for the couple. The popular adage that "like mates like," however, is sociologically sound (in terms of class, education, interests) but at the emotional level it is also true that "opposites attract." This is the meshing of need, which answers the not-infrequent question, "What did he ever see in her?" or "Why did she choose him?" (Winch, 1958). During periods of crisis or role stress the equilibrium established by the mutual need pattern may be disturbed. This is the point at which couples reach for help.

Because I perceive the call for help in marital discord as a crisis situation, concepts from crisis theory are emphasized. The work of Lydia Rapoport (1967, 1970) is especially helpful in this connection. The need for intervention as early as possible, while people are more accessible, is stressed, as is the planned use of time.

It is suggested that the minister should explain during the first contact with the couple (unless an immediate referral is indicated) that two further meetings will be offered them, to decide whether he can be of help. At the same time they are told that the decision will be a three-way one. I suggest to the group members that if no progress takes place after three sessions, and they are faced with a stalemate, consultation or referral should be seriously considered.

Role theory concepts (Spiegel, 1968; Biddle, 1979) are found to be particularly adaptable to the needs of the professionals. A tentative evaluation of each partner's major role functioning provides a practical direction for helping. Effective role functioning, as opposed to role retrogression, unfilled roles, or role ambiguity, are discussed in order to identify the assets and limitations in the individuals, in the marriage, and in their social milieu.

The application of principles to practice is an integral aspect of the course. The second session therefore uses "homework" assigned in the first session—for example, the first interview with Dr. and Mrs. Fisher (Chapter 4) and the three Martin interviews (Chapter 3) may be offered.

Both initial interviews in these assigned cases show early client resistance, as many cases do. Some group members share their own difficulties in dealing with this, and suggestions are offered by others. The principle of responding to affect rather than to content is brought out; that is, the client's feelings are accepted and the negative statements are not responded to at this early point. The task of enlisting the resistant partner is thus seen as a necessary principle to get counseling under way. As the course progresses, case material is drawn on, to provide further discussion and clarification of the assessment and treatment process.

The third session focuses on the value of interdisciplinary collaboration and on when this is indicated. How to use the network of community resources effectively for consultation as well as for referral is emphasized as an essential part of the program. For the second hour of this session a psychiatrist is brought in to identify when the nonmedically trained counselor should make a referral to psychiatry. The need to know or to get to know at least two psychiatrists is stressed, in order to personalize the referral.

Subsequent Sessions

During the subsequent sessions the members bring up examples from their own experience, and common operational principles are identified by the leader or by a group member. Sometimes a recent interview is reported on fully, and the next counseling steps are discussed. A summarized case along with specific questions may be presented during another session by one or two of the members. In one way or another each member brings something to the group. The leader draws attention to patterns of interaction between a couple. For example, the frequently seen, competitive power struggle or the dominance/submission axis, ranging on a continuum from mild to severe, is pointed out as it emerges from the case material. Presented problems and precipitating factors are noted. Pervasiveness and duration of the problems are taken into account; task setting and alternative goals are discussed.

The minister's counseling role is considered. Techniques such as being an active listener, creating a nonjudgmental atmosphere, moving from support to confrontation, the pros and cons of advice giving, task setting with limited goals, and referral when appropriate, are all linked to the cases presented.

In examining the counselor-client interaction, I have found the members of these groups particularly nondefensive when their role as counselor is questioned by a group member or by the leader.

It is sometimes necessary to make clear that the minister-counselor's nonjudgmental and accepting role is not in conflict with his or her role as preacher. A congregation can at times be morally criticized and admonished but this is not directed at any one individual or family. In counseling, the noncritical nonjudgmental attitude in no way condones inappropriate behavior. For instance, one can say to an unhappy promiscuous teen-ager, "I understand your troubles, but I am concerned about what may happen to you."

In discussing premarriage counseling, someone usually brings up the situation where the girl is pregnant and the couple don't really want to get married but feel pressure to do so from one or both families. The leader asks, "Is pregnancy a sufficient reason for marriage?" Everyone gets into the act. One will say, "Yes, I marry them. The chances are that they will grow together and become responsible as they both face the child they have brought into the world." Another will say, "It's a mistake to bring an unwanted child into a marriage, especially where the couple do not really love each other."

Someone will suggest a referral to an adoption agency, or that the girl have an abortion. One minister said, "If I don't marry them, I know that the man down the street will." A Reform rabbi disagreed; he would refuse to marry the couple unless they received counseling, so that they would achieve a better understanding of each other in the hope that the marriage would have a better chance to last. If not, he would advise them to break off and make other plans for the baby.

It was fascinating for me to see the conservative Anglican defend the Reform rabbi on this issue. Usually a consensus develops that the couple should be faced with the alternatives in a noncritical, nonjudgmental way.

The couple are thus given the opportunity to think through and discuss the pros and cons of marriage at this point, before assuming that marriage is the best solution.

At another session a minister reported that a wife had come to him in distress a few days before. She had not spoken to her husband for a week. In the discussion the question was raised about seeing one partner alone. A member objected that this could be a way of separating a couple still further and could increase the risk of taking sides. Another member pointed out that if the couple is seen together, the interaction can be observed and the adverse effect each has on the other can be brought to their attention.

The importance of keeping marital quarrels current, of helping couples not drag in everything that hurt or irritated them over the past ten years or so, is stressed (Bach & Wyden, 1968).

The leader brings out that angry feelings are part of the human condition, that it is better to clear the battle smoke at the time rather than bring the fight into the bedroom or, as often happens, continue it indirectly by "taking it out" on the children.

I emphasize that they, as ministers, possess a built-in asset in that they represent the "good father" figure, and permission from them to tolerate imperfections in one's mate may be very therapeutic. In addition, in the area of sex, permission from them to relax, and encouraging couples to enjoy each other physically, can have a positive impact on the couple if sexual dissatisfactions have come up.

When we discuss infidelity, I raise the question, "Is this a valid reason for divorce?" Also, "Is there a guilty party?" This again results in lively discussion and exposes differences of opinion in the group. It is brought out that the "injured" spouse may have contributed to the infidelity, as is illustrated in the case of the Victors in Chapter 2. It is also recognized that a long-lasting extramarital relationship should be distinguished from a passing "affair" (Strean, 1980).

The Use of Role Playing.

In a session on child rearing, we act out a brief sociodrama* concerning the not uncommon complaint of a wife about the husband who comes home and

---

*This is usually a general situation which is set up beforehand, and acted out in role playing. The term differs from psychodrama, of Moreno fame, where an actual life situation and the person's behavior are acted out in front of the group, as a therapeutic experience. [Moreno, 1972]

hides behind the newspaper, leaves her to discipline the children when they get out of hand, and then blames her for the consequences. She brings him to the minister, having made an appointment ahead of time, urging that her husband be given a good lecture.

We role-play the "lecture," and of course it is a shambles. The "wife" is asked how she feels when the role playing is finished, and she tells the group, "I feel I won. I feel virtuous, and that I've been taken advantage of." Then we ask the "husband" how he feels after the role playing. He feels resentful, greatly misunderstood, angry with his "wife" for dragging him into this, and disappointed with the minister who took her side.

We then take another couple and another minister and the role-playing interview proceeds. "She" is told to keep on talking, to pour out all her complaints nonstop. "He" is told to be quietly bored but to make an attempt to show his resentment. He tries to get a word in edgewise, but this is impossible.

Here we "cut" and ask, what the minister/counselor should do now? Should he allow this to go on or should he intervene? We go back to the scene before I said "cut." Now the minister, quick to take a cue, interrupts, "Just a minute, madam," he says, "it seems to me you're complaining that your husband doesn't talk. I notice he tries to get a word in, but can't manage to."

"Well," she responds, "I talk to him so much because *he* doesn't talk." He says, "I give up because she doesn't stop." The negative interaction and feedback are explained to the couple, and they are now asked to try it again, but this time they are to behave differently.

The "woman" becomes quieter. The "husband" does come on to say that if she will ask him directly for some advice about anything, including the children, or if she will take him more seriously when he does offer an opinion, he will try, as he does want to help out and quiet her down.

Sometimes a minister who volunteered to role-play finds he is a little uncomfortable and gets stumped; he can use a little help. I may stand behind him, and whisper a suggestion or two.

In any case, this type of learning is a lot of fun, and teaches the participants how to use a technique which is different from their usual approach.

Accepting Limited Goals

One of the features that comes out repeatedly in my work with ministers is their tendency to overgive. Working with time limits is a particular challenge to this group. On more than one occasion I have said to a minister, "You know what? Pack your trunk—not your suitcase—and move in with the family, because the way you're becoming involved in all aspects of their problems, you can hardly do less." Then I add, I hope facetiously, "Don't forget there's a family next door, and remember, you have a family, too."

I have sometimes thought that my main contribution to this group was probably showing them what *not* to do and when to draw on other community resources in order to keep them from becoming overinvolved in the many demands on them in marriage and family counseling.

ORGANIZING PREMARRIAGE PROGRAMS

There were some unexpected and worthwhile "spin-offs" from these courses. In several of the churches and synagogues, some of the members of the course developed their own premarriage program. This possibility is discussed before the group disbands and it is pointed out that it may be difficult for the minister to be the leader for young people in his own congregation, whom he knows well and who know each other well. Several congregations may get together and use a resource person. Another suggestion has been the use of a series of resource persons. This approach may be used flexibly in five or six sessions, combining the lecture and discussion methods. For continuity, the minister may be present in this less intimate series.

I recommend that the religious aspect be kept in the background, particularly in the beginning sessions. In drawing on outside resources, one might start with an accountant on budgeting, or an interior decorator on home furnishing. In other words, one often has to get in by the back door!

Over the years I have acted as opening speaker for some of the programs organized by former "students." One member initiated a six-session Institute for Brides and Grooms which was offered to engaged couples from a variety of religious centers. I was the opening speaker at the first session twice a year for a period of thirteen years!

Staffed by volunteers, this institute regularly drew in fifteen to twenty couples twice a year. The committee kept in touch with the couples and maintained a friendly contact with them and their family additions over the years. They underlined for me something I have known for a long time, that volunteers are an underused resource in most communities. This is a subject of much interest to me, one, however, beyond the scope of this book.

Epilogue

Preparation for marriage has only been touched on in these last two chapters. It is still largely an uncharted area. There is much to be learned and to be done in helping young people face the increasing complexities of modern life. Internal conflicts and problems within the family have always been with us, sometimes unheeded, sometimes absorbed by the extended family in a more stable environment. Until well into the nineteenth century, when the Industrial Revolution got under way, the North American family tended to be a comprehensive unit, largely meeting its own economic, social, and emotional needs.

Professional marriage counseling was quite unknown to previous generations. It has arisen in response to the pressures and tensions engendered by the massive technological, social, and economic challenges to the present-day family.

In recent years many approaches designed to assist and strengthen the family in the process of adaptation have been and are being developed and tested out. Meanwhile, it is incumbent on the marriage counselor to keep a finger on the pulse of the community beyond the office or agency walls and outside the covers of the latest book.

In our day the institution of marriage is being placed in the dock. It is being questioned, even rejected, in many quarters. Alternative lifestyles are pressing forward and competing for social acceptance. The direction for the institution of marriage is uncertain.

Yet the family in one form or another will survive. Times change, mores change, but the need for commitment to this, the most central of human relationships between man, woman, and their young, remains.

References and
Suggested Readings

ACKERMAN, N. *The psychodynamics of family life.* New York: Basic Books, Inc., 1958.

ACKERMAN, N., BEATMAN, F. & SHERMAN, S.N. (Eds.) *Expanding theory and practice in family therapy.* New York: Family Service Association of America, 1967.

ALDOUS, J. *Family careers: Developmental changes in families.* New York: John Wiley & Sons, 1978.

AXALINE, V. *Play therapy.* Cambridge, Mass.: Riverside Press, 1947.

BACH, G.K., & WYDEN, P. *The intimate enemy.* New York: William Morrow & Son, 1968.

BADER, E., MICROYS, G., SINCLAIR, C., WILLET, E., & CONWAY, B. Do marriage preparation programs really work? A Canadian experience. In *Journal of Marital and Family Therapy,* April 1980, **6**, (2).

BALINT, M. *The doctor, his patient, and the illness.* London: Pitman Medical Publishing Co. Ltd., 1957.

BALINT, M. & BALINT, E. *Psychotherapeutic techniques in medicine.* London: Tavistock Publications, 1961.

BALL, M. Issues of violence in family casework. *Social Casework,* January 1977, **58**, (1), 3–12.

BANDLER, R., GRINDER, J., & SATIR, V. *Changing with families.* Palo Alto: Science & Behavior Books, 1976.

BANE, M.J.O. Marital disruption and the lives of children. *Journal of Social Issues*, 1976, **32**, 103–117.

BARDILL, D.R. & RYAN, F.J. *Family Group Casework*. Washington, D.C.: National Association of Social Workers, 1973.

BARNETT, R.C. & BARUCH, G.K. Women in the middle years: A critique of research and theory. *Psychology of Women Quarterly,* 1978, 3, 187–197.

BARRIER, D. & FREEMAN, D.R. Some implications for social work practitioners of the new divorce legislation. *Intervention,* Journal of the Corporation of Social Workers of the Province of Quebec, Summer, 1969.

BARTEN, H.H., (Ed.) *Children and their parents in brief therapy.* New York: Behavioral Publications, 1973.

BECK, D. Research findings on the outcome of marital counselling. *Social Casework*, March 1975, **56**, (3).

BELL, R.R. *Premarital sex in a changing society.* Englewood Cliffs, N.J.: Prentice-Hall, 1966.

BELLIVEAU, N., & RICHTER, L. *Understanding human sexual inadequacy.* Boston: Little, Brown & Co., 1970.

BENEDEK, T. Parenthood as a developmental phase. *Journal of the American Psychoanalytic Association*, 1959, **7**, 389–417.

BERENSON, D. Alcohol and the family system. In P.J. Guerin, Jr. (Ed.), *Family therapy.* New York: Gardner Press, 1976.

BERNARD, J. Change and stability in sex norms and behavior. *Journal of Social Issues*, 1976, **32**, 207–223.

BERNE, E. *Games people play.* New York: Grove Press, 1964.

BIDDLE, B.J. *Role Theory.* New York: Academic Press, 1979.

BOTT, E. Conjugal roles and social networks. In N.W. Bell & E.F. Fogel (Eds.), *A modern introduction to the family.* New York: The Free Press, 1968.

BOWEN, M. Alcoholism and the family system. In *The Family*, 1974, **1**, (1) 2–25. New Rochelle, N.Y.: Centre for Family Learning.

_____. Family reaction to death. In P.J. Guerin, Jr. (Ed.), *Family therapy.* New York: Gardner Press,1976.

_____. *Family therapy in clinical practice.* New York: Jason Aronson, 1978

BRANDWEIN, R.A. Women and children last: The social situation of divorced mothers and their families. *Journal of Marriage and the Family*, 1974, **36**, 498–514.

BRECHENSER, D.M. Brief psychotherapy using transactional analysis. *Social Casework*, March 1972, **53**, 173–176.

BRODERICK, C. B. & BERNARD, J. (Eds.) *The individual, sex and society: A SIECUS handbook for teachers and counsellors.* Baltimore: Johns Hopkins Press, 1969.

BRUNER, J.S. Play is serious business. *Psychology Today*, January 1975.

BURKE, R.J. & WEIR, T. Some personality differences between members of one-career and two-career families. *Journal of Marriage and the Family*, 1976, **38**, 453–459.

CARTER, R.D. & THOMAS, E.J.A. Modification of problematic marital communication using corrective feedback and instruction. *Behavior Therapy*, 1973, **4**, 100–109.

CHILMAN, C.S. *Growing up poor*. Washington, D.C.: U.S. Dept. of Health, Education and Welfare, 1966.

_____. Teen-age pregnancy: A research review. *Social Work*, November 1979, **24**, (6).

COHEN, P.C. & KRAUSE, M.D. *Casework with the wives of alcoholics*. New York: Family Service Association of America, 1971.

COOK, A.H. *The working mother*. Ithaca, N.Y.: New York State School of Industrial and Labor Relations, Cornell University, 1975.

COOKERLEY, J.R. Evaluating different approaches to marriage counselling. In David H.L. Olson (Ed.), *Treating relationships*. Lake Mills, Iowa: Graphic Publishing Co. Inc., 1976.

DAVIS, D.I. Alcoholics Anonymous and family therapy. *Journal of Marital and Family Therapy,* January 1980, **6**, (1), 65–73.

DESPERT, J.L. *Children of divorce*. New York: Doubleday-Dolphin, 1962.

DEUTSCH, F. & MURPHY, W.F. *The clinical interview*. New York: International Universities Press, 1955.

DICKS, H.V. *Marital tensions*. London: Routledge and Kegan Paul, 1967.

DUVALL, E. *Family development*. Philadelphia: J.B. Lippincott, 1971.

_____. *Marriage and family development,* 5th ed. Philadelphia: J.B. Lippincott, 1977.

ELLIS, A. *The art and science of love*. New York: Signet Books, 1972.

EPSTEIN, N.B. & WESTLEY, W.A. *Silent majority*. San Francisco: Jossey-Bass, 1970.

ERIKSON, E.H. *Identity and the life cycle,* vol. 1. New York: International Universities Press, 1959.

_____. *Identity, youth and crisis*. New York: W.W. Norton, 1968.

EYSENCK, H.J.F. The effects of psychotherapy: An evaluation. *Journal of Consulting Psychology,* October 1952, **16**, 319–323.

FISHER, E.O. *Help for today's troubled marriages*. New York: Award Books, 1970.

_____. *Divorce: The new freedom, A guide to divorcing and divorce counseling*. New York: Harper & Row, 1974.

FISHMAN, P.M. Interaction: The work women do. *Social Problems*, 1978, **25**, 397–406.

FLYNN, J. Recent findings related to wife abuse. *Social Casework*, January 1977, **58**, 13–20.

FRAIBERG, S. *The magic years.* New York: Scribners, 1959.

FRANK, J. The role of hope in psychotherapy. *International Journal of Psychiatry*, May 1968, **5**, 394.

FREEMAN, D.R. Counselling engaged couples in small groups. *Social Work*, October 1965, **10**, (4). Reprinted in Munson, *Social Work with Families*, 314–321.

_____. Social work counselling—Short-term crisis intervention. *Canadian Counsellor*, Journal of the Canadian Guidance and Counselling Association, January 1968, **2**, (1).

_____. The use of the telephone in marital crisis. *Intervention*, Bulletin of the Corporation of Professional Social Workers of the Province of Quebec, Summer 1972, **38**, 14–21.

FRIED, B. *The middle-age crisis,* rev. ed. New York: Harper & Row, 1976.

FREUD, A. *The ego and mechanisms of defence*, 3rd printing. New York: International Universities Press, 1950.

FUCHS, E. *The second season: Life, love and sex—Women in the middle years.* Garden City, N.Y.: Anchor Press/Doubleday, 1977.

GARCEA, R.A. & IRWIN, O. A family agency deals with the problems of dropouts. *Social Casework*, 1962, **43**, (2), 71–75.

GARRETT, A. Transference in casework. In Cora Kasins (Ed.), *Principles and techniques of casework*. New York: Family Service Association of America, 1950.

GERMAIN, C. General systems theory and ego psychology: An ecological perspective. *Social Service Review*, December 1978, **52**, (4), 535–552.

GESELL, A.S., ILG, F.L., & AMES, L.B. *Infant and child in the culture of today*, rev. ed. New York: Harper's, 1974.

GINOTT, H. *Between parent and child*. New York: McGraw-Hill, 1968.

_____. *Between parent and teen-ager*. New York: Brunner/Mazel, 1969.

GLENDENING, S. E. & WILSON, A. J. Experiments in group premarriage counseling. *Social Casework*, 1972, **53**, 551–562.

GLICK, P.C. The family life cycle. *American Sociological Review*, April 1947, **12**.

_____. *American Families*. New York: John Wiley & Sons, 1957.

GOLAN, N. *Treatment in crisis situations*. New York: The Free Press, 1978.

GOCHROS, H.L. Sexual problems in social work practice. *Social Work*, 1971, 163–165.

GOCHROS, H.L. & SCHULTZ, L. (Eds.) *Human sexuality and social work*. New York: Association Press, 1972.

GOODE, W.J. *Women in divorce*. New York: The Free Press, 1975.

GREENE, B. *The psychotherapies of marital disharmony*. New York: The Free Press, 1965.

_____. *A clinical approach to marital problems*. Springfield, Ill: C.C. Thomas, 1970.

GREER, S. E. & D'ZURILLA, T. J. Behavioral approaches to marital discord and conflict. *Journal of Marriage and Family Counseling*, 1975, **1**, 299–315.

GURMAN, A.S. The effects and effectiveness of marital therapy: A review of outcome research. *Family Process*, June 1973, **12**, (2), 145–170.

GURMAN, A.S. & KNISKERN, D.P. Research on marital and family therapy: Progress, perspective and prospect. In S.L. Garfield & A.E. Bergin (Eds.), *Handbook of psychotherapy and behavioral change: An empirical analysis,* 2nd ed. New York: John Wiley & Sons, 1978.

_____. (Eds.) *Handbook of family therapy.* New York: Brunner/Mazel, 1981.

HALEY, J. *Changing families: A family therapy reader.* New York: Grune & Stratton, 1971.

_____. *Strategies of psychotherapy.* New York: Grune & Stratton, 1972.

_____. *Problem-solving therapy: New strategies for effective family therapy.* San Francisco: Jossey-Bass, 1976.

HALPERN, H. *No strings attached: A guide to a better relationship with your grown-up child.* New York: Simon & Schuster, 1979.

HARDY, M.E., & CONWAY, M.E. *Role Theory.* New York: Appleton-Century-Crofts, 1978

HAYNES, J.M. Divorce mediator: A new role. *Social Work*, January 1978.

HEARN, G. (Ed.) *The general systems approach: Contributions to an holistic conception of social work.* New York: Council on Social Work Education, 1969.

HEPWORTH, D.H. Early removal of resistance in task-centered casework. *Social Work*, July 1979.

HILGARD, E. & BOWER, G. *Theories of learning*, 4th ed. New York: Appleton-Century-Crofts, 1974.

HILL, R. *Family development in three generations.* New York: Schenkman, 1970.

HOFFMAN, L.W. & NYE, F.I. *Working mothers.* San Francisco: Jossey-Bass, 1974.

HOLLIS, F. *Casework: A psychosocial therapy.* New York: Random House, 1964.

HUNT, M.M. *The world of the formerly married.* New York: McGraw-Hill, 1966.

HUNT, M.M. & HUNT, B. *The divorce experience.* New York: McGraw-Hill, 1977.

HURDLE, J.F. You can enjoy sex after seventy. *Sexology*, April 1971, **37**, 49–51.

IRVING, H.H. *Divorce mediation: The rational alternative.* Toronto: Personal Library Publishers, 1980.

JACKSON, D.D. Family rules: The marital quid pro quo. *Archives of General Psychiatry*, 1965, **2**, 589.

JEHU, D. *Learning theory and social work.* London: Routledge and Kegan Paul, 1967

KAPLAN, H.S. *The new sex therapy: Active treatment of sexual dysfunction.* New York: Brunner/Mazel, 1974.

_____. *Disorders of sexual desire: And other new concepts and techniques in sex therapy*. New York: Brunner/Mazel, 1979.

KESHET, H.F. & ROSENTHAL, K.M. Fathering after marital separation. *Social Work*, January 1978.

KOMAROVSKY, M. *Blue collar marriage*. New York: Random House, 1964.

_____. *Dilemmas of masculinity*. New York: W. W. Norton, 1976.

LANTZ, J. *Family and marital therapy: A transactional approach*. New York: Appleton-Century-Crofts, 1978

LEITENBERG, H. Positive reinforcement and extinction procedures. In W.S. Agras (Ed.), *Behavior modification: Principles and clinical applications*. Boston: Little, Brown, 1972.

LEVINSON, D. *The seasons of a man's life*. New York: Alfred A. Knopf, Ltd., 1978.

LEVY, J. & MONROE, R. *The happy family*. New York: Alfred A. Knopf, 1938.

LORING, R.K. & OTTO, H.A. (Eds.) *New life options: The working woman's resource book*. New York: McGraw-Hill, 1976.

MACE, D.R. The minister's role in marriage preparation. *Pastoral Psychology*, 1952, **3**, 45–48.

_____. *Getting ready for marriage*. Nashville, Tenn: Abingdon Press, 1972.

MACE, D.R. & MACE, V. Marriage enrichment: A preventive group approach for couples. In D.H.L. Olson (Ed.), *Treating relationships*. Lake Mills, Iowa: Graphic Publishing Co., 1976.

MAIER, H.W. *Three theories of child development*, 3rd ed. New York: Harper & Row, 1978.

MESSINGER, L., WALKER, K.N., & FREEMAN, S.J.J. Preparation for re-marriage following divorce: The use of group techniques. *American Journal of Orthopsychiatry*, April 1978, **48**, (2).

MEYER, C. Individualizing the multi-problem family. *Social Casework*, May 1968, 267–272.

MINUCHIN, S. *Families of the slums*. New York: Basic Books, 1967

_____. The plight of the poverty-stricken family in the U.S.A. *Child Welfare*, March 1970, **44**, 124–130.

_____. *Families and family therapy*. Cambridge, Mass.: Harvard University Press, 1974.

MINUCHIN, S. & MONTALVO, B. Techniques for working with disorganized low income families. In Jay Haley (Ed.), *Changing families*. New York: Grune & Stratton, 1971.

MORENO, J.L. *Psychodrama*. 4th ed. Beacon, N.C.: Beacon House, 1972.

MORLEY, W.E. Theory of crisis intervention. *Pastoral Psychology*, April 1970. pp. 1–6.

MORROW, W.R. & GOCHRAS, H.L. Misconceptions regarding behavior modification. *Social Work Review*, 1970, **44**, (3), 293–307.

MUDD, E.H. Premarital counseling. In S. Liebman (Ed.), *Understanding your patient*. Philadelphia: Lippincott, 1957.

MUNSON, C.E. (Ed.) *Social work with families—Theory and practice*. New York: The Free Press, 1980.

NASH, E. M. Premarital counseling. In J. P. Lemmens & K. E. Krantz (Eds.), *The adolescent experience: A counseling guide to social and sexual behavior*. New York: Macmillan, 1970.

OATES, W.E. & ROWATT, W. *Before you marry them: A premarital guidebook for pastors*. Nashville, Tenn.: Broadman Press, 1975.

OTTO, H.A. & OTTO, R. *Total sex*. New York: New American Library, Signet Books, 1972.

PAOLINO, T.J. & McCRADY, B. *Marriage and marital therapy: Psychoanalytic, behavioral and systems theory perspectives*. New York: Brunner/Mazel, 1978

PAPPS, P. The Greek chorus and other techniques of paradoxical therapy. *Family Process*. March 1980, 45–57.

PARAD, H.J. (Ed.) *Crisis intervention: Selected readings*. New York: Family Service Association of America, 1965.

PAUL, N. The role of mourning and empathy in conjoint marital therapy. In G. Zuk & I. Boszormenyi-Nagy (Eds.), *Family therapy and disturbed families*. Palo Alto, Cal.: Science and Behavior Books, 1967.

PERLMAN, H.H. *Social casework: A problem-solving process*. Chicago: University of Chicago Press, 1957.

_____. Some notes on the waiting list. *Social Casework*, 1963, **44**, (4).

RAKOFF, V.M. Cultural Differences and the Work Ethic. In S.C. Feinstein, et. al. (Eds.), *Adolescent Psychiatry*, vol. 8. Chicago: University of Chicago Press, 1980.

RAPOPORT, L. The state of crisis: Some theoretical considerations. In H.J. Parad, (Ed.), *Crisis intervention: Selected readings*. New York: Family Service Association of America, 1965.

_____. Crisis-oriented short-term casework. *The Social Service Review*, 1967, **41**, (1), 38.

_____. Crisis intervention as a mode of brief treatment. In R.W. Roberts & R.H. Nee (Eds.), *Theories of social casework*. Chicago: University of Chicago Press, 1970.

RAPOPORT, R. Normal crises, family structure, and mental health. *Family Process*, 1963, **2**, (1). Reprinted in Parad, 1965.

RAPOPORT, R. & ROBERT, N. *Dual-career families re-examined*. New York: Harper & Row, 1976.

REID, W.J. & EPSTEIN, L. *Task-centered casework*. New York: Columbia University Press, 1972.

REID, W.J. & SHYNE, A.W. *Brief and extended casework*. New York: Columbia University Press, 1969.

RHODES, S. A developmental approach to the life cycle of the family. *Social Casework*, May 1977, **58**, (5), 301–311.

RODGERS, R.H. Toward a theory of family development. *Journal of Marriage and The Family,* August 1964, **26**.

_____. *Family interaction and transaction: The developmental approach*. Englewood Cliffs, N.J.: Prentice-Hall, 1973.

ROGERS, C. *Encounter Groups*. New York: Harper & Row, 1970.

_____. *Becoming partners: Marriage and its alternatives*. New York: Delacorte Press, 1972.

RUBIN, H.H. & NEWMAN, B. *Active sex life after sixty*. New York: Arco Publishing Co., 1969.

RUBIN, L.B. *Women of a certain age*. New York: Harper & Row, 1979.

RUSSELL, A. Limitations of family therapy. *Clinical Social Work Journal*, 1976, **4**, (2).

RUTLEDGE, A. L. *Premarital counseling*. Cambridge, Mass.: Schenkman Co., 1966.

SATIR, V., STACHEWIAR, J. & TASCHMAN, H.A. *Helping families to change*, 3rd printing. New York: Jason Aronson, 1977.

SCHERZ, F.H. Crisis of adolescence in family life. *Social Casework*, April 1967, **48**, 209–215.

_____. Maturational crisis and parent-child interaction. *Social Casework*, 1971, **52**, 362–369.

SCHLESINGER, B. (Ed.) *Sexual behavior in Canada: Patterns and problems*. Toronto: University of Toronto Press, 1977.

SCHLESINGER, B. & MULLEN, R.A. Sexuality and the aged: Taboos and misconceptions must give way to reality. In B. Schlesinger (Ed.), *Sexual behavior in Canada,* Toronto: University of Toronto Press, 1977.

SCHLESINGER, B. & TODRES, R. Motherless families. An increasing societal pattern. *Child Welfare*, September 1976, **55**, 553–558.

SCHMIDT, D.D. & MESSNER, E. The role of the family physician in the crisis of impending divorce. *Journal of Family Practice*, April 1975, **2**, 99–102.

SCHUMM, W.R. & DENTON, W. Trends in pre-marriage counselling. *Journal of Marital and Family Therapy*, October 1979, **5**, (4).

SCHWARTZ, W. Social group work: The interactionist approach. In J. B. Turner (Ed.), *Encyclopedia of Social Work*, vol. 2. New York: National Association of Social Workers, 1977.

SHULMAN, L. *The skills of helping individuals and groups*. Itasca, Ill.: Peacock Publishers, 1979.

SMALLEY, R.E. The functional approach to casework practice. In R.W. Roberts & R.H. Nee (Eds.), *Theories of social casework*. Chicago: University of Chicago Press, 1970.

SOROKIN, P., ZIMMERMAN, C.C., & GALTIN, C.J. *A systematic source book in rural sociology*, Vol. 2. Minneapolis: University of Minnesota Press, 1931.

SPENCE, D. & LONNER, T. The empty nest: A transition with motherhood. *The Family Coordinator*, 1971, **20**, 369–375.

SPIEGEL, J. The resolution of role conflict within the family. In N.W. Bell & E.F. Vogel (Eds.), *The family*. New York: The Free Press, 1968.

STEINBERG, J.L. Towards an interdisciplinary commitment: A divorce lawyer proposes attorney-therapist marriages or at least, an affair. *Journal of Marital and Family Therapy*, July 1980, 259–268.

STEINGLASS, P. Experimenting with family treatment approaches to alcoholism, 1950–1975, A review. *Family Process*, 1975, **15**, 96–123.

STREAN, H.S. *The extramarital affair*. New York: The Free Press, 1980.

STUART, R.B. An operant interpersonal program for couples. In D.H.L. Olson (Ed.), *Treating relationships*. Lake Mills, Iowa: Graphic Publishing Co., 1976.

THOMAS, E.J. *Marital communication and decision making: Analysis, assessment and change*. New York: The Free Press, 1977.

TURNER, F.J. (Ed.) *Social work treatment: Interlocking theoretical approaches,* 2nd ed. New York: The Free Press, 1979.

VINCENT, C.E. (Ed.) *Sexual marital health: The physician as consultant*. New York: McGraw-Hill, 1973.

VISHER, E.B. & VISHER, J.S. *Step-families: A guide to working with step-parents and step-children*. New York: Brunner/Mazel, 1979.

VOGEL, E.F. & BELL, N.W. The emotionally disturbed child as the family scapegoat. In N.W. Bell & E.F. Vogel (Eds.)., *The family*. New York: The Free Press, 1968.

WALKER, K.N. & MESSINGER, L. Re-marriage after divorce: Dissolution and reconstruction of family boundaries. *Family Process*, June 1979, **18**.

WALKER, K.N., ROGERS, J., & MESSINGER, L. Re-marriage after divorce: A review. *Social Casework*, May 1977, **58**, (5), 276–285.

WALLACE, J. & KELLY, J. B. Divorce counseling: A community service for families in the midst of divorce. *American Journal of Orthopsychiatry*, 1977, **47**, 4–22.

WALLERSTEIN, J.S. & KELLY, J.B. Children and divorce: A review. *Social Work*, November 1979, **24**, (6), 472.

WATTENBERG, E. & REINHARDT, H. Female-headed families: Trends and implications. *Social Work*, November 1979, **24**, (6), 460–467.

WATZLAWICK, P. *The language of change: Elements of therapeutic communication*. New York: Basic Books, 1978

_____. A review of the double-bind theory. *Family Process*, March 1963, **2**, (1).

WATZLAWICK, P., BEAVIN, J., & JACKSON, D. *Pragmatics of human communication.* New York: W.W. Norton, 1967.

WATZLAWICK, P., WEAKLAND, J., & FISH, R. *Changes.* New York: W.W. Norton, 1974.

WEAKLAND, J.H., FISCH, R., WATZLAWICK, P., & BODIN, A.M. Brief therapy: Focused problem resolution. *Family Process*, June 1974, **13**, 141–167.

WEISS, R.S. *Marital separation.* New York: Basic Books, 1975.

_____. The emotional impact of marital separation. *Journal of Social Issues*, 1976, **32**, 135–145.

WHITE, B.L. *The first three years of life.* Englewood Cliffs, N.J.: Prentice-Hall, 1975.

WINCH, R.F. *Mate Selection: A Study of Complementary Needs.* New York: Harper, 1958.

WOLBERG, L.R. *Short-term psychotherapy.* New York: Grune & Stratton, 1967.

WOLPE, J. *The practice of behavior therapy.* New York: Pergamon Press, 1969.

WYDEN, P. & WYDEN, B. *Inside the sex clinic: A candid inquiry.* New York: World Publishing Co., 1971.

YANKELOVITCH, D. *The new morality: A profile of American youth in the seventies.* New York: McGraw-Hill, 1974.